# FANBOYS
## vs. ZOMBIES

## Volume Two
## Appetite for Destruction

**ROSS RICHIE** Chief Executive Officer • **MATT GAGNON** Editor-in-Chief • **FILIP SABLIK** VP-Publishing & Marketing • **LANCE KREITER** VP-Licensing & Merchandising • **PHIL BARBARO** Director of Finance
**BRYCE CARLSON** Managing Editor • **DAFNA PLEBAN** Editor • **SHANNON WATTERS** Editor • **ERIC HARBURN** Editor • **CHRIS ROSA** Assistant Editor • **STEPHANIE GONZAGA** Graphic Designer
**KASSANDRA HELLER** Production Designer • **JASMINE AMIRI** Operations Coordinator • **DEVIN FUNCHES** E-Commerce & Inventory Coordinator • **BRIANNA HART** Executive Assistant

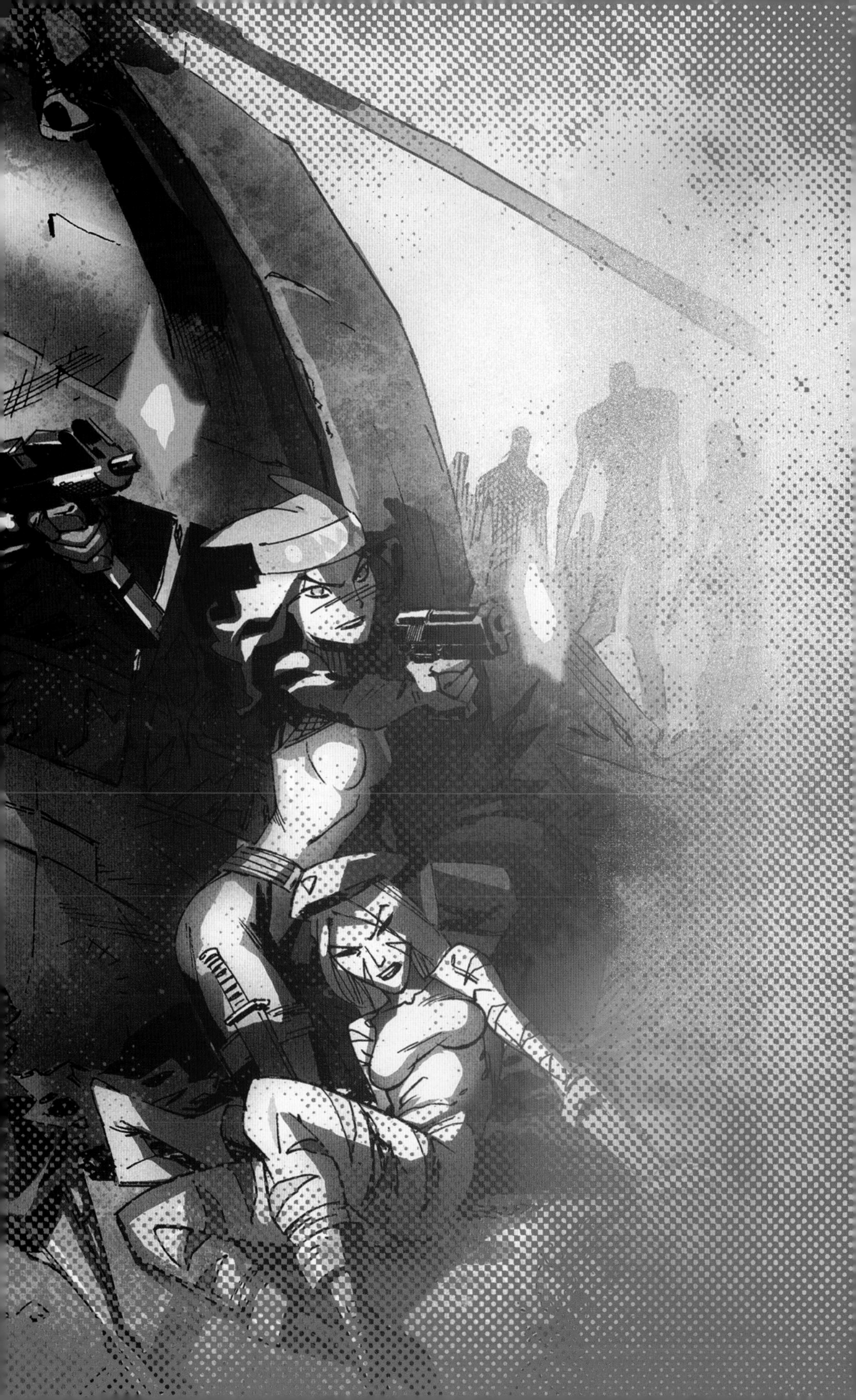

WRITTEN BY
SAM HUMPHRIES

ART BY
JERRY GAYLORD
AND
BRYAN TURNER

INK ASSISTS BY
PENELOPE
GAYLORD

COLORS BY
MIRKA ANDOLFO
WITH
ANDREA DOTTA,
FELIPE SOBREIRO
AND
GABRIEL CASSATA

COVER BY
KHARY
RANDOLPH
COLORS BY
EMILIO
LOPEZ

LETTERS BY
ED
DUKESHIRE

EDITOR
ERIC HARBURN

MANAGING EDITOR
BRYCE CARLSON

DESIGNER
KASSANDRA HELLER

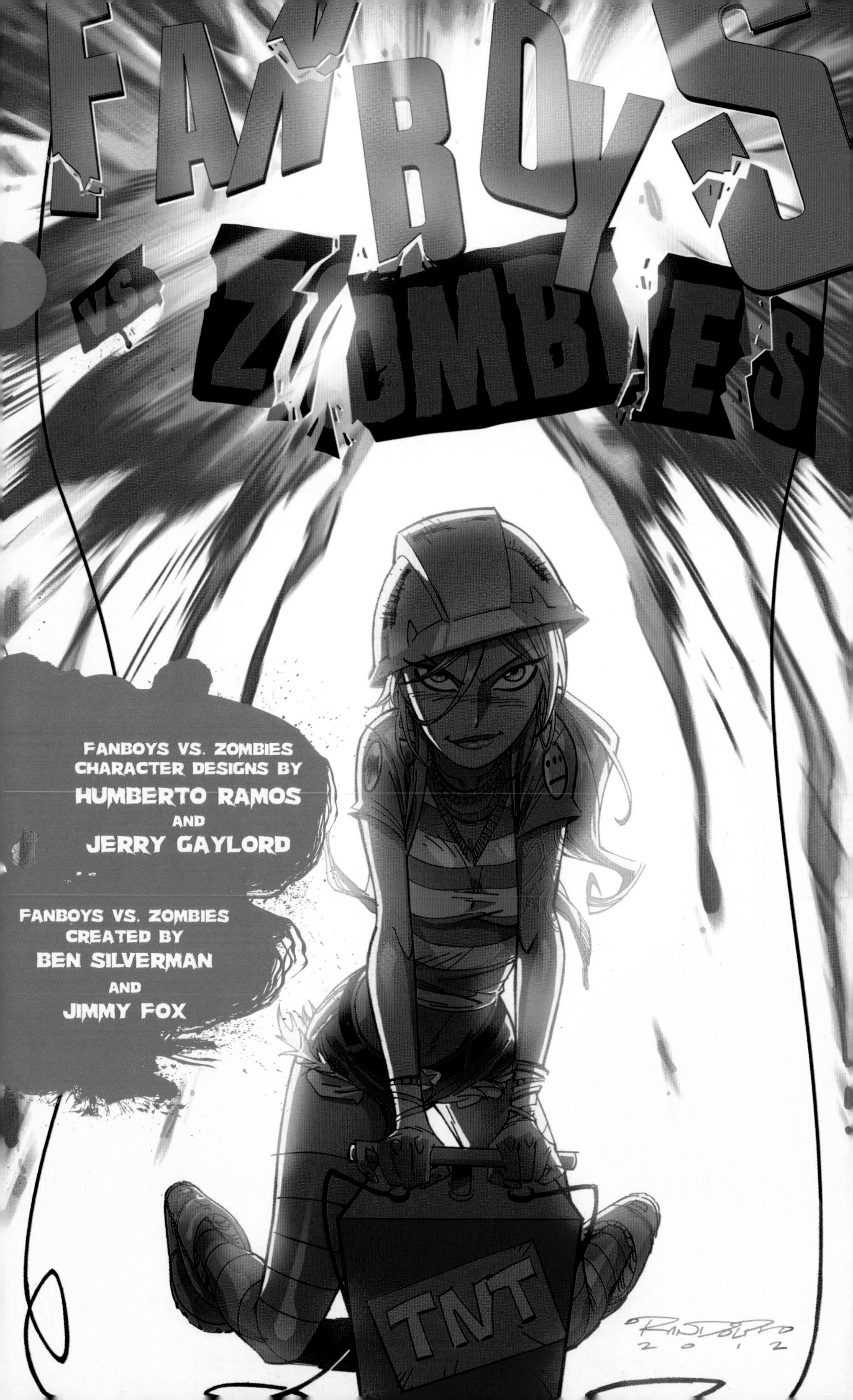
FANBOYS
VS.
ZOMBIES
TNT

FANBOYS VS. ZOMBIES
CHARACTER DESIGNS BY
HUMBERTO RAMOS
AND
JERRY GAYLORD

FANBOYS VS. ZOMBIES
CREATED BY
BEN SILVERMAN
AND
JIMMY FOX

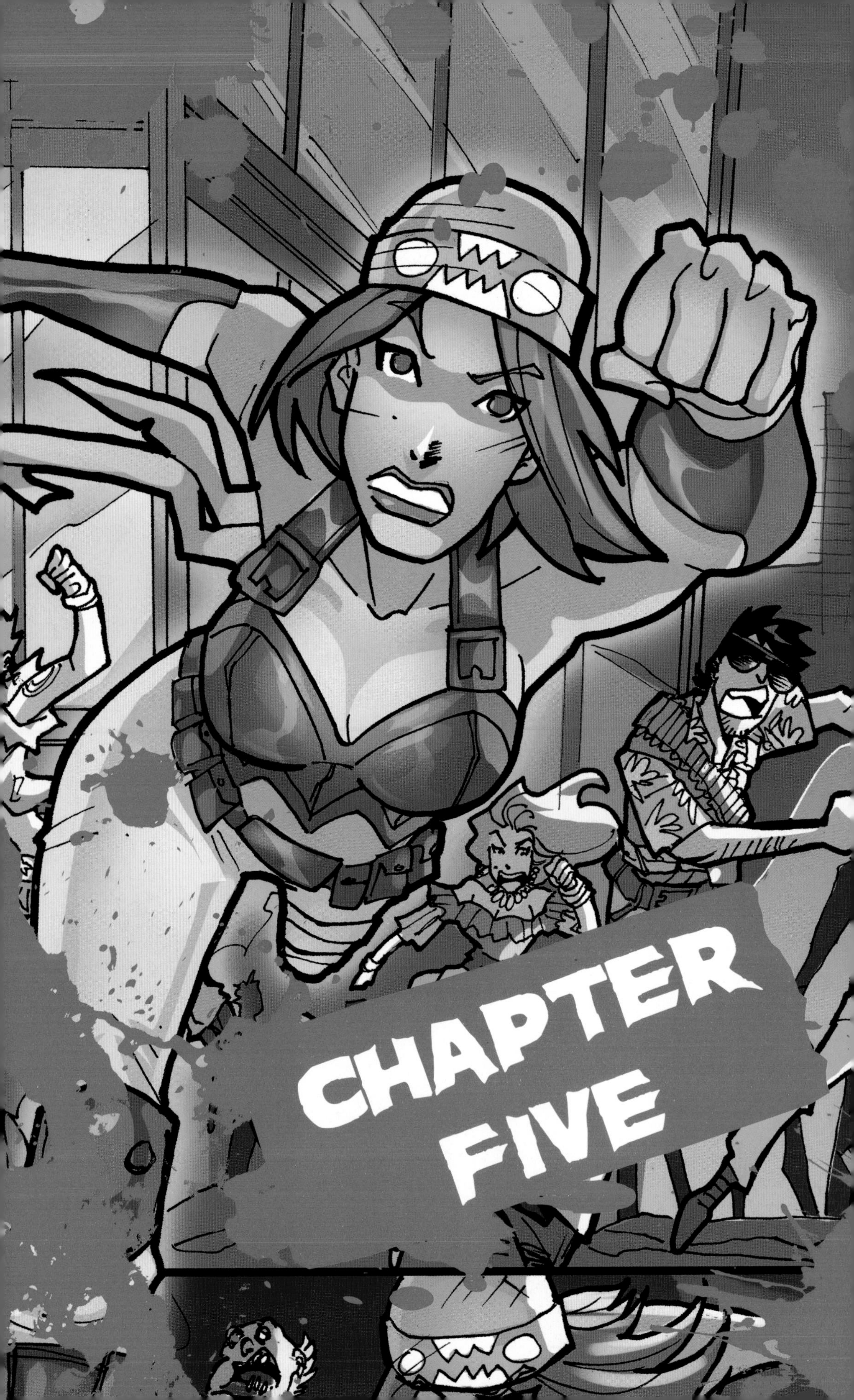
CHAPTER
FIVE

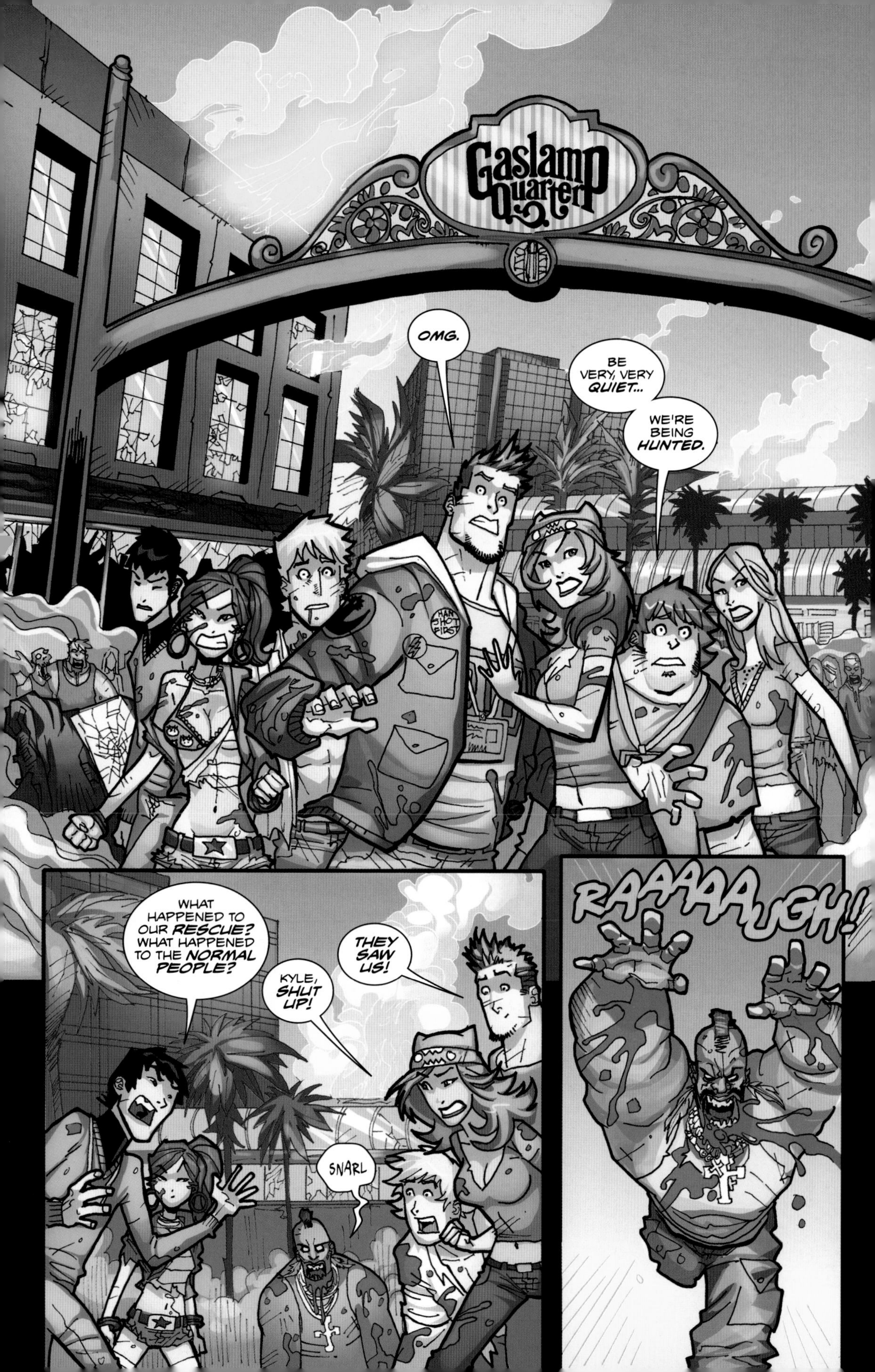

Gaslamp Quarter
OMG.
BE VERY, VERY QUIET...
WE'RE BEING HUNTED.
WHAT HAPPENED TO OUR RESCUE? WHAT HAPPENED TO THE NORMAL PEOPLE?
KYLE, SHUT UP!
THEY SAW US!
SNARL
RAAAAAUGH!

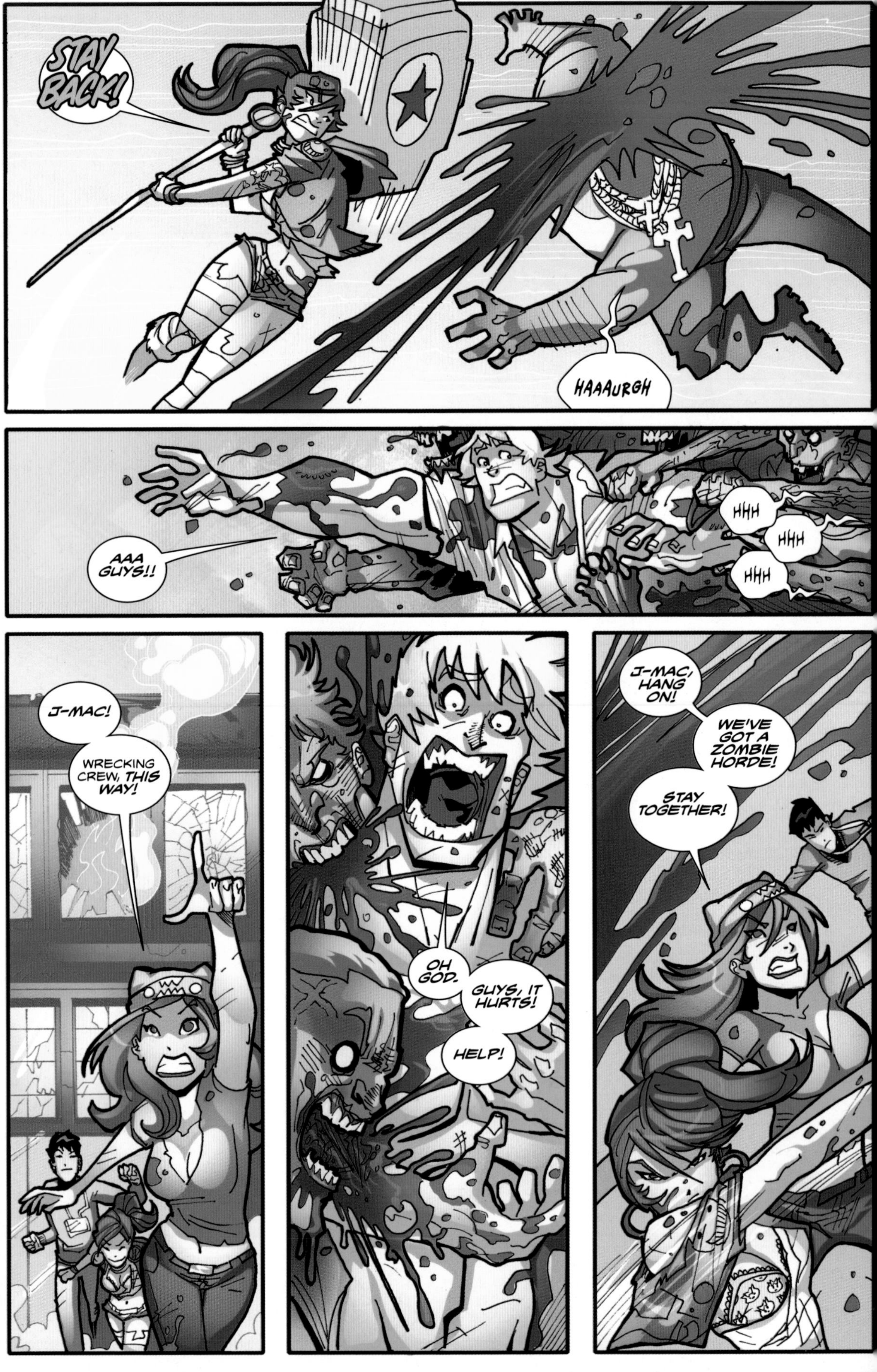
STAY BACK!
HAAAURGH
AAA GUYS!!
HHH
HHH
HHH
J-MAC!
WRECKING CREW, THIS WAY!
OH GOD.
GUYS, IT HURTS!
HELP!
J-MAC, HANG ON!
WE'VE GOT A ZOMBIE HORDE!
STAY TOGETHER!

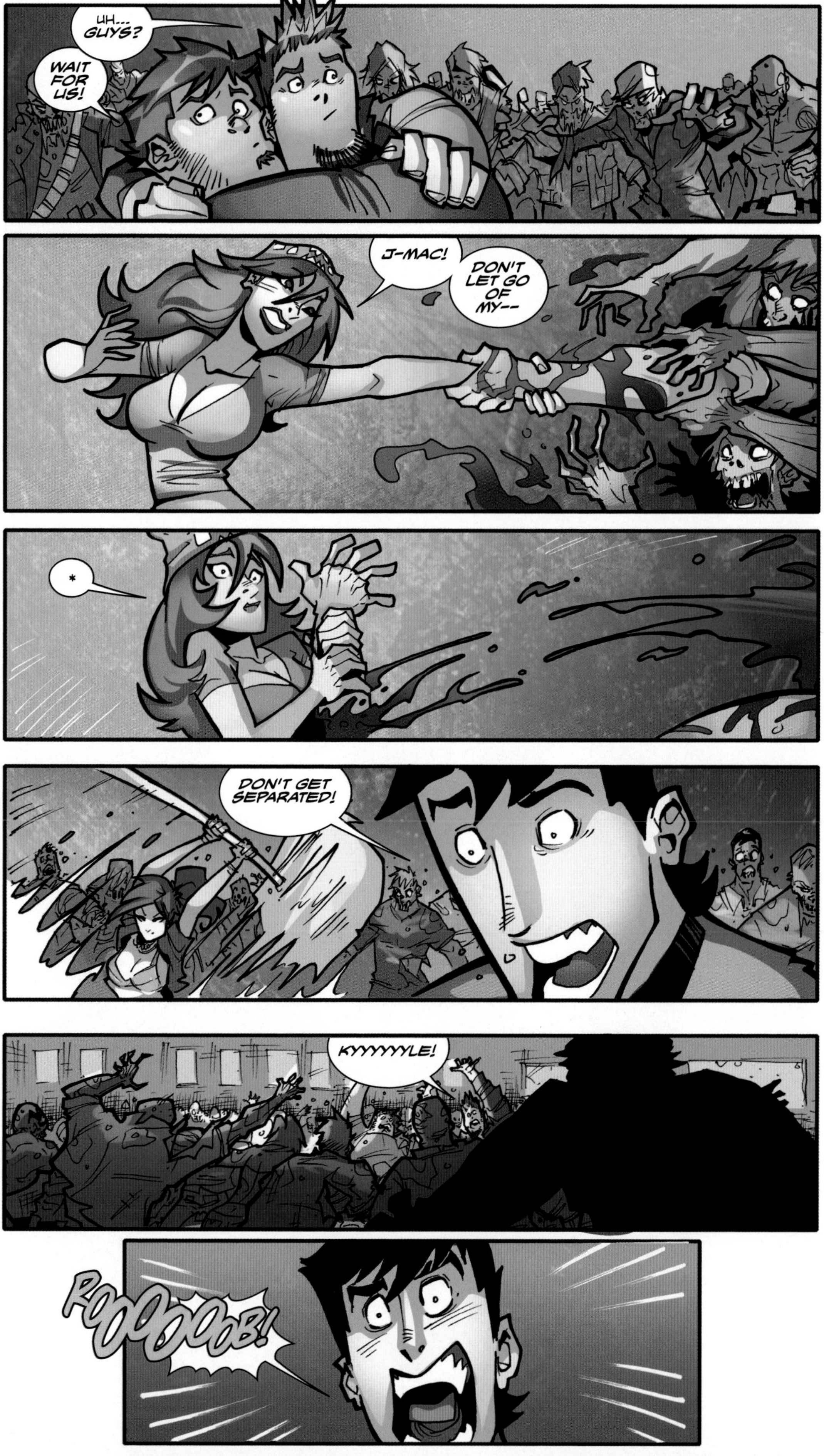
UH... GUYS?
WAIT FOR US!
J-MAC!
DON'T LET GO OF MY--
*
DON'T GET SEPARATED!
KYYYYYYLE!
ROOOOOOOB!

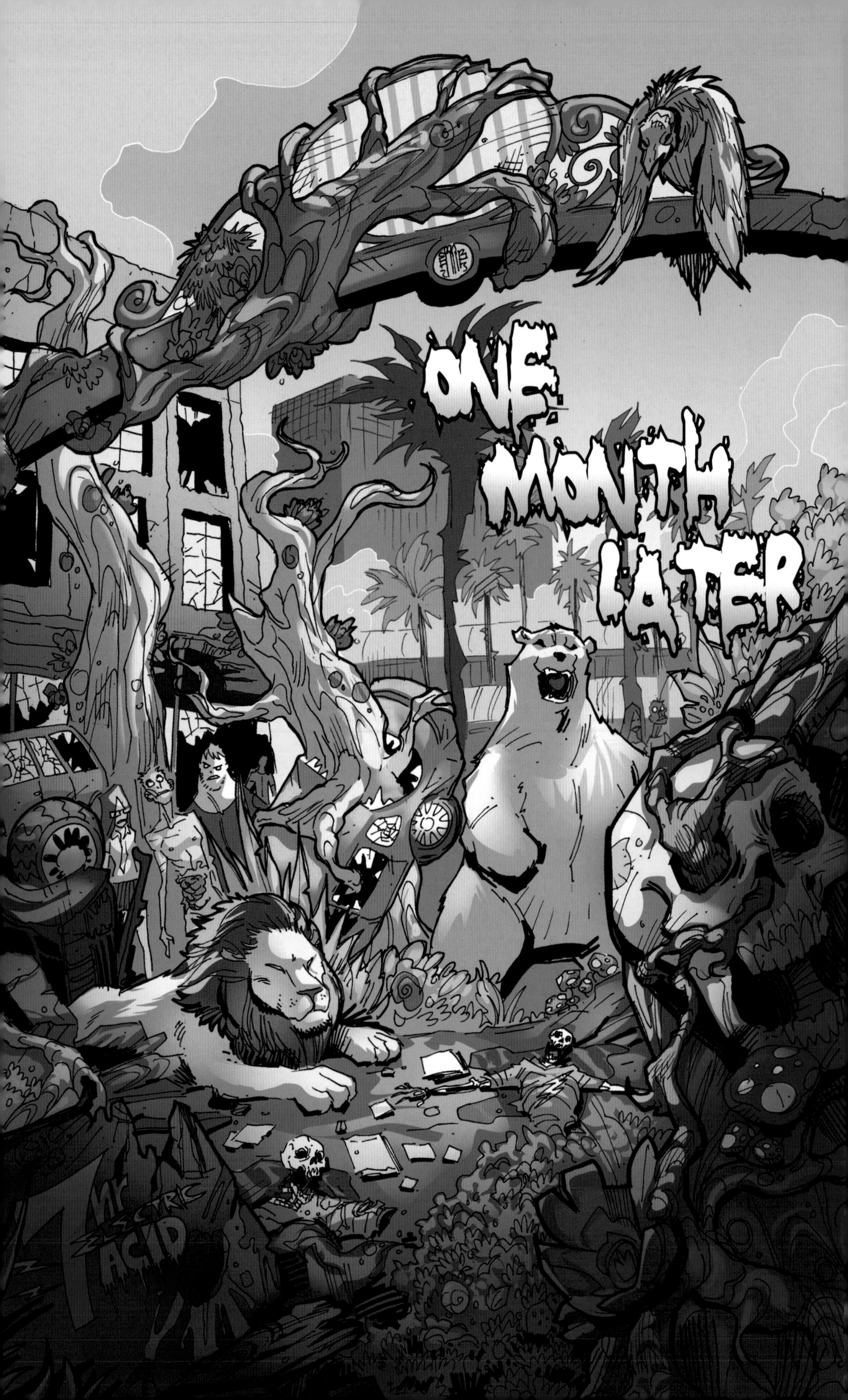
ONE MONTH LATER

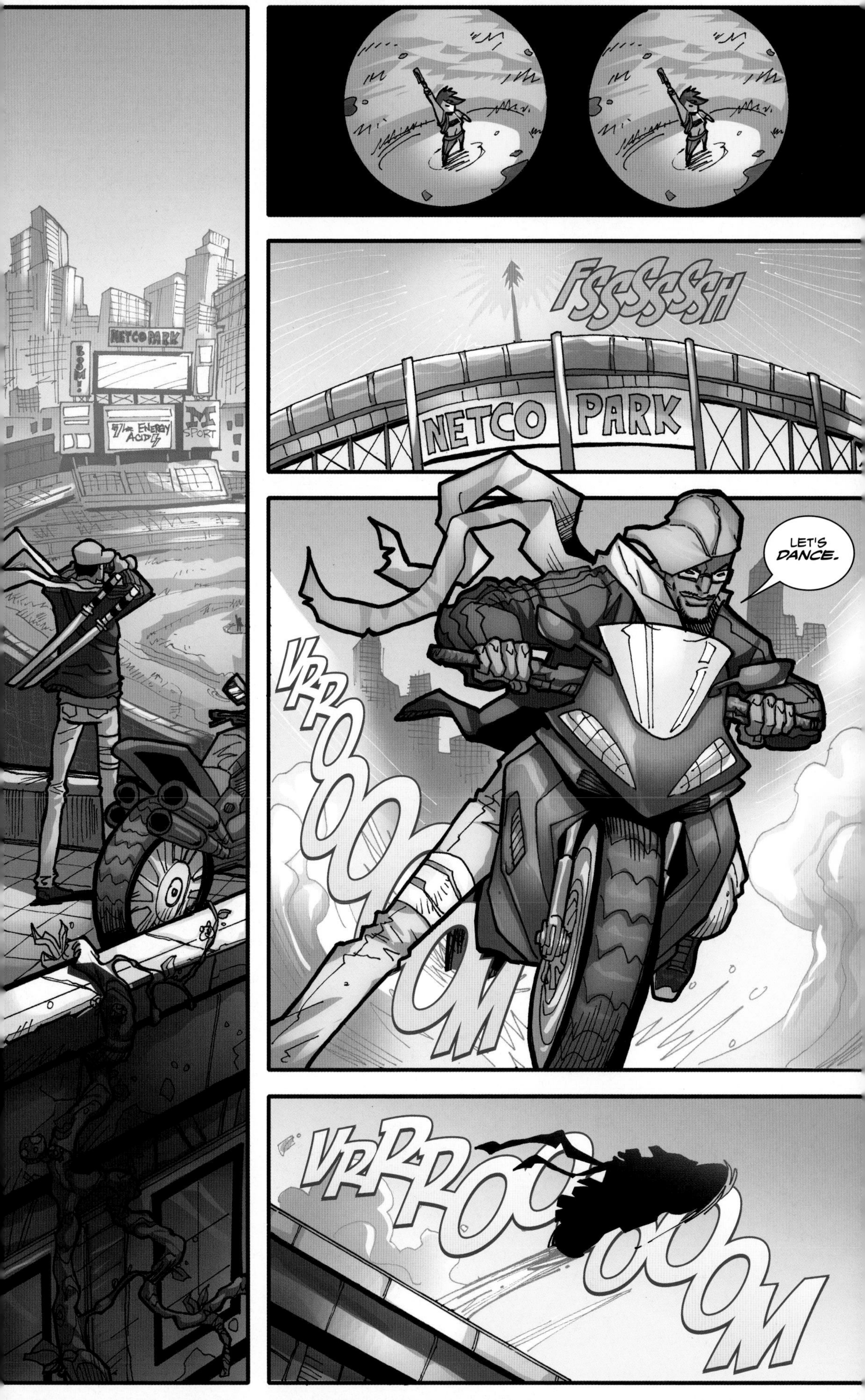
NETCO PARK
BOOM!
ENERGY ACID
M SPORT
FSSSSSSH
NETCO PARK
VRROOOOOM
LET'S DANCE.
VRRROOOOOOM

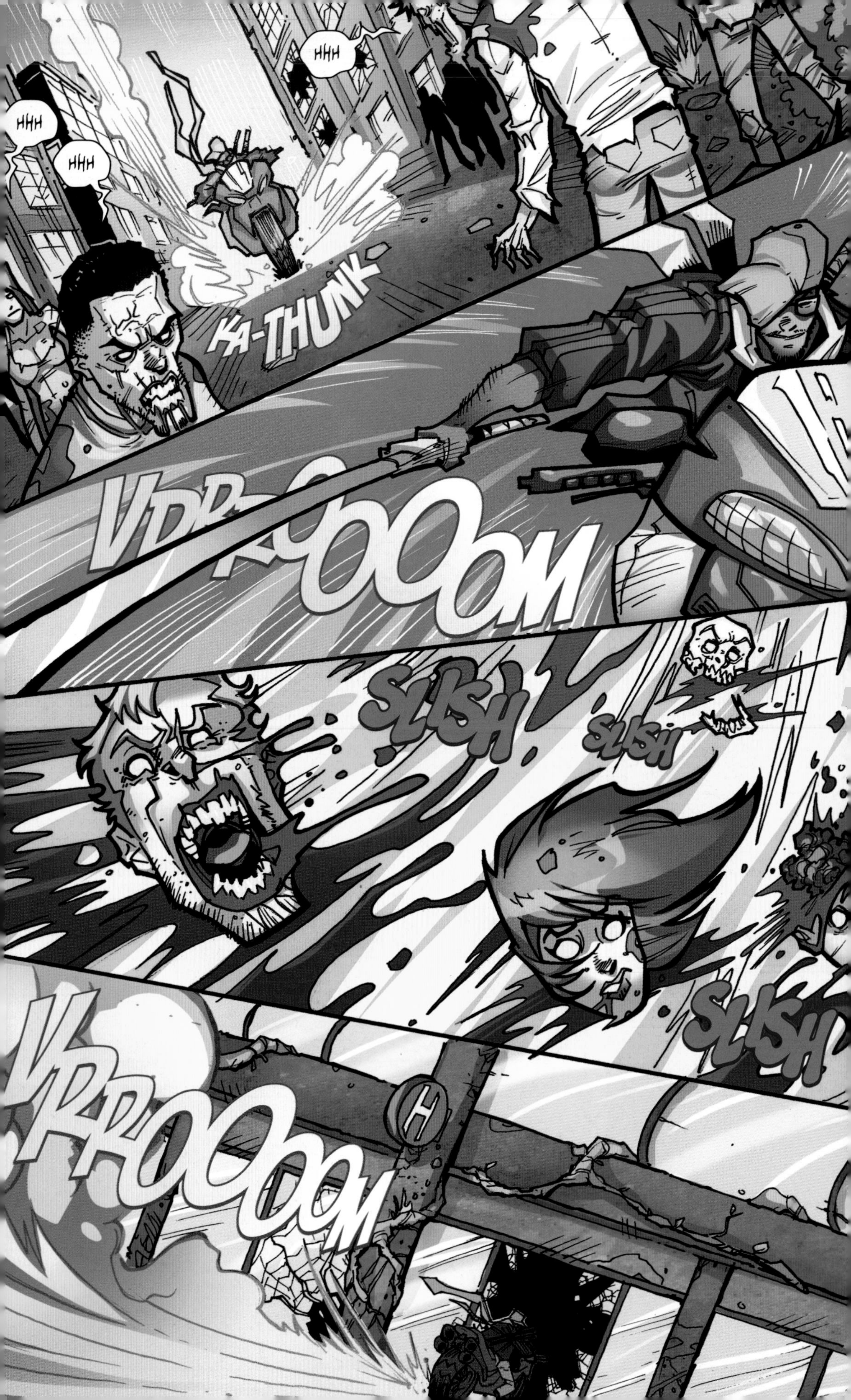
HHH
HHH
HHH
KA-THUNK
VDROOOOM
SLISH
SLISH
SLISH
VRROOOOM

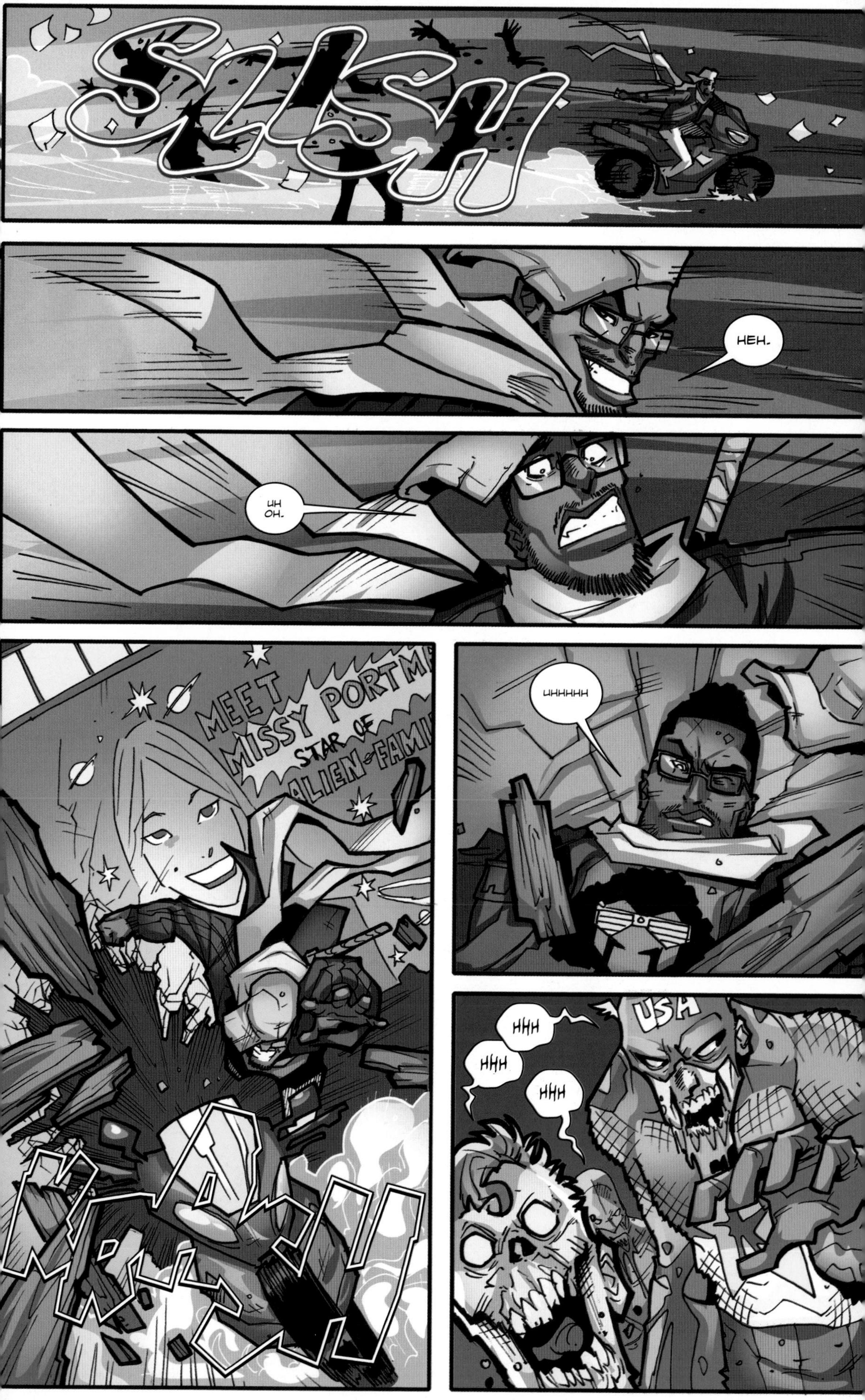
SLISH
HEH.
UH OH.
MEET MISSY PORTM
STAR OF
ALIEN FAMI
UHHHHH
HHH
HHH
HHH
USA

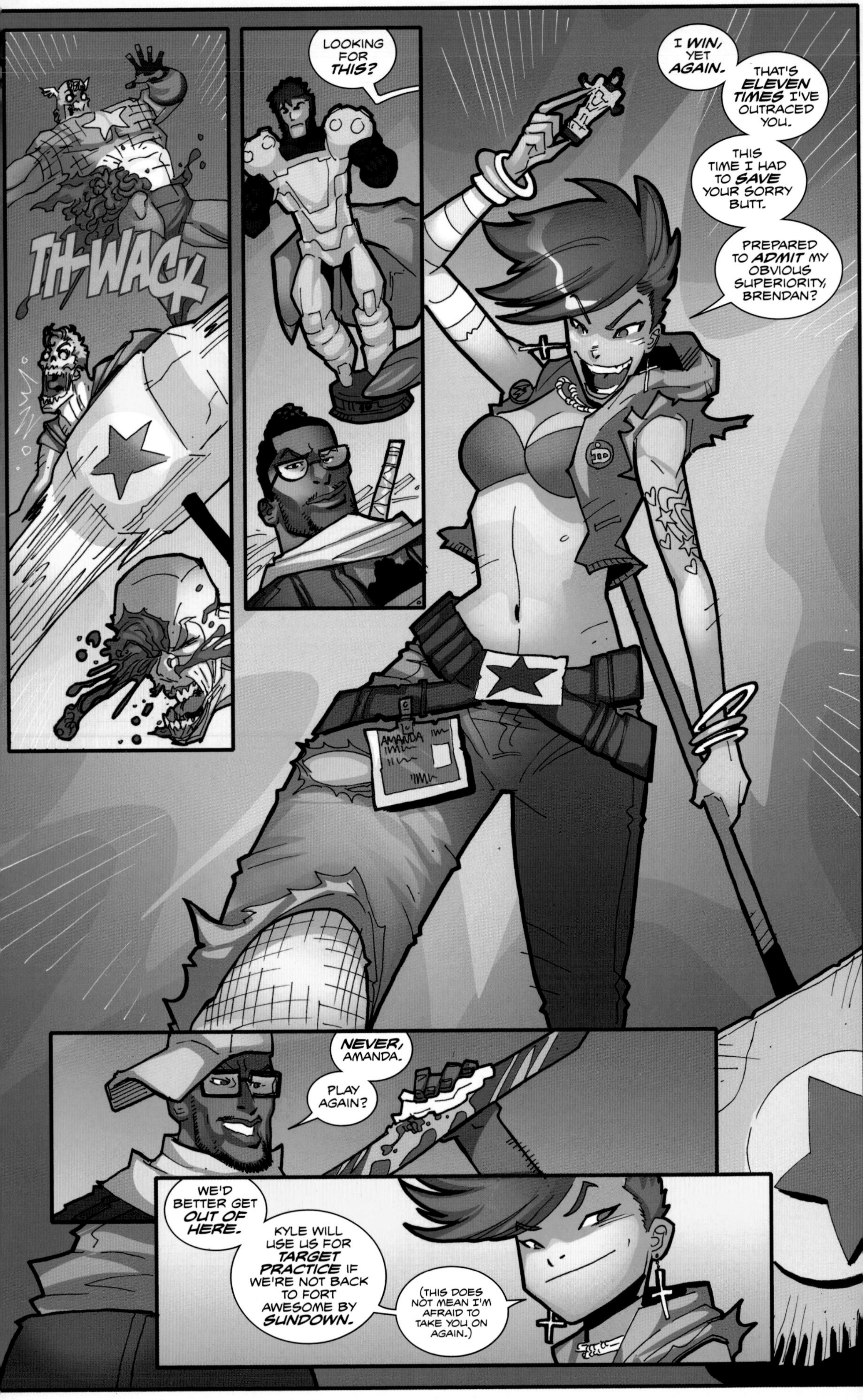
TH-WACK
LOOKING FOR THIS?
I WIN, YET AGAIN.
THAT'S ELEVEN TIMES I'VE OUTRACED YOU.
THIS TIME I HAD TO SAVE YOUR SORRY BUTT.
PREPARED TO ADMIT MY OBVIOUS SUPERIORITY, BRENDAN?
AMANDA
NEVER, AMANDA.
PLAY AGAIN?
WE'D BETTER GET OUT OF HERE.
KYLE WILL USE US FOR TARGET PRACTICE IF WE'RE NOT BACK TO FORT AWESOME BY SUNDOWN.
(THIS DOES NOT MEAN I'M AFRAID TO TAKE YOU ON AGAIN.)

KA-BLAM

Hilton

FORT AWESOME
HOME OF THE
WRECKING CREW
ZOMBIES GO HOME!

YOUR MOVE, *CREEP.*

CHIPS

the office crew VOL 1

CLARKSVILLE

FALSE BLOOD BOXSET

CLARKSVILLE

FALSE BLOOD BOXSET

KA-BLAM

THE *UK* VERSION WAS BETTER.

OH!

SORRY, I DIDN'T SEE YOU COME IN.

HAVEN'T SEEN YOU IN *A* WHILE.

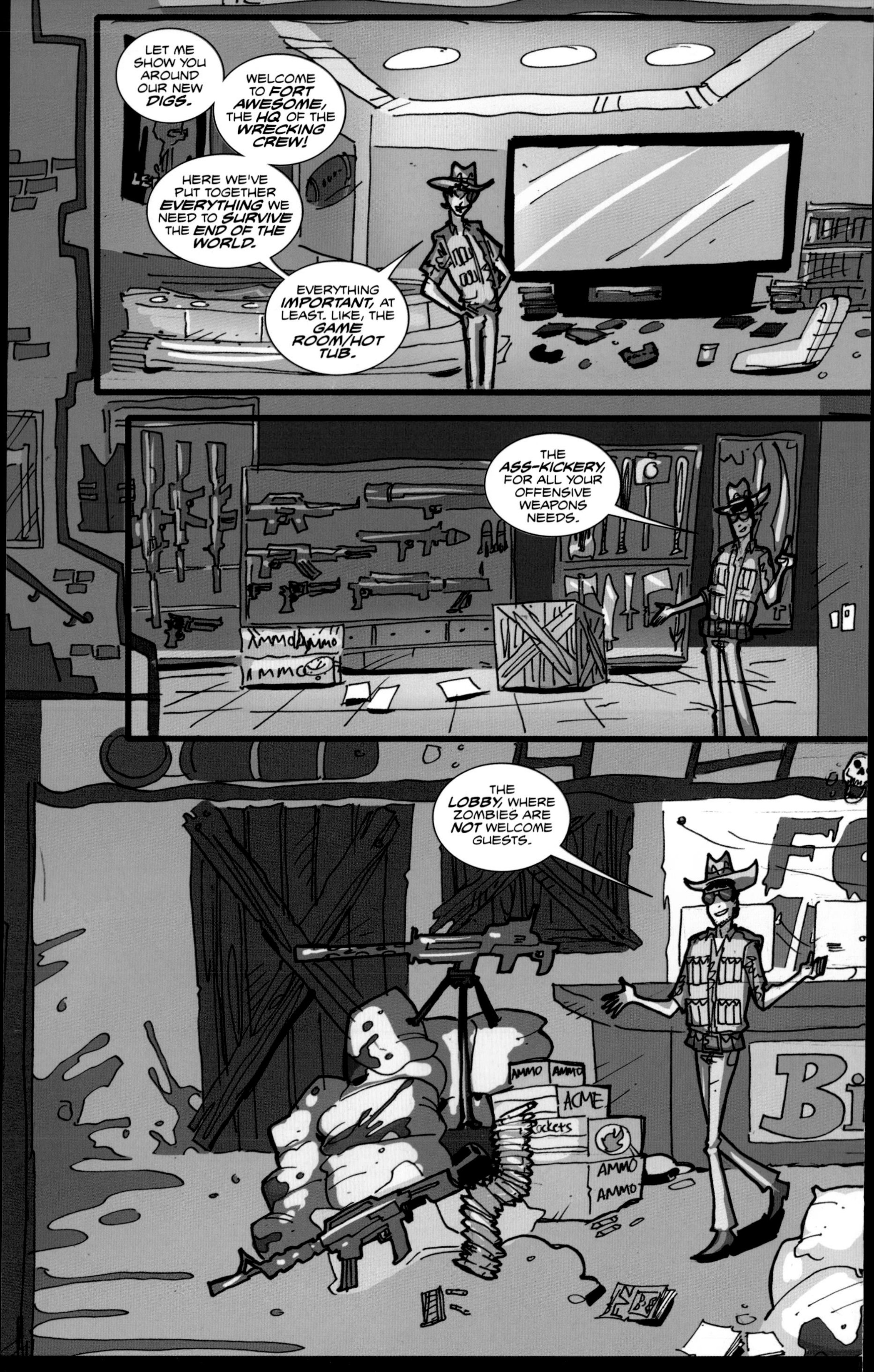
LET ME SHOW YOU AROUND OUR NEW DIGS.
WELCOME TO FORT AWESOME, THE HQ OF THE WRECKING CREW!
HERE WE'VE PUT TOGETHER EVERYTHING WE NEED TO SURVIVE THE END OF THE WORLD.
EVERYTHING IMPORTANT, AT LEAST. LIKE, THE GAME ROOM/HOT TUB.
THE ASS-KICKERY, FOR ALL YOUR OFFENSIVE WEAPONS NEEDS.
AMMO AMMO
AMMO
THE LOBBY, WHERE ZOMBIES ARE NOT WELCOME GUESTS.
AMMO AMMO
ACME
Rockets
AMMO
AMMO

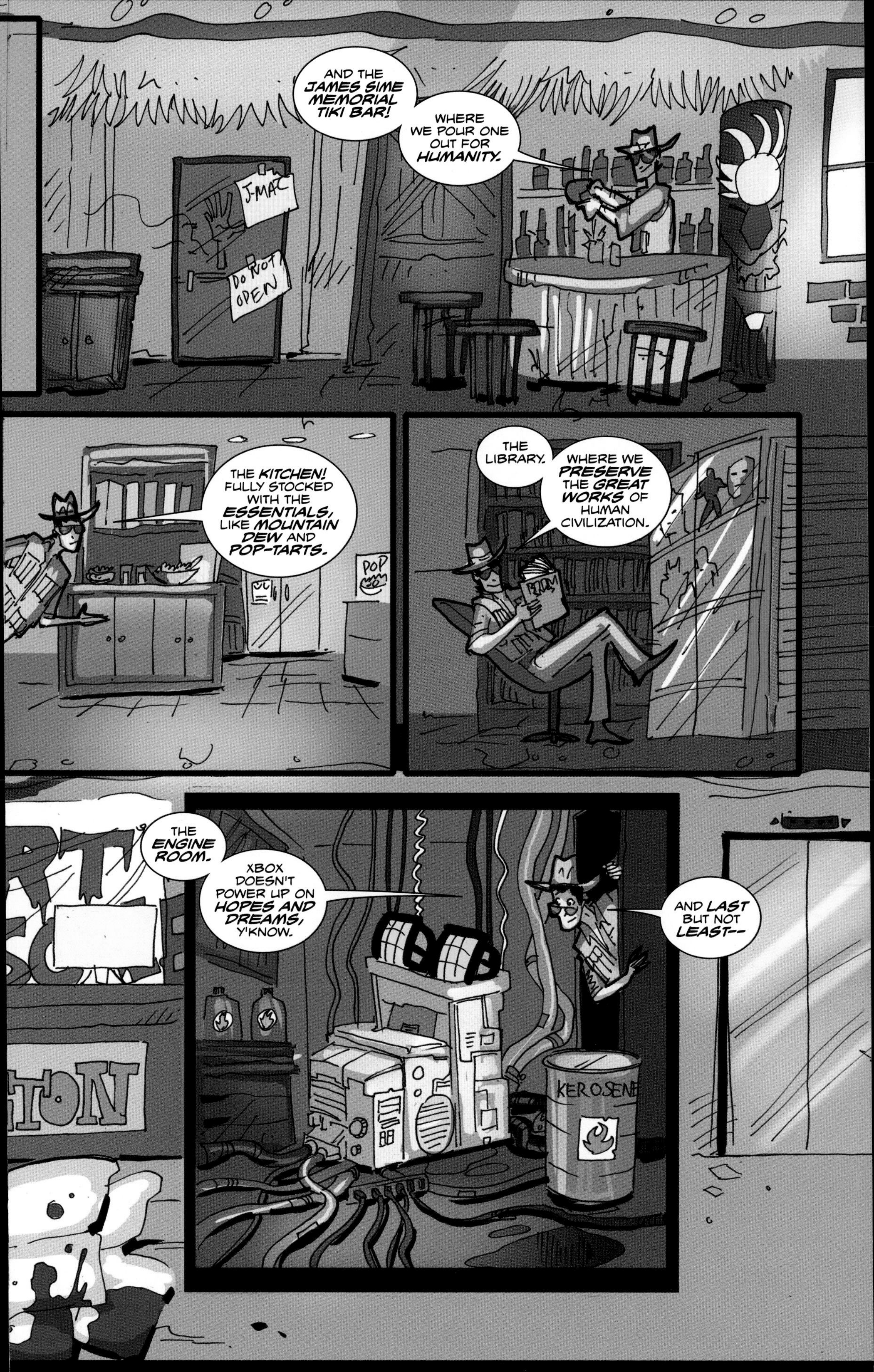
AND THE JAMES SIME MEMORIAL TIKI BAR!
WHERE WE POUR ONE OUT FOR HUMANITY.
J-MAC
DO NOT OPEN
THE KITCHEN! FULLY STOCKED WITH THE ESSENTIALS, LIKE MOUNTAIN DEW AND POP-TARTS.
POP
THE LIBRARY.
WHERE WE PRESERVE THE GREAT WORKS OF HUMAN CIVILIZATION.
THE ENGINE ROOM.
XBOX DOESN'T POWER UP ON HOPES AND DREAMS, Y'KNOW.
KEROSENE
AND LAST BUT NOT LEAST--

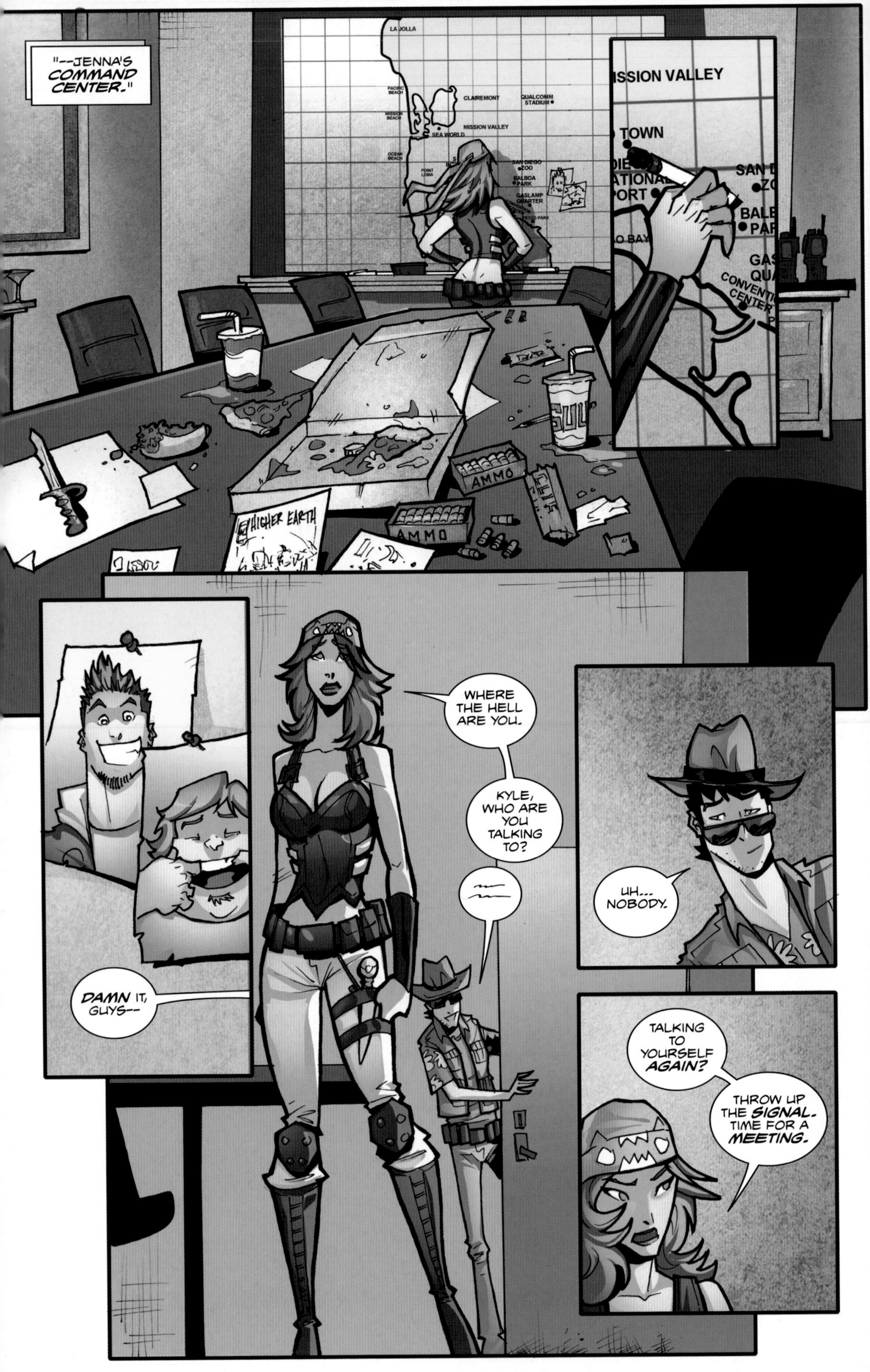
"--JENNA'S COMMAND CENTER."
LA JOLLA
PACIFIC BEACH
CLAIREMONT
QUALCOMM STADIUM
MISSION BEACH
SEA WORLD
MISSION VALLEY
OCEAN BEACH
POINT LOMA
SAN DIEGO ZOO
BALBOA PARK
GASLAMP QUARTER
MISSION VALLEY
TOWN
CONVENTION CENTER
AMMO
AMMO
HIGHER EARTH
WHERE THE HELL ARE YOU.
KYLE, WHO ARE YOU TALKING TO?
UH... NOBODY.
DAMN IT, GUYS--
TALKING TO YOURSELF AGAIN?
THROW UP THE SIGNAL. TIME FOR A MEETING.

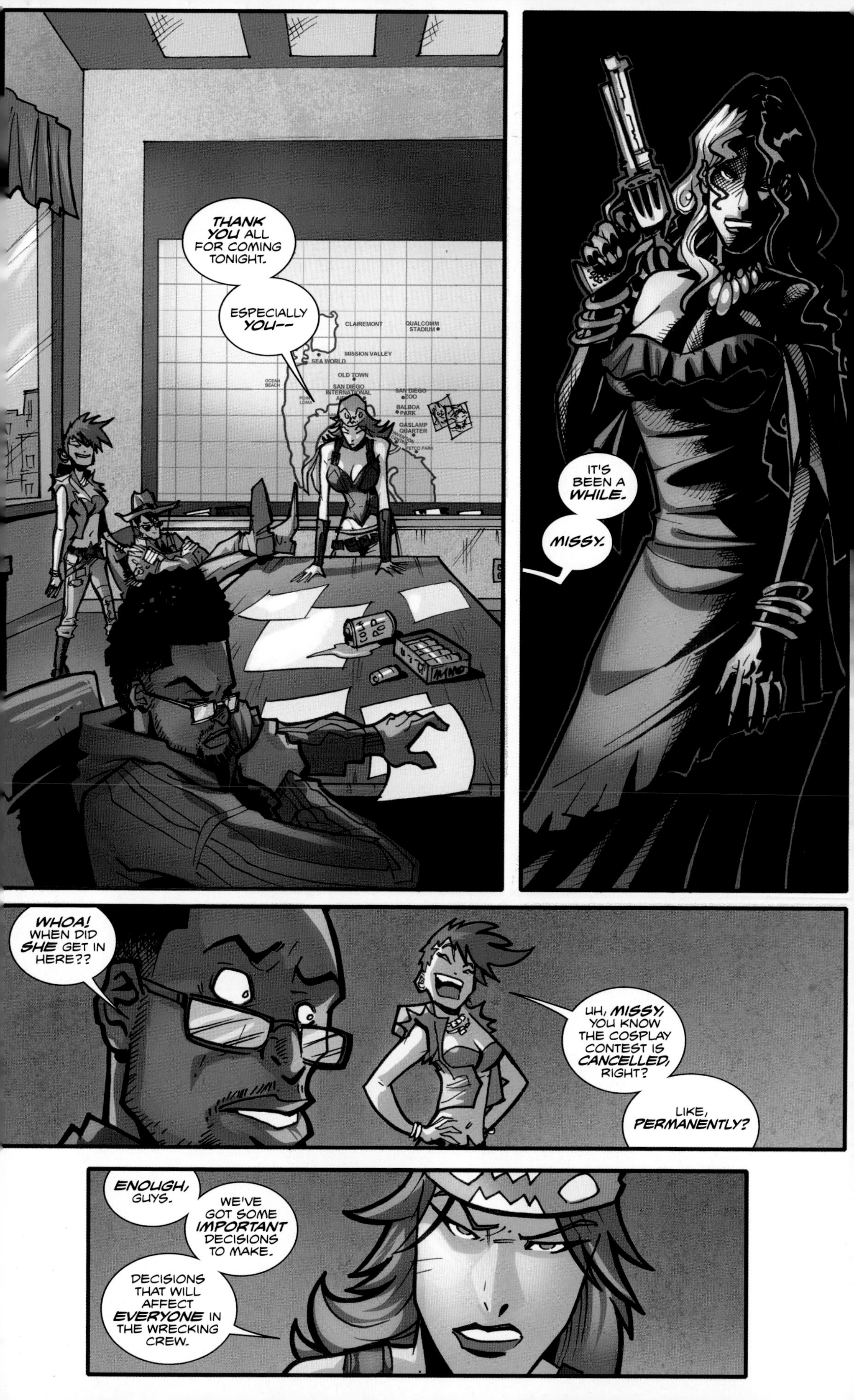

THANK YOU ALL FOR COMING TONIGHT.
ESPECIALLY YOU--
CLAIREMONT
QUALCOMM STADIUM
MISSION VALLEY
SEA WORLD
OLD TOWN
OCEAN BEACH
SAN DIEGO ZOO
BALBOA PARK
GASLAMP QUARTER
PETCO PARK
IT'S BEEN A WHILE.
MISSY.
WHOA! WHEN DID SHE GET IN HERE??
UH, MISSY, YOU KNOW THE COSPLAY CONTEST IS CANCELLED, RIGHT?
LIKE, PERMANENTLY?
ENOUGH, GUYS.
WE'VE GOT SOME IMPORTANT DECISIONS TO MAKE.
DECISIONS THAT WILL AFFECT EVERYONE IN THE WRECKING CREW.

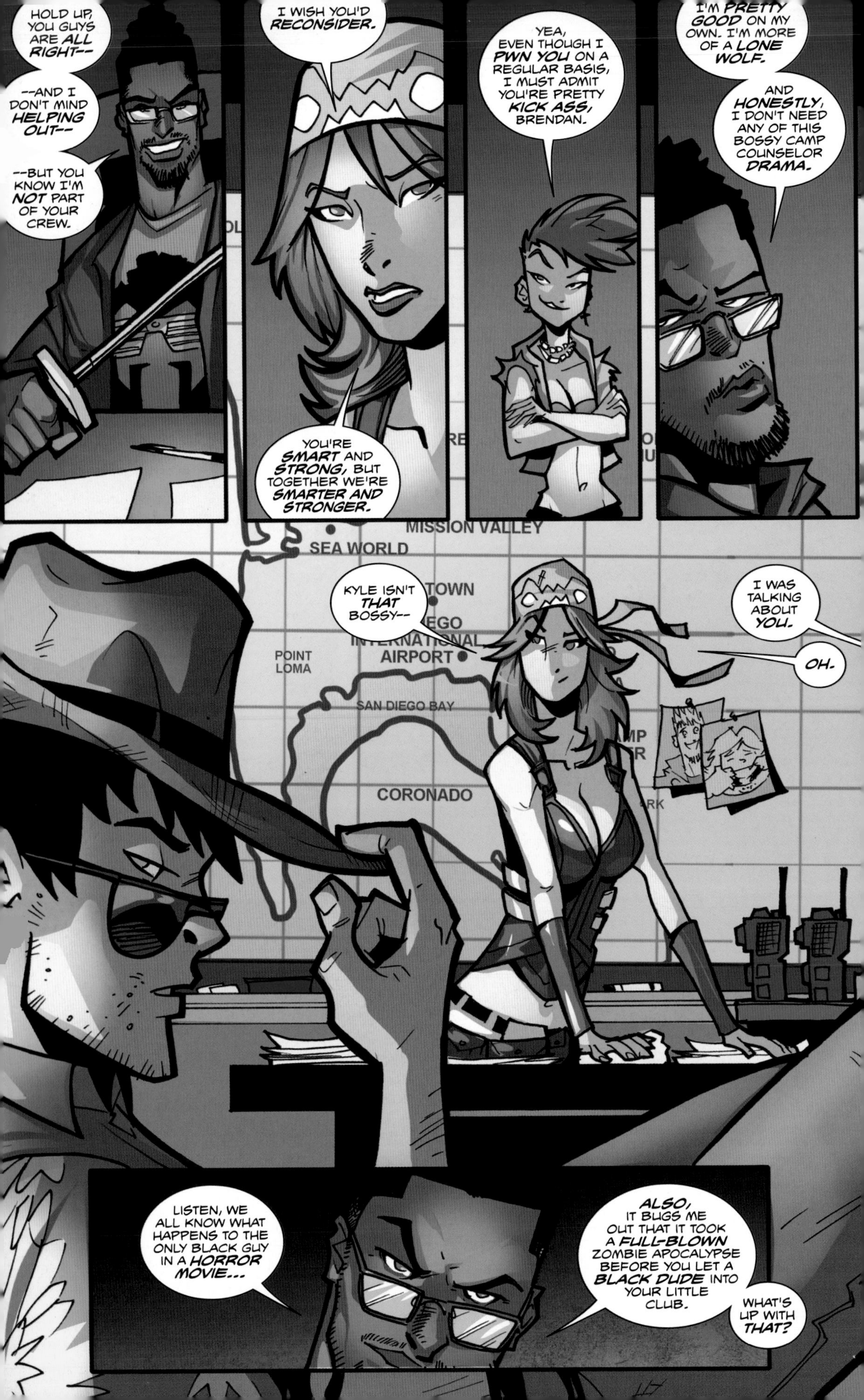

HOLD UP, YOU GUYS ARE ALL RIGHT--
--AND I DON'T MIND HELPING OUT--
--BUT YOU KNOW I'M NOT PART OF YOUR CREW.
I WISH YOU'D RECONSIDER.
YOU'RE SMART AND STRONG, BUT TOGETHER WE'RE SMARTER AND STRONGER.
YEA, EVEN THOUGH I PWN YOU ON A REGULAR BASIS, I MUST ADMIT YOU'RE PRETTY KICK ASS, BRENDAN.
I'M PRETTY GOOD ON MY OWN. I'M MORE OF A LONE WOLF.
AND HONESTLY, I DON'T NEED ANY OF THIS BOSSY CAMP COUNSELOR DRAMA.
MISSION VALLEY
SEA WORLD
POINT LOMA
AIRPORT
SAN DIEGO BAY
CORONADO
KYLE ISN'T THAT BOSSY--
I WAS TALKING ABOUT YOU.
OH.
LISTEN, WE ALL KNOW WHAT HAPPENS TO THE ONLY BLACK GUY IN A HORROR MOVIE...
ALSO, IT BUGS ME OUT THAT IT TOOK A FULL-BLOWN ZOMBIE APOCALYPSE BEFORE YOU LET A BLACK DUDE INTO YOUR LITTLE CLUB.
WHAT'S UP WITH THAT?

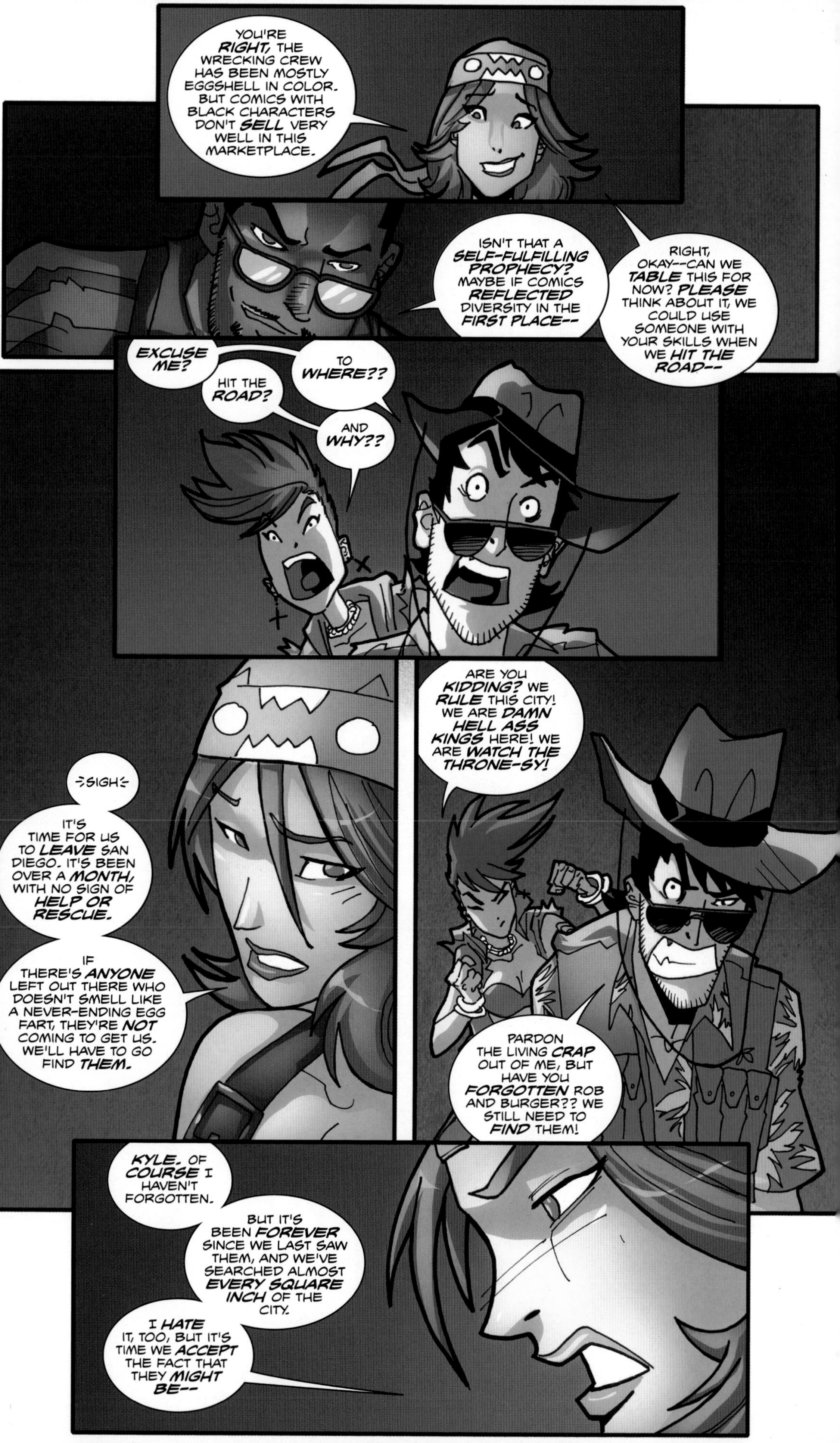

YOU'RE RIGHT, THE WRECKING CREW HAS BEEN MOSTLY EGGSHELL IN COLOR. BUT COMICS WITH BLACK CHARACTERS DON'T SELL VERY WELL IN THIS MARKETPLACE.
ISN'T THAT A SELF-FULFILLING PROPHECY? MAYBE IF COMICS REFLECTED DIVERSITY IN THE FIRST PLACE--
RIGHT, OKAY--CAN WE TABLE THIS FOR NOW? PLEASE THINK ABOUT IT, WE COULD USE SOMEONE WITH YOUR SKILLS WHEN WE HIT THE ROAD--
EXCUSE ME?
HIT THE ROAD?
TO WHERE??
AND WHY??
-SIGH-
IT'S TIME FOR US TO LEAVE SAN DIEGO. IT'S BEEN OVER A MONTH, WITH NO SIGN OF HELP OR RESCUE.
IF THERE'S ANYONE LEFT OUT THERE WHO DOESN'T SMELL LIKE A NEVER-ENDING EGG FART, THEY'RE NOT COMING TO GET US. WE'LL HAVE TO GO FIND THEM.
ARE YOU KIDDING? WE RULE THIS CITY! WE ARE DAMN HELL ASS KINGS HERE! WE ARE WATCH THE THRONE-SY!
PARDON THE LIVING CRAP OUT OF ME, BUT HAVE YOU FORGOTTEN ROB AND BURGER?? WE STILL NEED TO FIND THEM!
KYLE. OF COURSE I HAVEN'T FORGOTTEN.
BUT IT'S BEEN FOREVER SINCE WE LAST SAW THEM, AND WE'VE SEARCHED ALMOST EVERY SQUARE INCH OF THE CITY.
I HATE IT, TOO, BUT IT'S TIME WE ACCEPT THE FACT THAT THEY MIGHT BE--

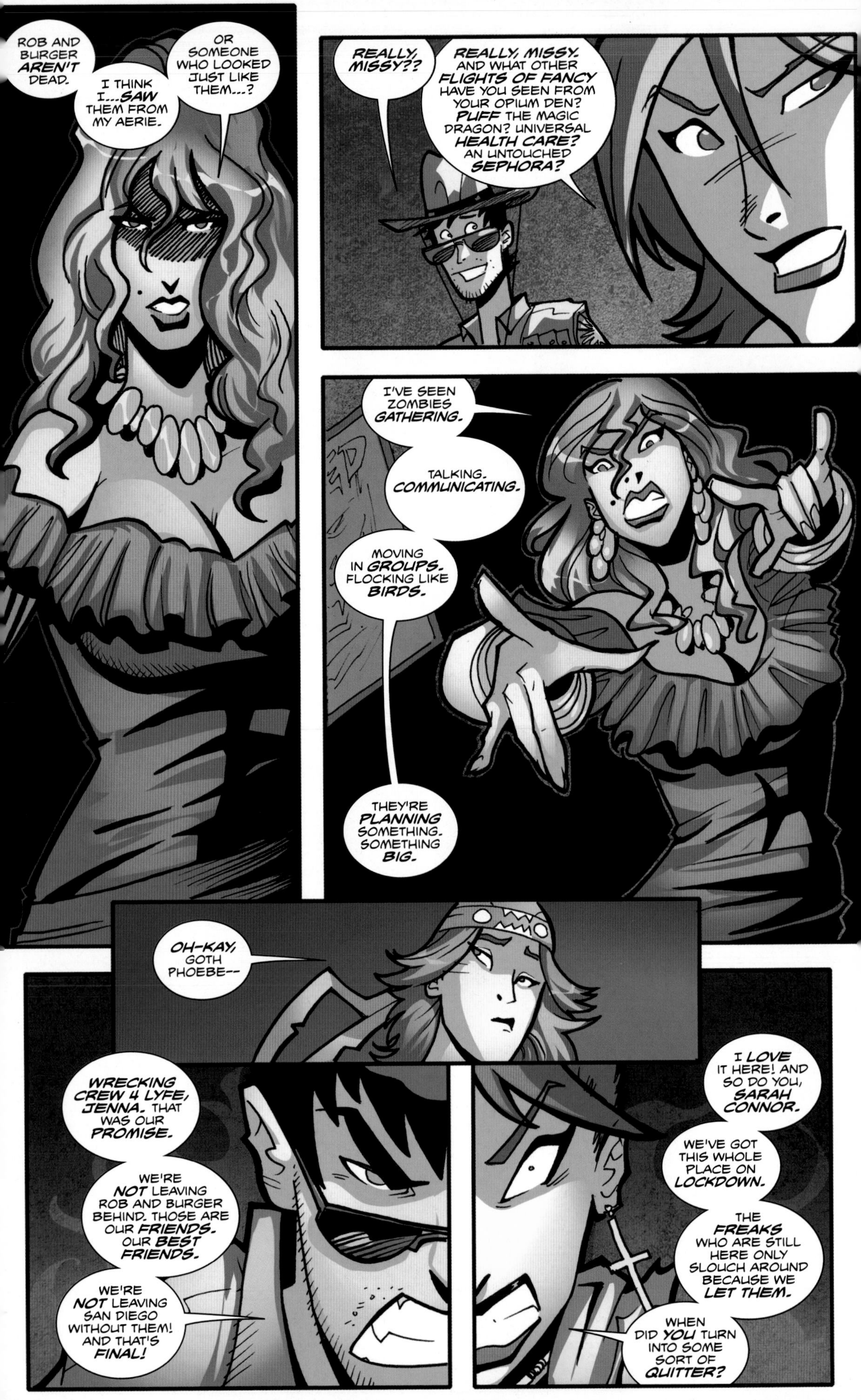

ROB AND BURGER AREN'T DEAD.
I THINK I...SAW THEM FROM MY AERIE.
OR SOMEONE WHO LOOKED JUST LIKE THEM...?
REALLY, MISSY??
REALLY, MISSY. AND WHAT OTHER FLIGHTS OF FANCY HAVE YOU SEEN FROM YOUR OPIUM DEN? PUFF THE MAGIC DRAGON? UNIVERSAL HEALTH CARE? AN UNTOUCHED SEPHORA?
I'VE SEEN ZOMBIES GATHERING.
TALKING. COMMUNICATING.
MOVING IN GROUPS. FLOCKING LIKE BIRDS.
THEY'RE PLANNING SOMETHING. SOMETHING BIG.
OH-KAY, GOTH PHOEBE--
WRECKING CREW 4 LYFE, JENNA. THAT WAS OUR PROMISE.
WE'RE NOT LEAVING ROB AND BURGER BEHIND. THOSE ARE OUR FRIENDS. OUR BEST FRIENDS.
WE'RE NOT LEAVING SAN DIEGO WITHOUT THEM! AND THAT'S FINAL!
I LOVE IT HERE! AND SO DO YOU, SARAH CONNOR.
WE'VE GOT THIS WHOLE PLACE ON LOCKDOWN.
THE FREAKS WHO ARE STILL HERE ONLY SLOUCH AROUND BECAUSE WE LET THEM.
WHEN DID YOU TURN INTO SOME SORT OF QUITTER?

AND WHAT ARE *YOU*, SOME SORT OF *PSYCHO*? OUR LUCK HAS *HELD OUT*, BUT IT CAN'T LAST *FOREVER*! THIS CITY IS CRAWLING WITH MORE AND MORE ZOMBIES *EVERY DAY*.

IT'S EVEN *WORSE* AT NIGHT.

THIS ISN'T A GAME WITH A *HIGH SCORE*. WE CAN'T *KILL* THEM ALL. WE *LEAVE*, OR FIGHT UNTIL WE *DIE*. THERE ARE NO *ACHIEVEMENTS* TO UNLOCK, NO LEADERBOARDS OF *KILL COUNTS*.

*371.*

OH, *WHAT*. LIKE YOU GUYS DON'T *KEEP TRACK*??

ALL *RIGHT*!

ALL RIGHT. IT'S BEEN A LONG... *MONTH*. LET'S *SLEEP* ON IT, OKAY?

KYLE, YOU'VE GOT *FIRST WATCH*.

WE'VE LITERALLY GOT A *BAJILLION* SAFE, SECURE ROOMS IN THIS BUILDING.

BRENDAN, I'D FEEL BETTER IF YOU STAYED *HERE* TONIGHT.

*YOU* TOO--

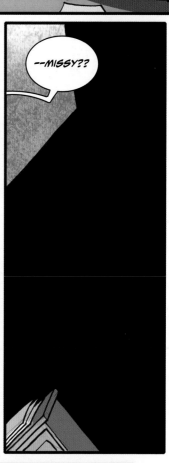

--MISSY??

*DAMN IT.*

THE *WORST PART* ABOUT THE END OF THE WORLD IS I CAN'T TELL *TMZ* WHAT A *SERIOUS WEIRDO* MISSY PORTMAN TURNED OUT TO BE.

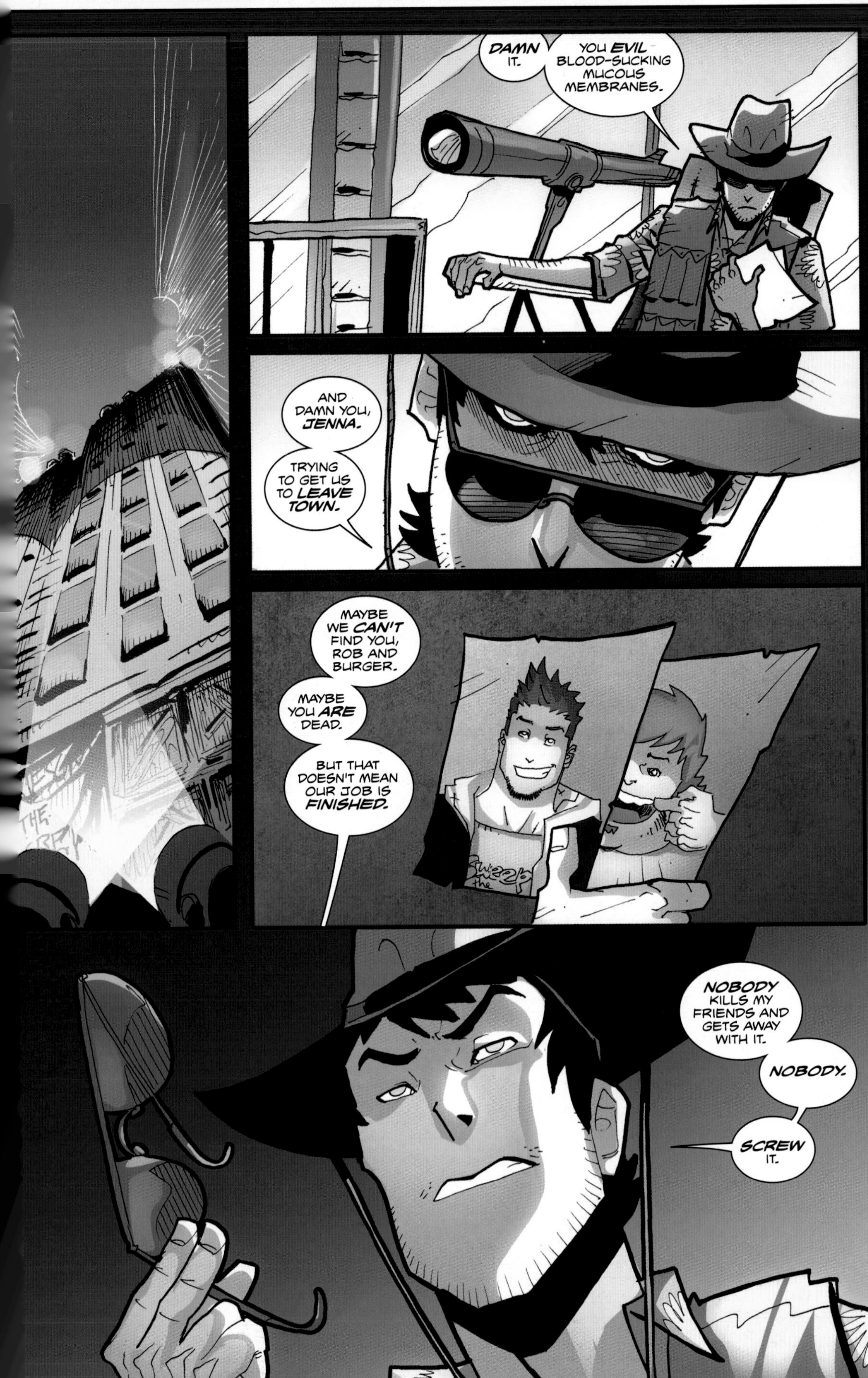
DAMN IT.
YOU EVIL BLOOD-SUCKING MUCOUS MEMBRANES.
AND DAMN YOU, JENNA.
TRYING TO GET US TO LEAVE TOWN.
MAYBE WE CAN'T FIND YOU, ROB AND BURGER.
MAYBE YOU ARE DEAD.
BUT THAT DOESN'T MEAN OUR JOB IS FINISHED.
NOBODY KILLS MY FRIENDS AND GETS AWAY WITH IT.
NOBODY.
SCREW IT.

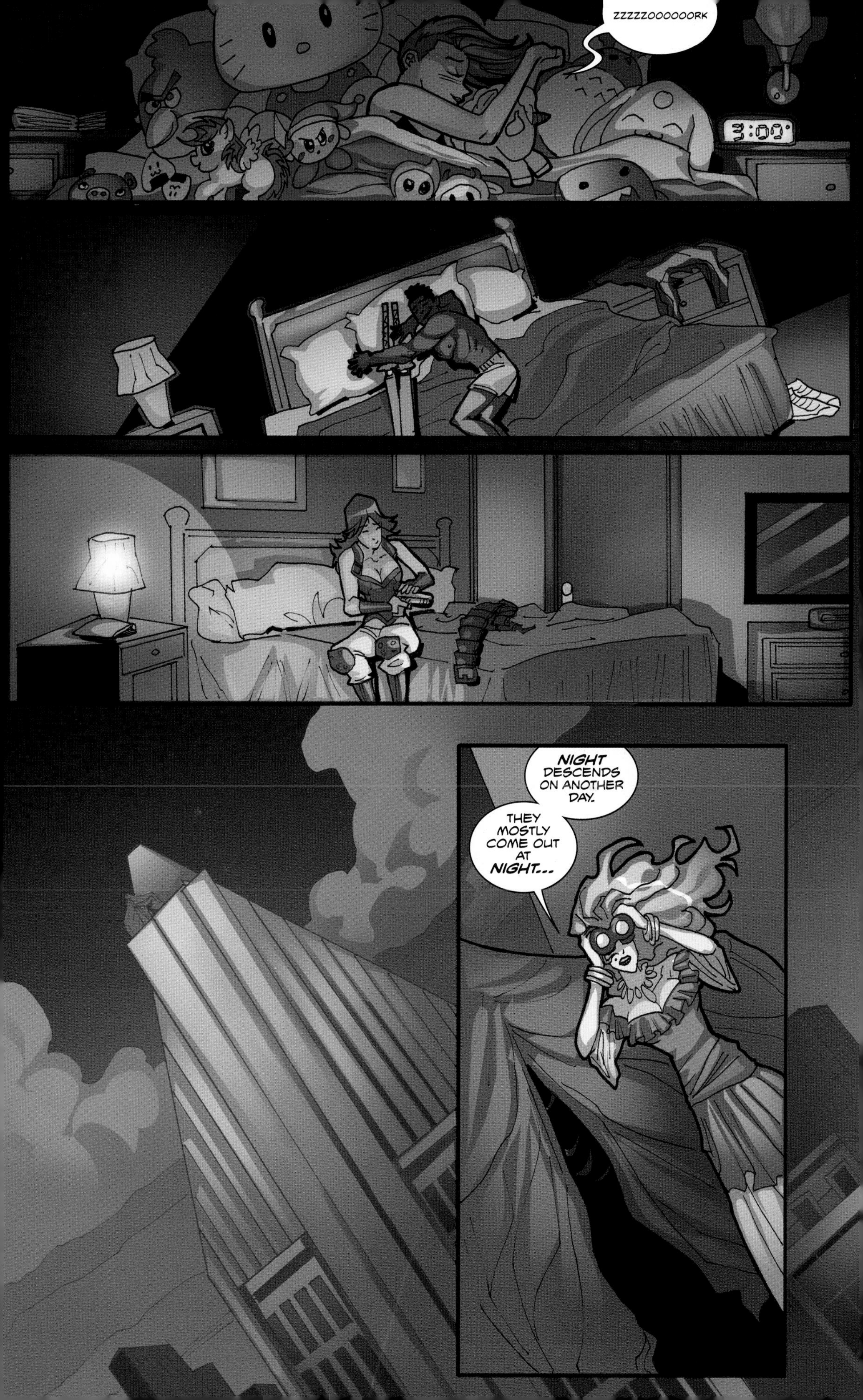
ZZZZZOOOOOORK
3:00
NIGHT DESCENDS ON ANOTHER DAY.
THEY MOSTLY COME OUT AT NIGHT...

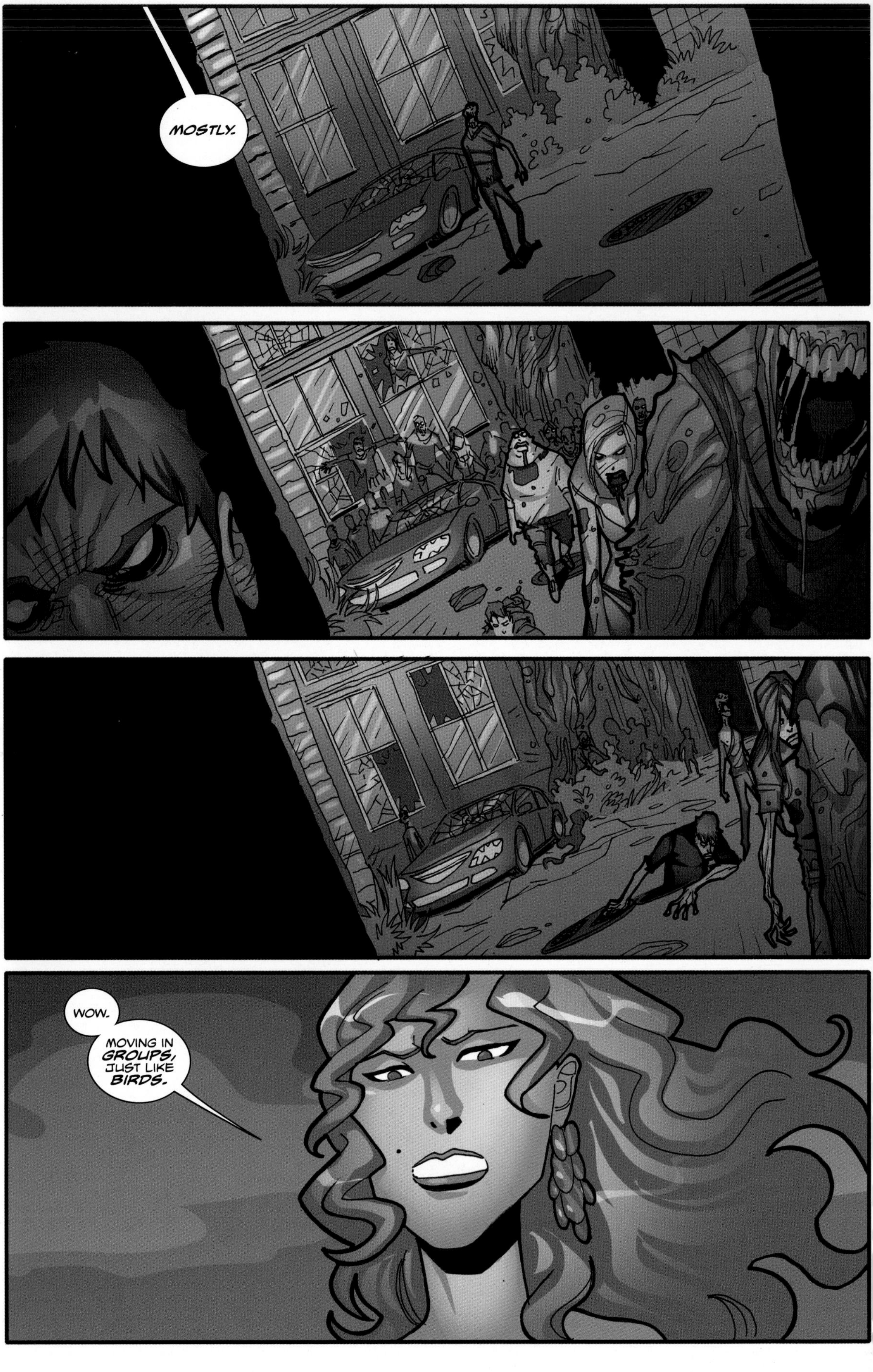
MOSTLY.
WOW.
MOVING IN GROUPS, JUST LIKE BIRDS.

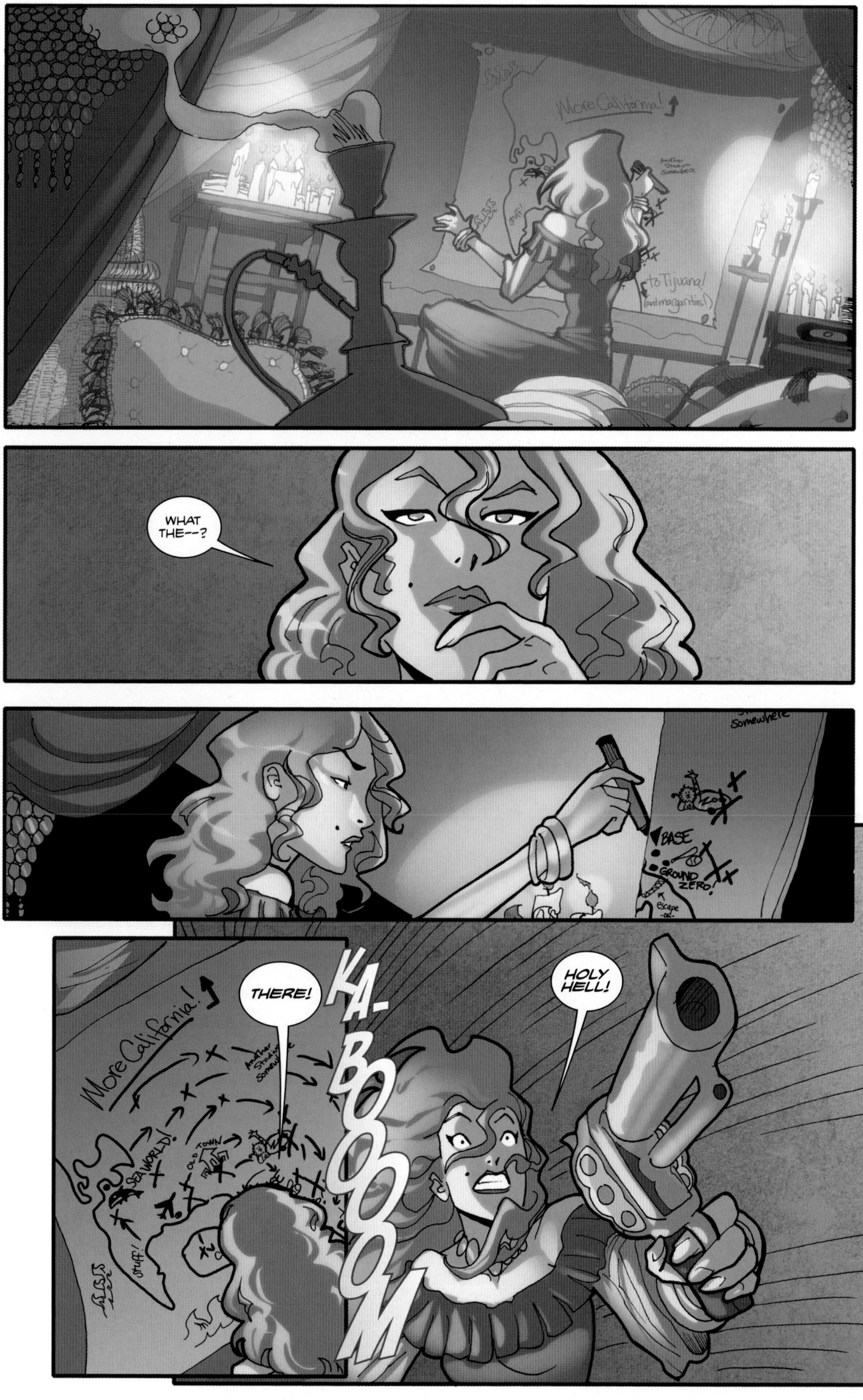
More California!
To Tijuana!
(and margaritas!)
WHAT THE--?
Somewhere
BASE
GROUND ZERO!
THERE!
KA-BOOOOOM
HOLY HELL!
More California!
SEA WORLD!
OLD TOWN
STUFF!

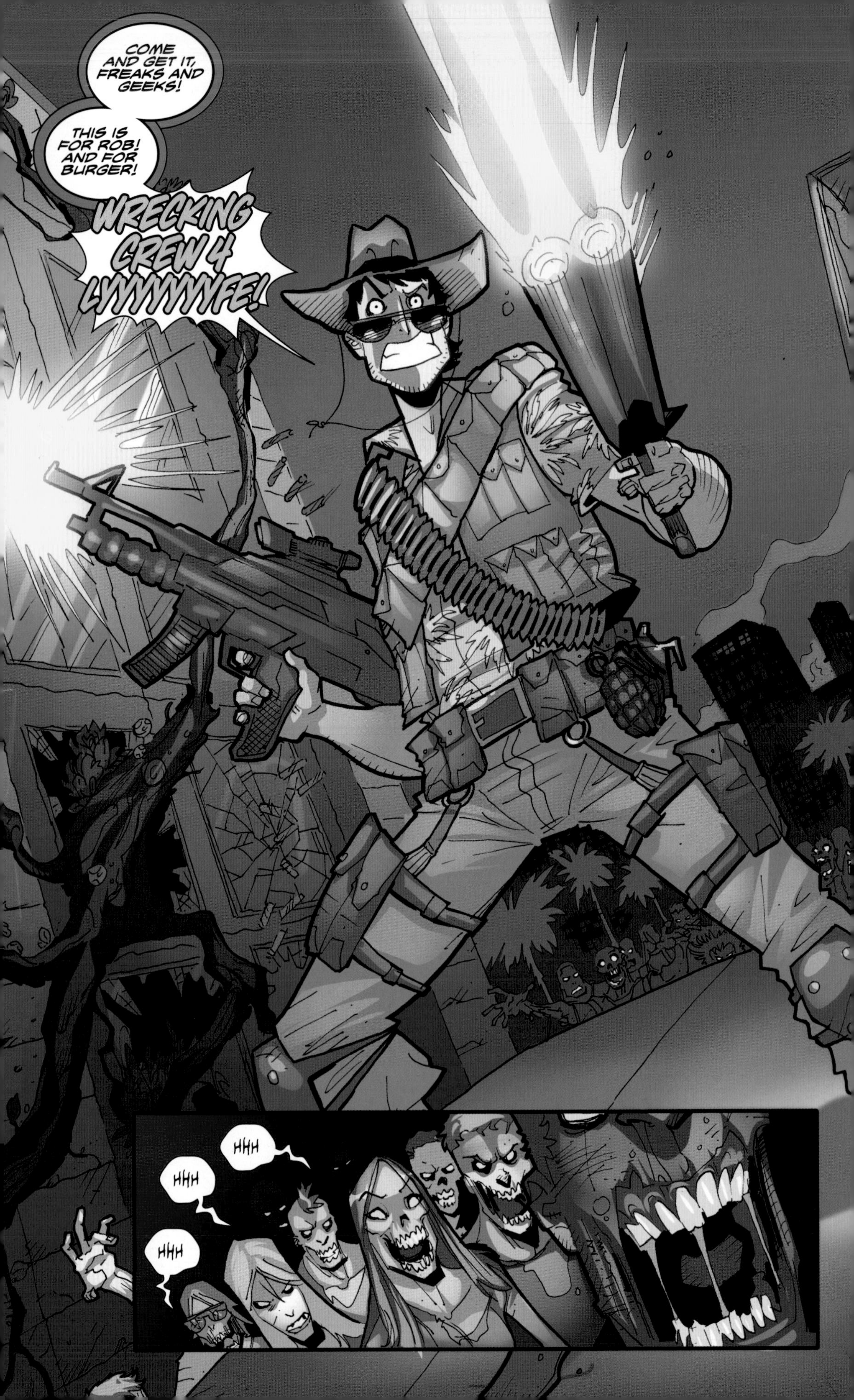
COME AND GET IT, FREAKS AND GEEKS!
THIS IS FOR ROB! AND FOR BURGER!
WRECKING CREW 4 LYYYYYYYFE!
HHH
HHH
HHH

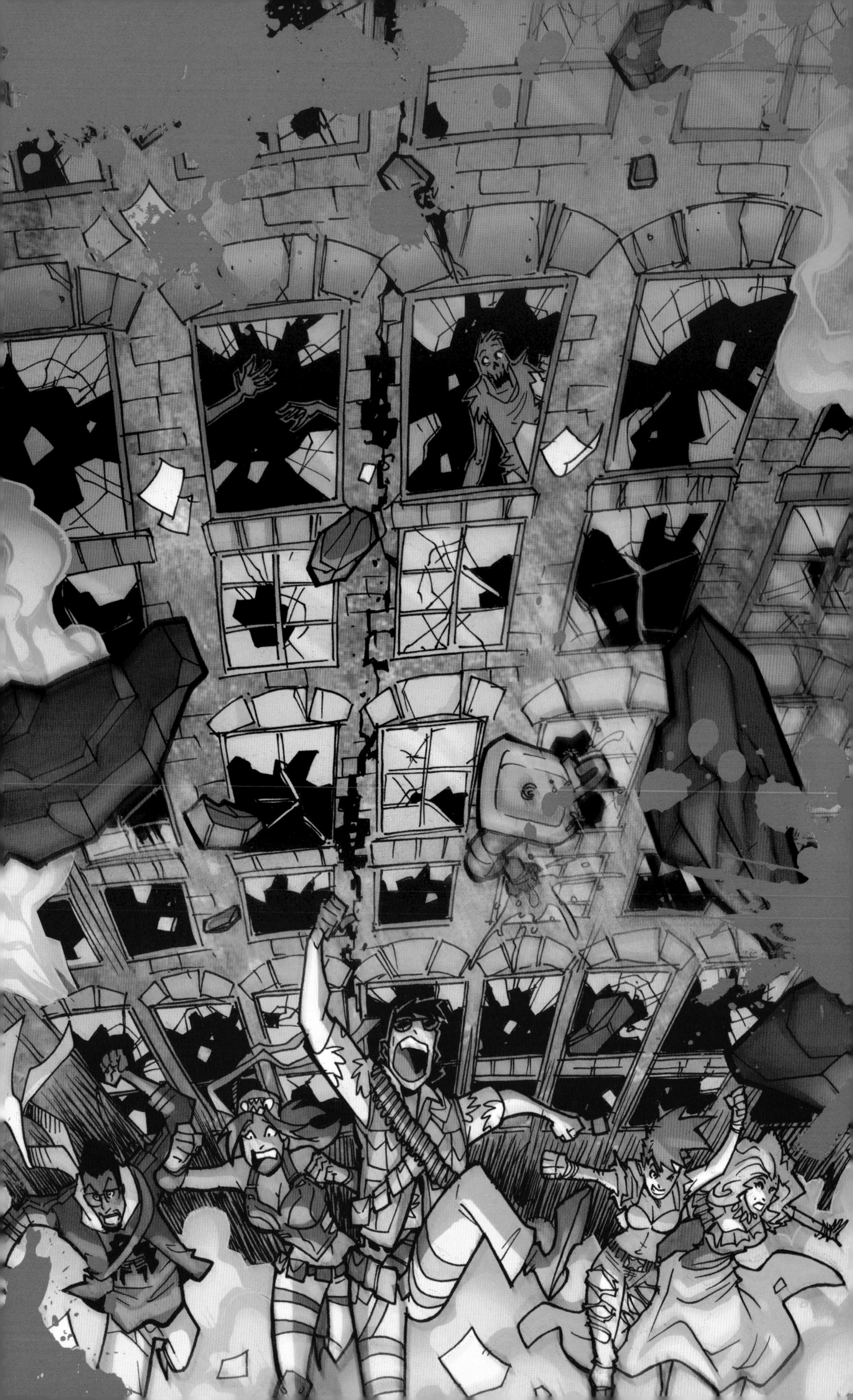

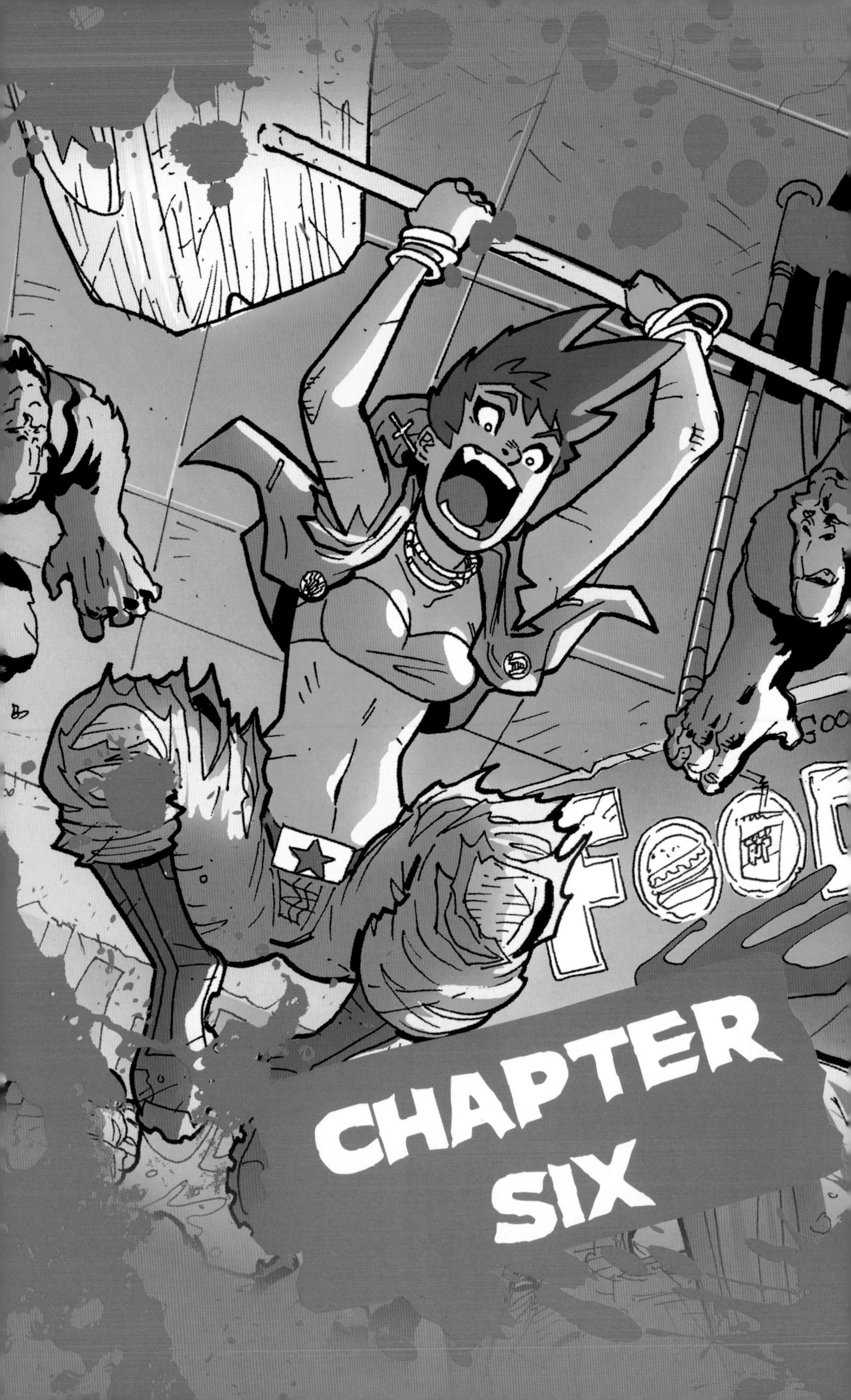

# CHAPTER SIX

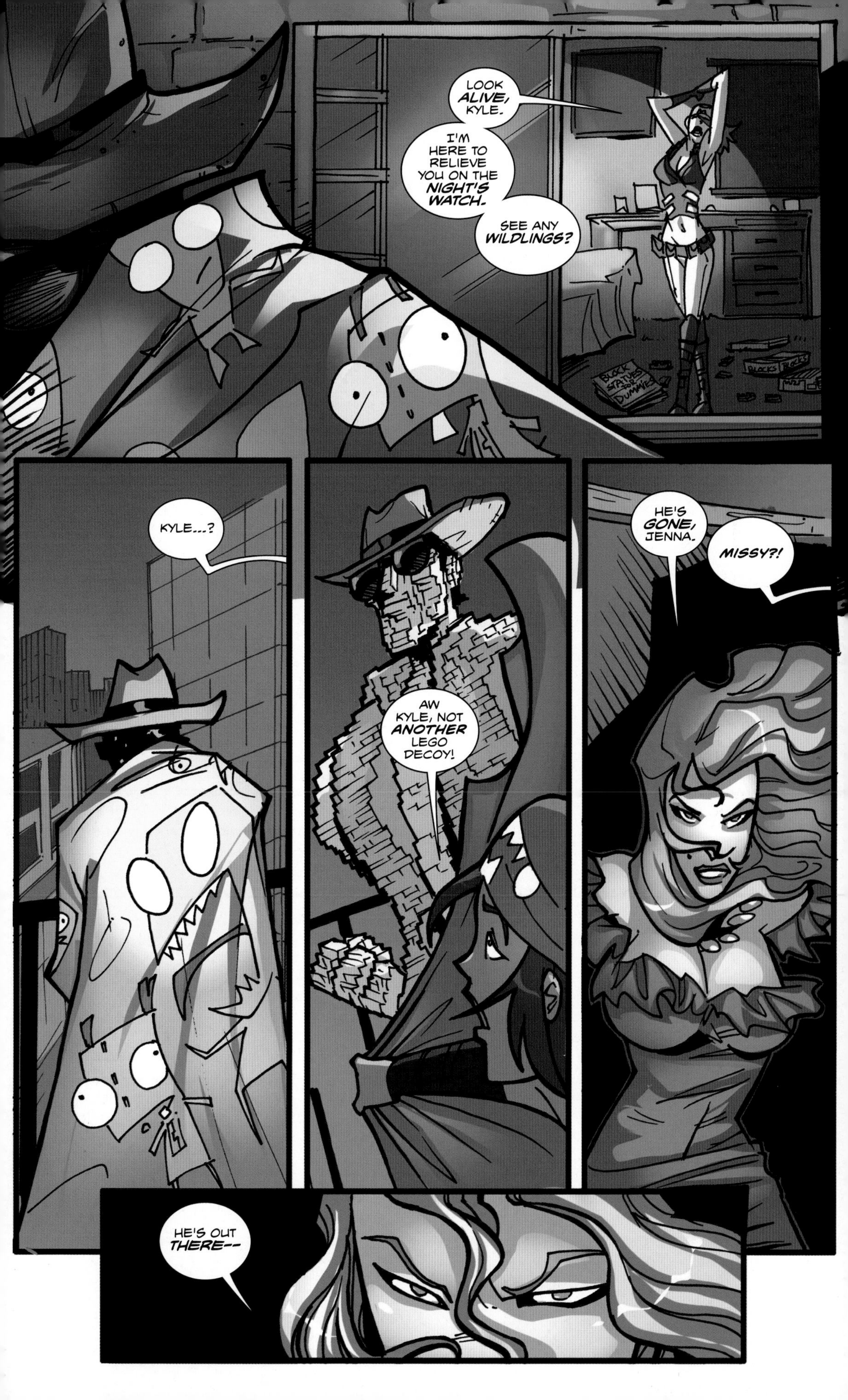
LOOK ALIVE, KYLE.
I'M HERE TO RELIEVE YOU ON THE NIGHT'S WATCH.
SEE ANY WILDLINGS?
BLOCK STATUES FOR DUMMIES
BLOCKS
BLOCKS
KYLE...?
AW KYLE, NOT ANOTHER LEGO DECOY!
HE'S GONE, JENNA.
MISSY?!
HE'S OUT THERE--

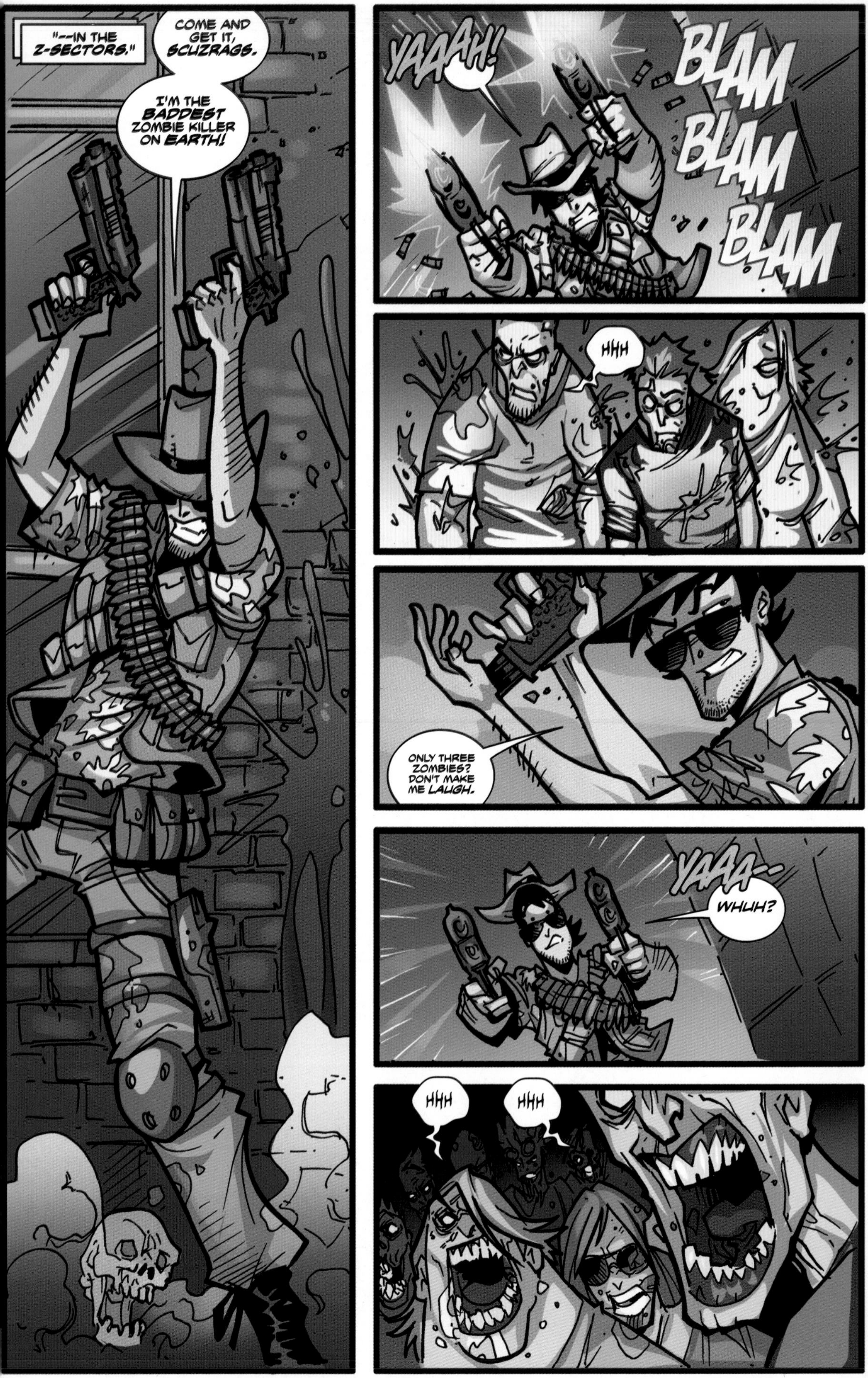
"--IN THE Z-SECTORS."
COME AND GET IT, SCUZRAGS.
I'M THE BADDEST ZOMBIE KILLER ON EARTH!
YAAAH!
BLAM BLAM BLAM
HHH
ONLY THREE ZOMBIES? DON'T MAKE ME LAUGH.
YAAA--
WHUH?
HHH
HHH

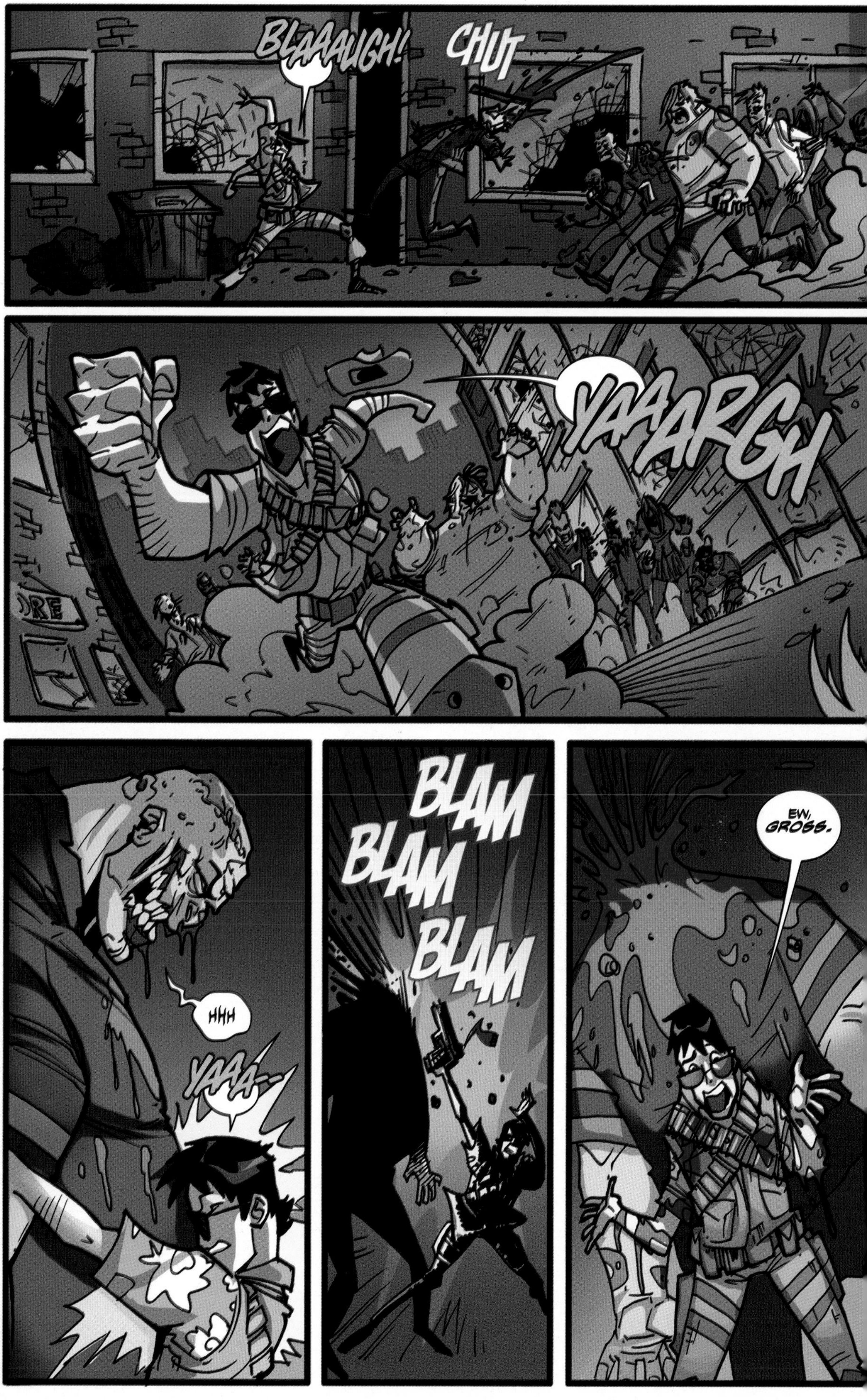
BLAAAUGH!
CHUT
YAAARGH
HHH
YAAA--
BLAM
BLAM
BLAM
EW, GROSS.

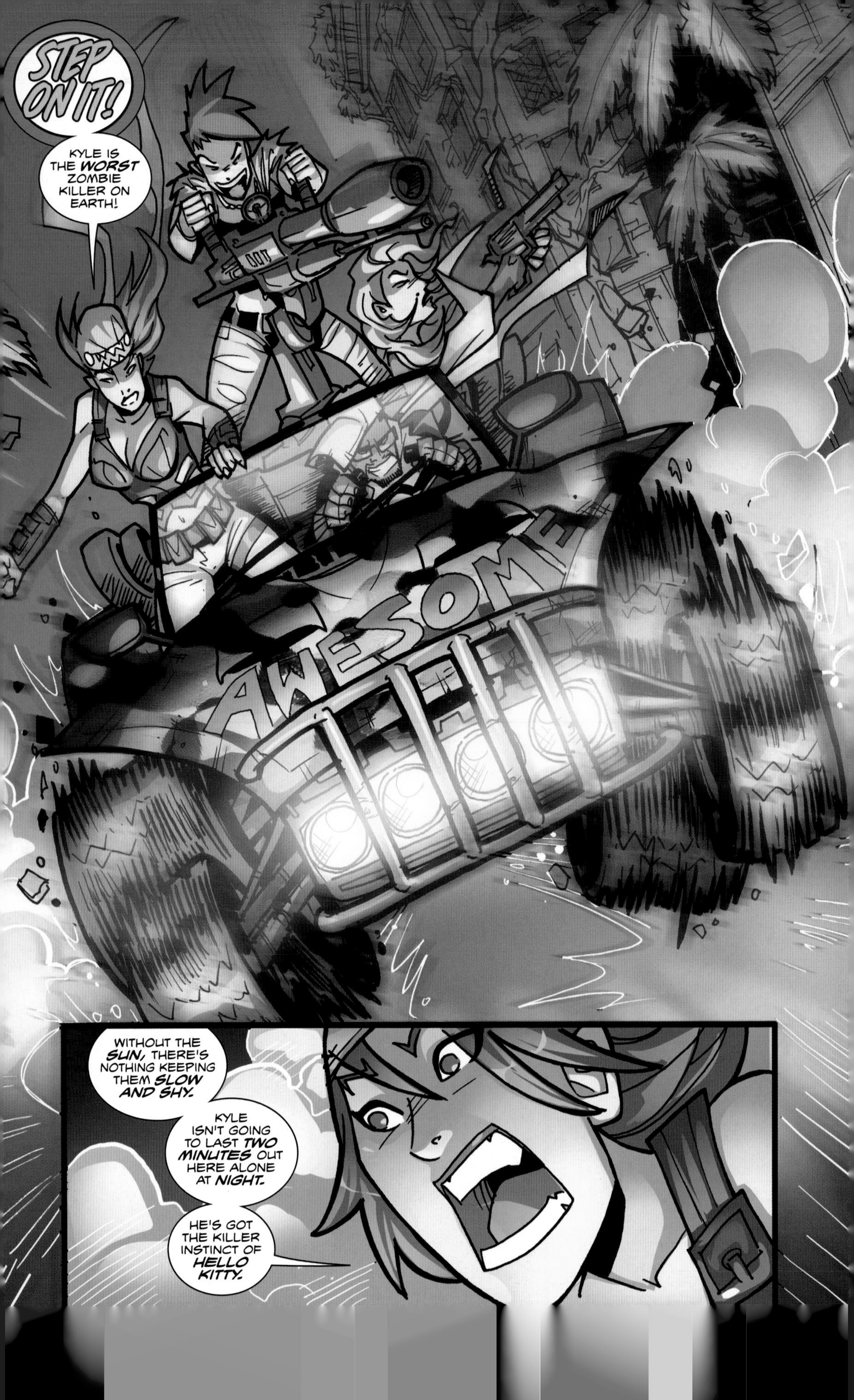
STEP ON IT!
KYLE IS THE WORST ZOMBIE KILLER ON EARTH!
AWESOME
WITHOUT THE SUN, THERE'S NOTHING KEEPING THEM SLOW AND SHY.
KYLE ISN'T GOING TO LAST TWO MINUTES OUT HERE ALONE AT NIGHT.
HE'S GOT THE KILLER INSTINCT OF HELLO KITTY.

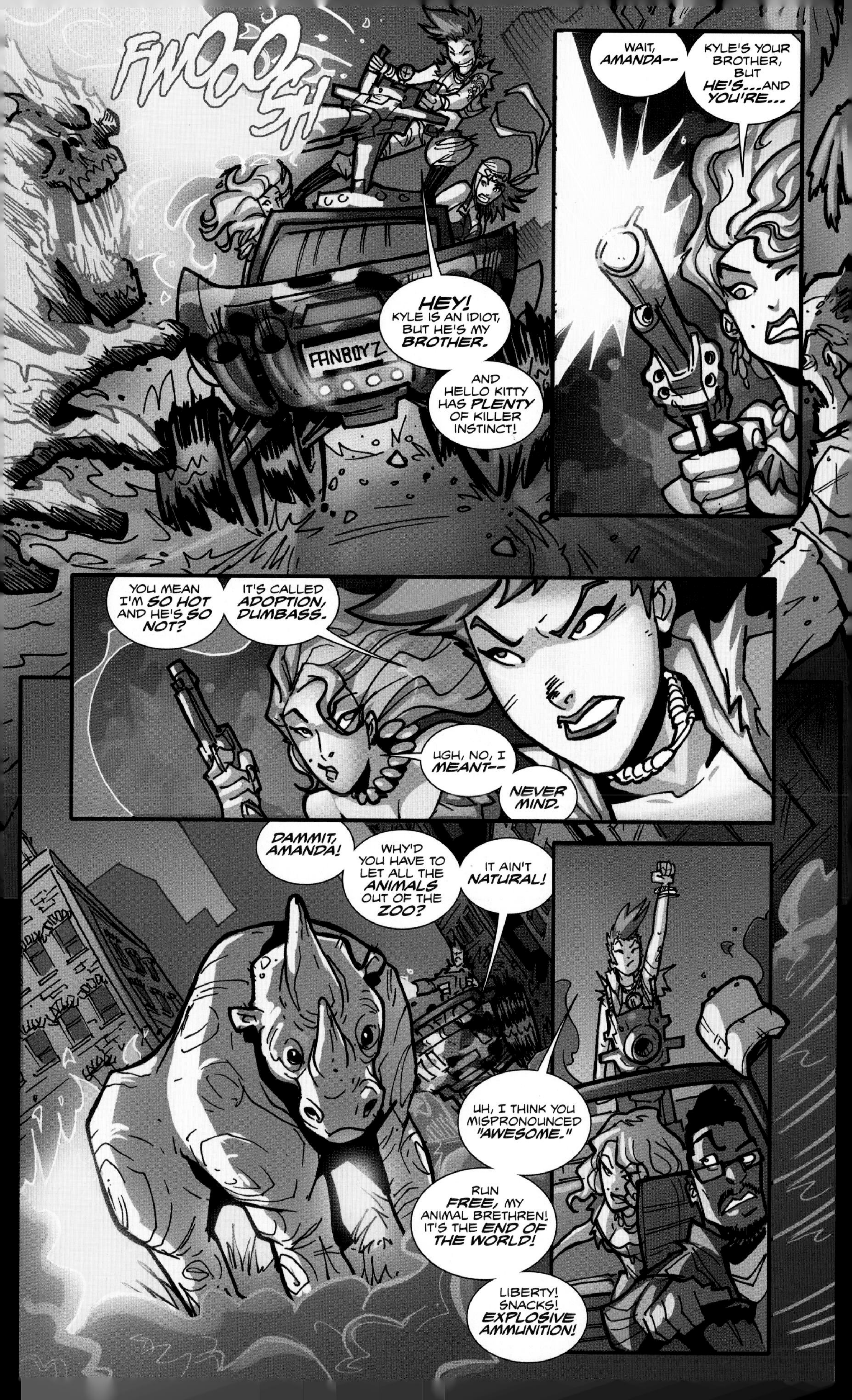
FWOOOOOSH
FANBOYZ
HEY! KYLE IS AN IDIOT, BUT HE'S MY BROTHER.
AND HELLO KITTY HAS PLENTY OF KILLER INSTINCT!
WAIT, AMANDA--
KYLE'S YOUR BROTHER, BUT HE'S...AND YOU'RE...
YOU MEAN I'M SO HOT AND HE'S SO NOT?
IT'S CALLED ADOPTION, DUMBASS.
UGH, NO, I MEANT--
NEVER MIND.
DAMMIT, AMANDA!
WHY'D YOU HAVE TO LET ALL THE ANIMALS OUT OF THE ZOO?
IT AIN'T NATURAL!
UH, I THINK YOU MISPRONOUNCED "AWESOME."
RUN FREE, MY ANIMAL BRETHREN! IT'S THE END OF THE WORLD!
LIBERTY! SNACKS! EXPLOSIVE AMMUNITION!

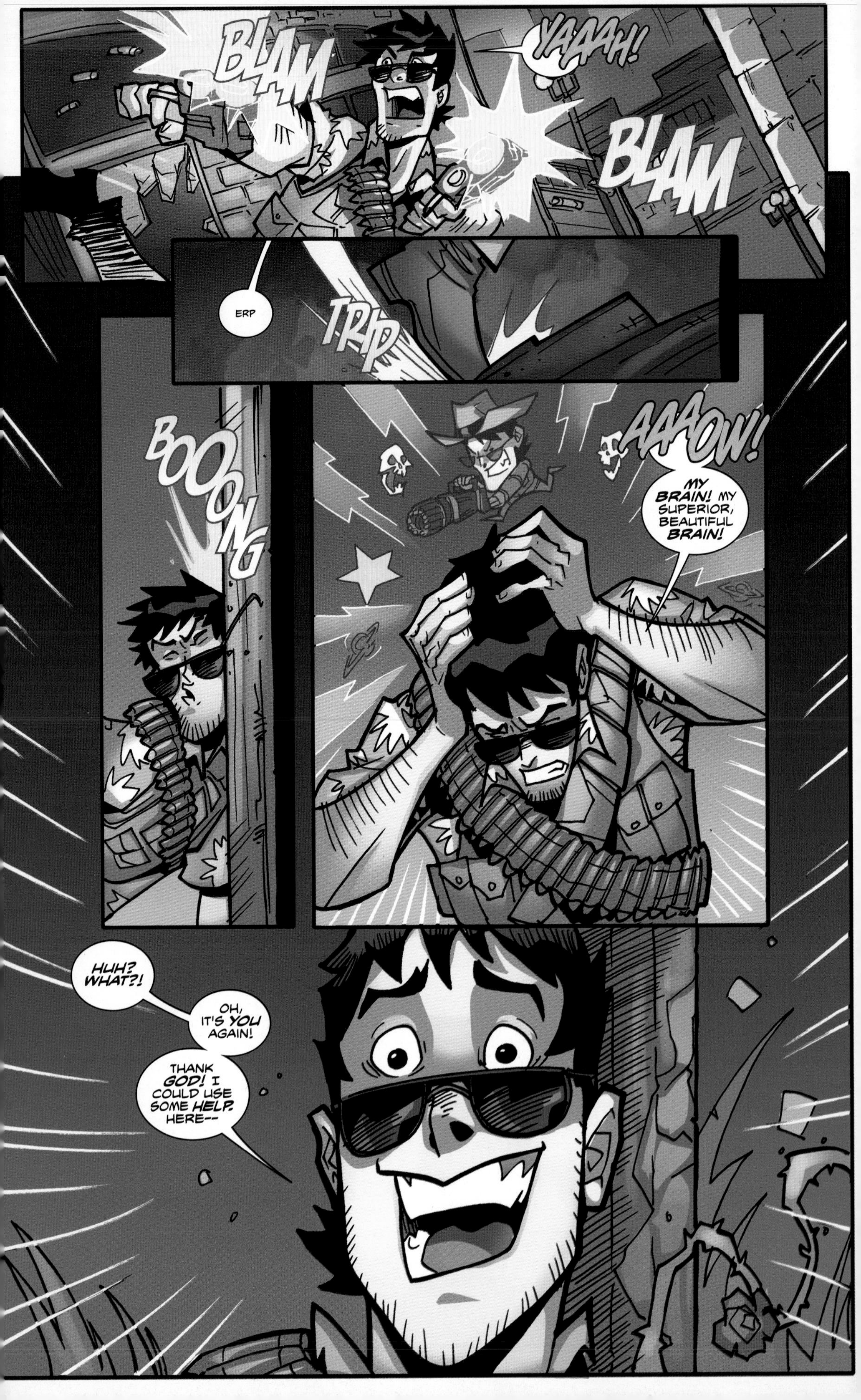
BLAM
YAAAH!
BLAM
ERP
TRIP
BOOOONG
AAAOW!
MY BRAIN! MY SUPERIOR, BEAUTIFUL BRAIN!
HUH? WHAT?!
OH, IT'S YOU AGAIN!
THANK GOD! I COULD USE SOME HELP HERE--

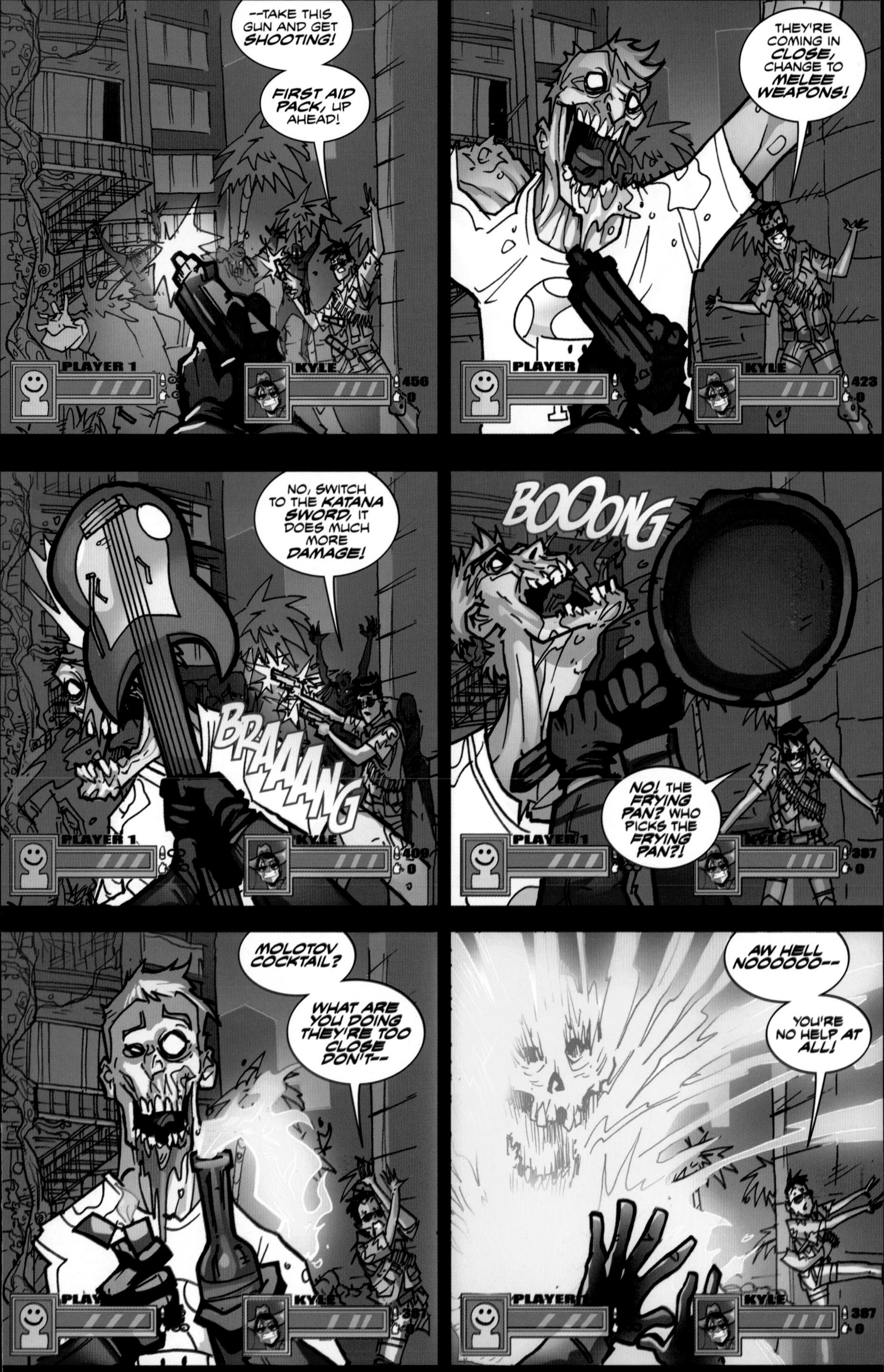
--TAKE THIS GUN AND GET SHOOTING!
FIRST AID PACK, UP AHEAD!
PLAYER 1
KYLE
456
0
THEY'RE COMING IN CLOSE, CHANGE TO MELEE WEAPONS!
PLAYER
KYLE
423
0
NO, SWITCH TO THE KATANA SWORD, IT DOES MUCH MORE DAMAGE!
BRAAAANG
PLAYER 1
KYLE
0
BOOOONG
NO! THE FRYING PAN? WHO PICKS THE FRYING PAN?!
PLAYER 1
387
0
MOLOTOV COCKTAIL?
WHAT ARE YOU DOING THEY'RE TOO CLOSE DON'T--
KYLE
AW HELL NOOOOOO--
YOU'RE NO HELP AT ALL!
PLAYER
KYLE
387
0

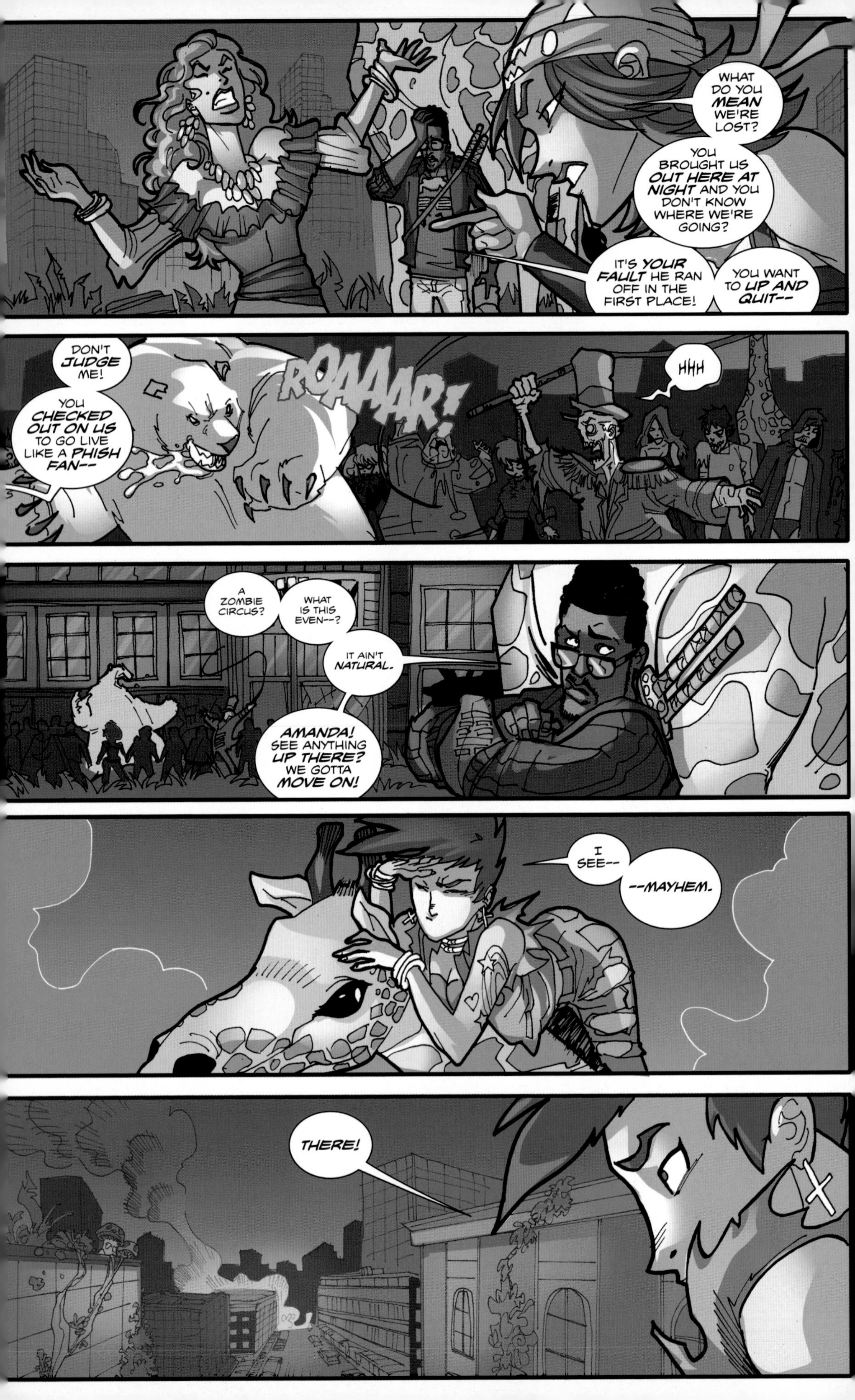
WHAT DO YOU MEAN WE'RE LOST?
YOU BROUGHT US OUT HERE AT NIGHT AND YOU DON'T KNOW WHERE WE'RE GOING?
IT'S YOUR FAULT HE RAN OFF IN THE FIRST PLACE!
YOU WANT TO UP AND QUIT--
DON'T JUDGE ME!
YOU CHECKED OUT ON US TO GO LIVE LIKE A PHISH FAN--
ROAAAAR!
HHH
A ZOMBIE CIRCUS?
WHAT IS THIS EVEN--?
IT AIN'T NATURAL.
AMANDA! SEE ANYTHING UP THERE? WE GOTTA MOVE ON!
I SEE--
--MAYHEM.
THERE!

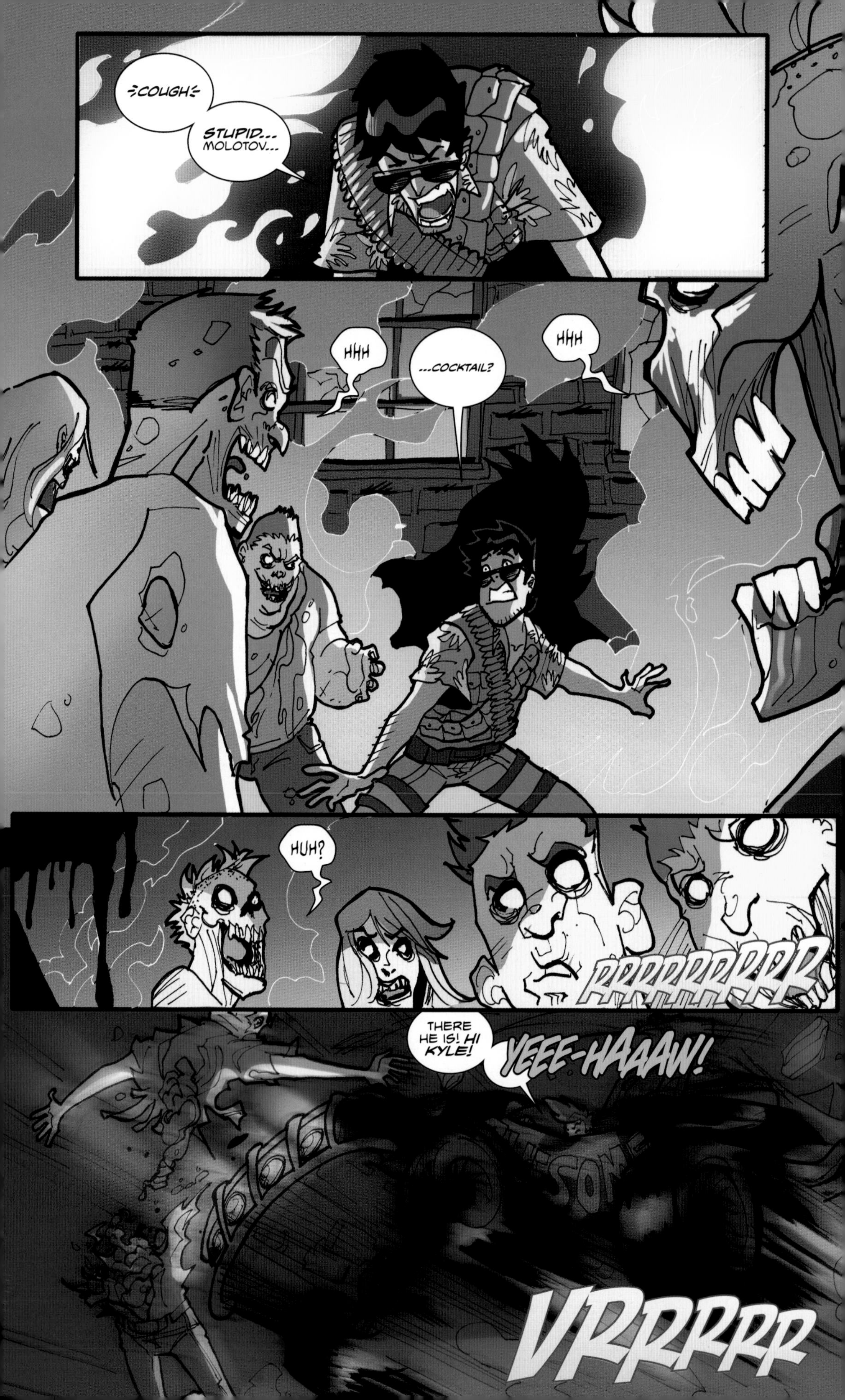

COUGH
STUPID... MOLOTOV...
HHH
...COCKTAIL?
HHH
HUH?
RRRRRRRRRR
THERE HE IS! HI KYLE!
YEEE-HAAAW!
VRRRRR

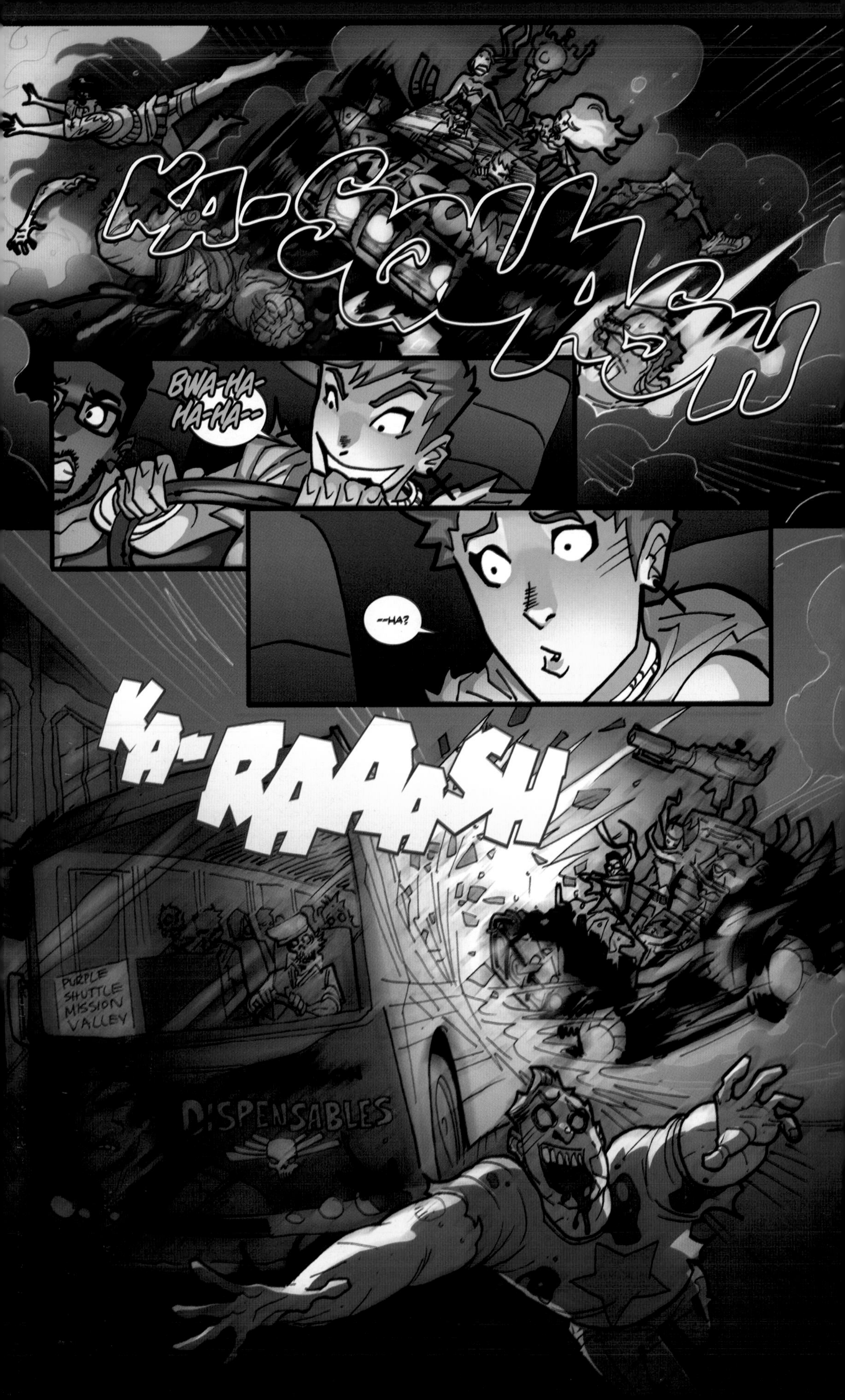
BWA-HA-HA-HA--
--HA?
KA-RAAASH
PURPLE SHUTTLE MISSION VALLEY
DISPENSABLES

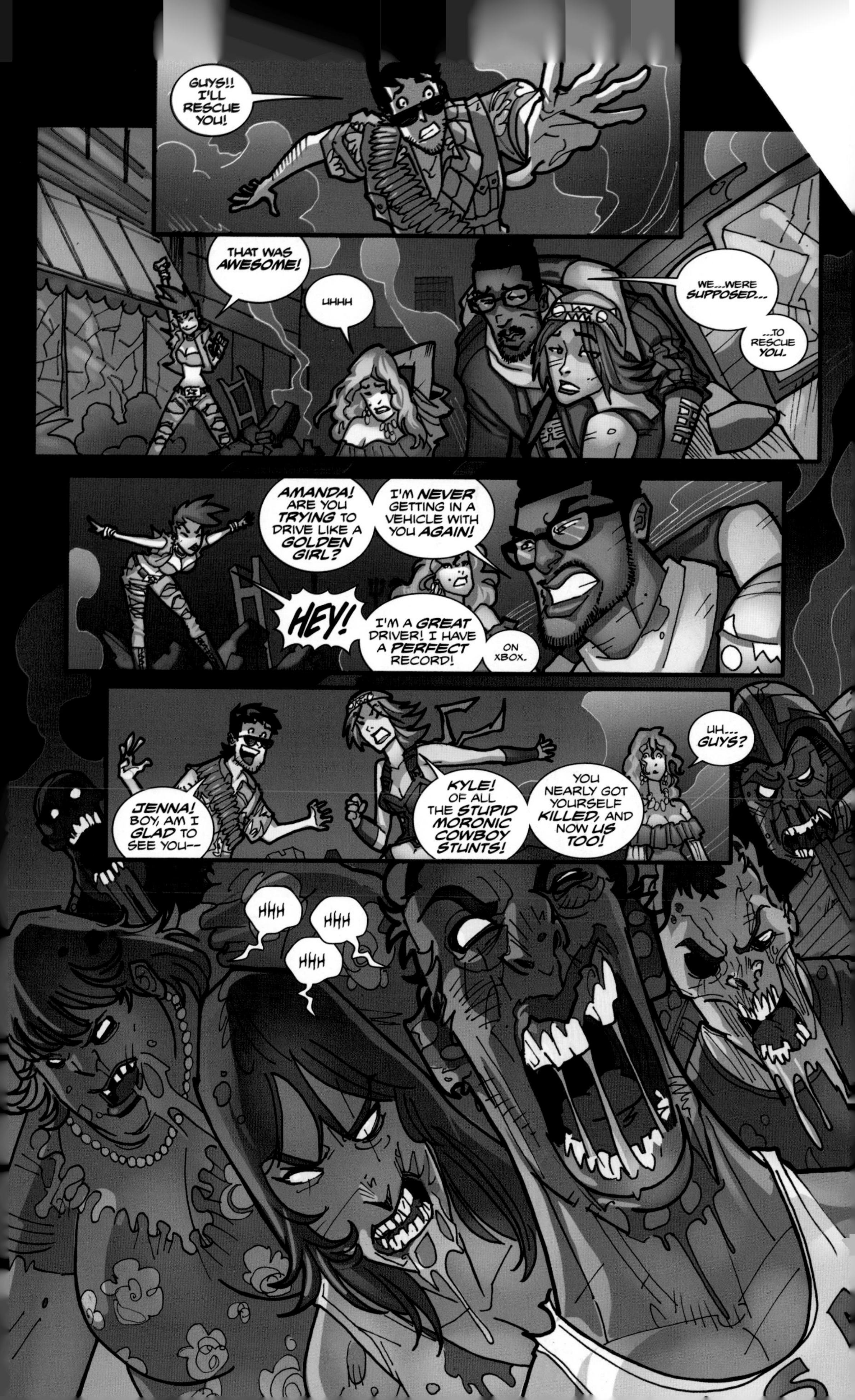
GUYS!! I'LL RESCUE YOU!
THAT WAS AWESOME!
UHHH
WE...WERE SUPPOSED...
...TO RESCUE YOU.
AMANDA! ARE YOU TRYING TO DRIVE LIKE A GOLDEN GIRL?
I'M NEVER GETTING IN A VEHICLE WITH YOU AGAIN!
HEY!
I'M A GREAT DRIVER! I HAVE A PERFECT RECORD!
ON XBOX.
JENNA! BOY, AM I GLAD TO SEE YOU--
KYLE! OF ALL THE STUPID MORONIC COWBOY STUNTS!
YOU NEARLY GOT YOURSELF KILLED, AND NOW US TOO!
UH... GUYS?
HHH
HHH
HHH

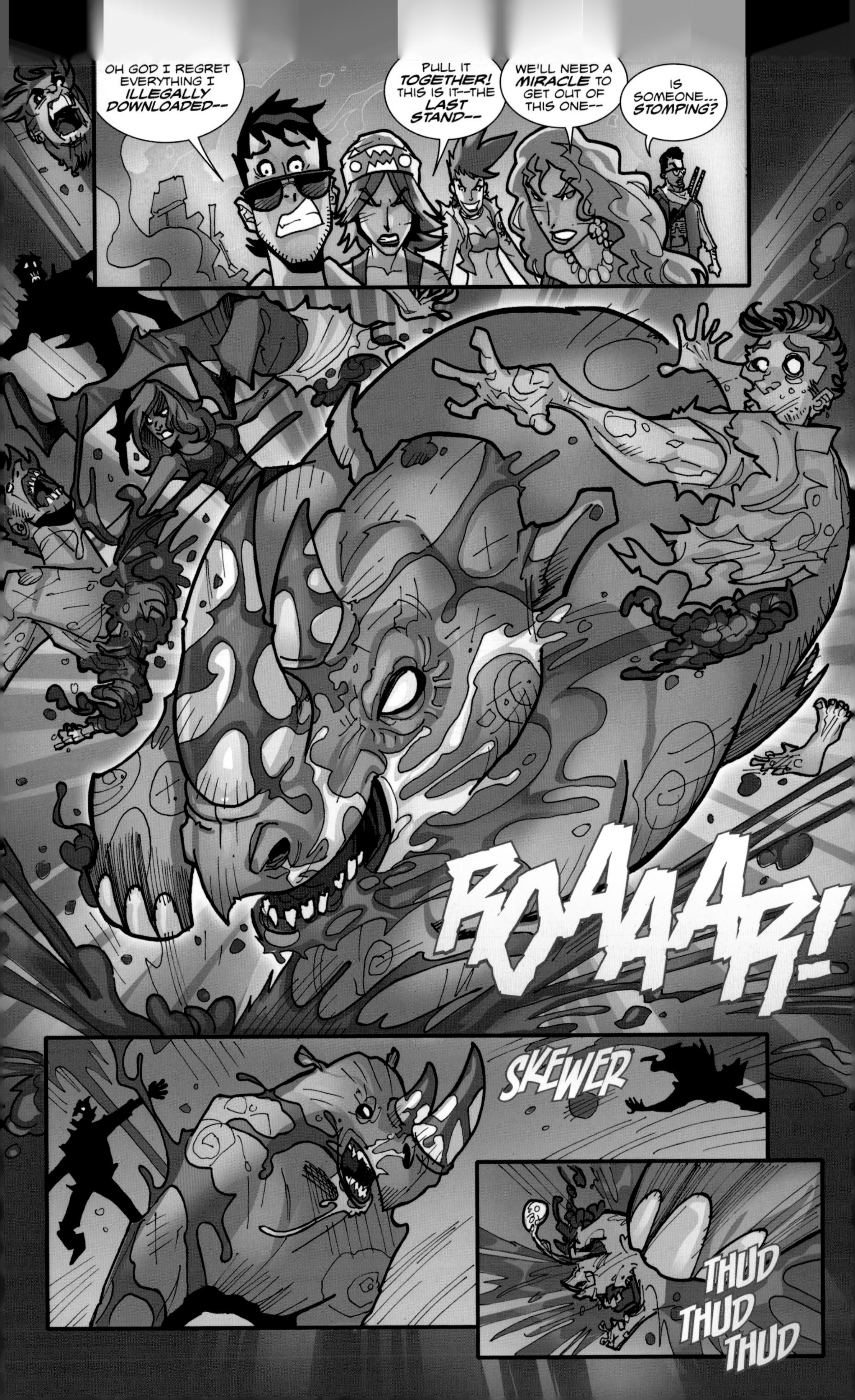
OH GOD I REGRET EVERYTHING I ILLEGALLY DOWNLOADED--
PULL IT TOGETHER! THIS IS IT--THE LAST STAND--
WE'LL NEED A MIRACLE TO GET OUT OF THIS ONE--
IS SOMEONE... STOMPING?
ROAAAR!
SKEWER
THUD
THUD
THUD

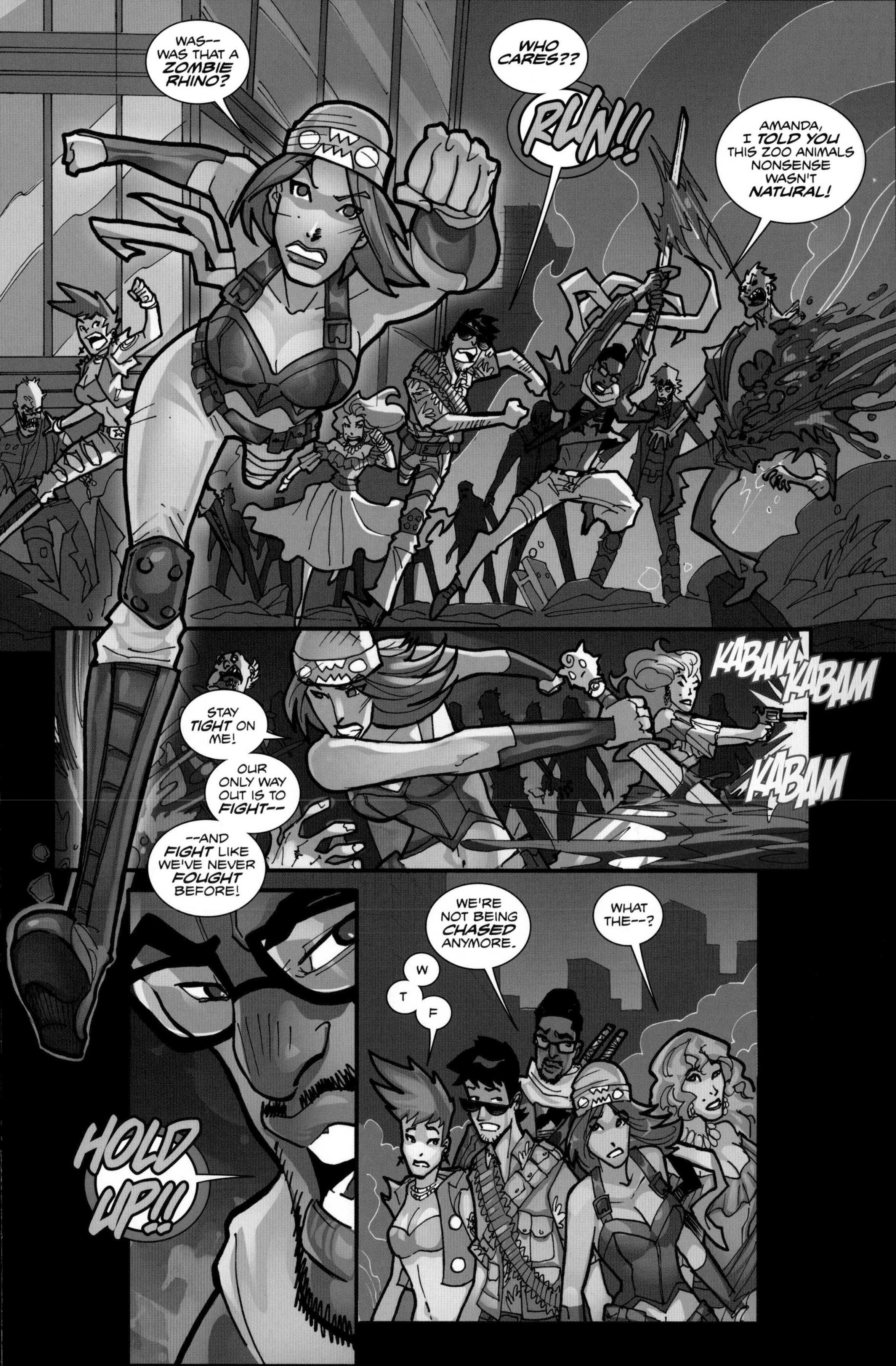
WAS-- WAS THAT A ZOMBIE RHINO?
WHO CARES??
RUN!!
AMANDA, I TOLD YOU THIS ZOO ANIMALS NONSENSE WASN'T NATURAL!
KABAM KABAM
KABAM
STAY TIGHT ON ME!
OUR ONLY WAY OUT IS TO FIGHT--
--AND FIGHT LIKE WE'VE NEVER FOUGHT BEFORE!
HOLD UP!!
WE'RE NOT BEING CHASED ANYMORE.
WHAT THE--?
W
T
F

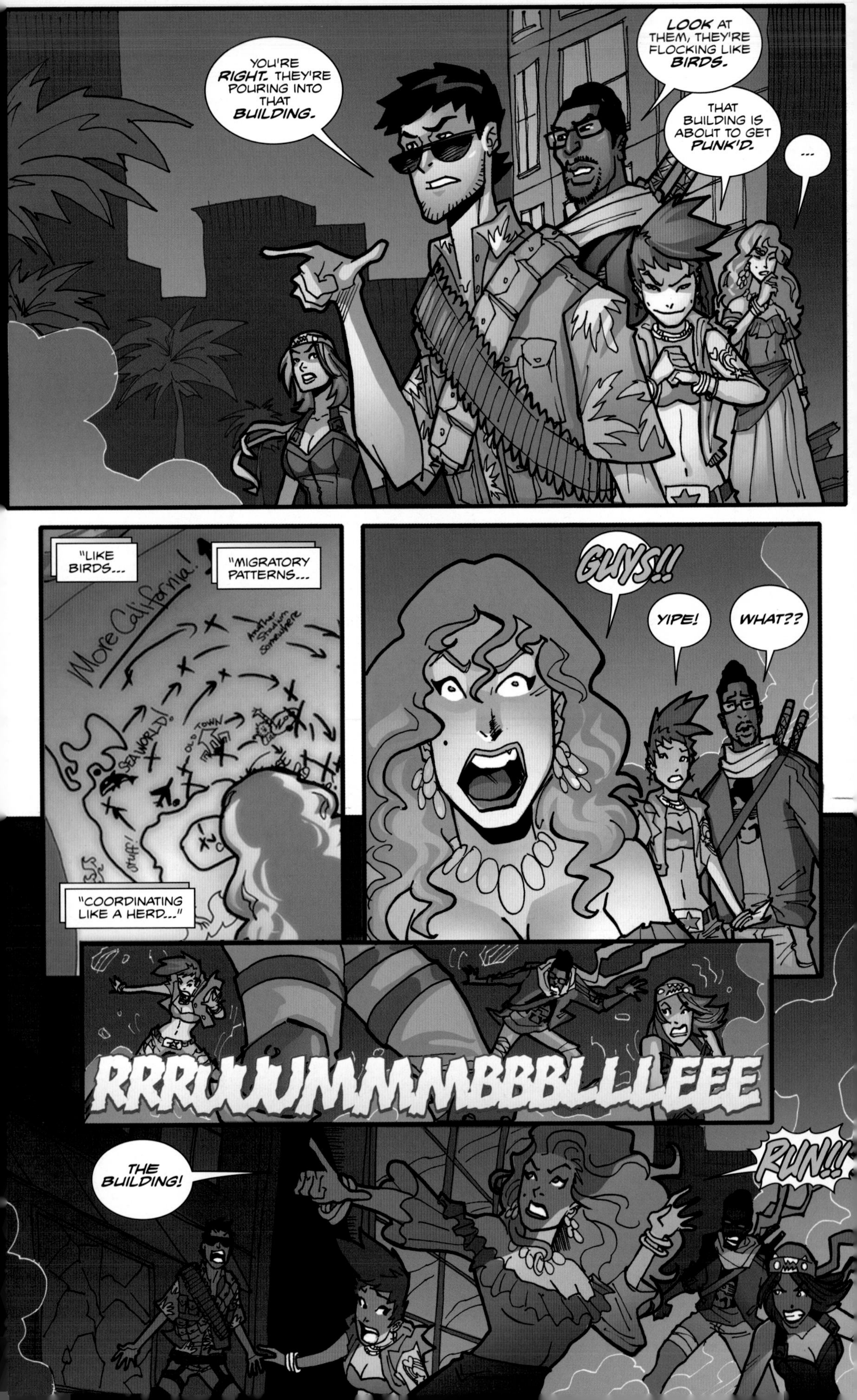

YOU'RE RIGHT. THEY'RE POURING INTO THAT BUILDING.
LOOK AT THEM, THEY'RE FLOCKING LIKE BIRDS.
THAT BUILDING IS ABOUT TO GET PUNK'D.
...
"LIKE BIRDS...
"MIGRATORY PATTERNS...
More California!
"COORDINATING LIKE A HERD..."
GUYS!!
YIPE!
WHAT??
RRRUUUMMMMBBBLLLEEE
THE BUILDING!
RUN!!

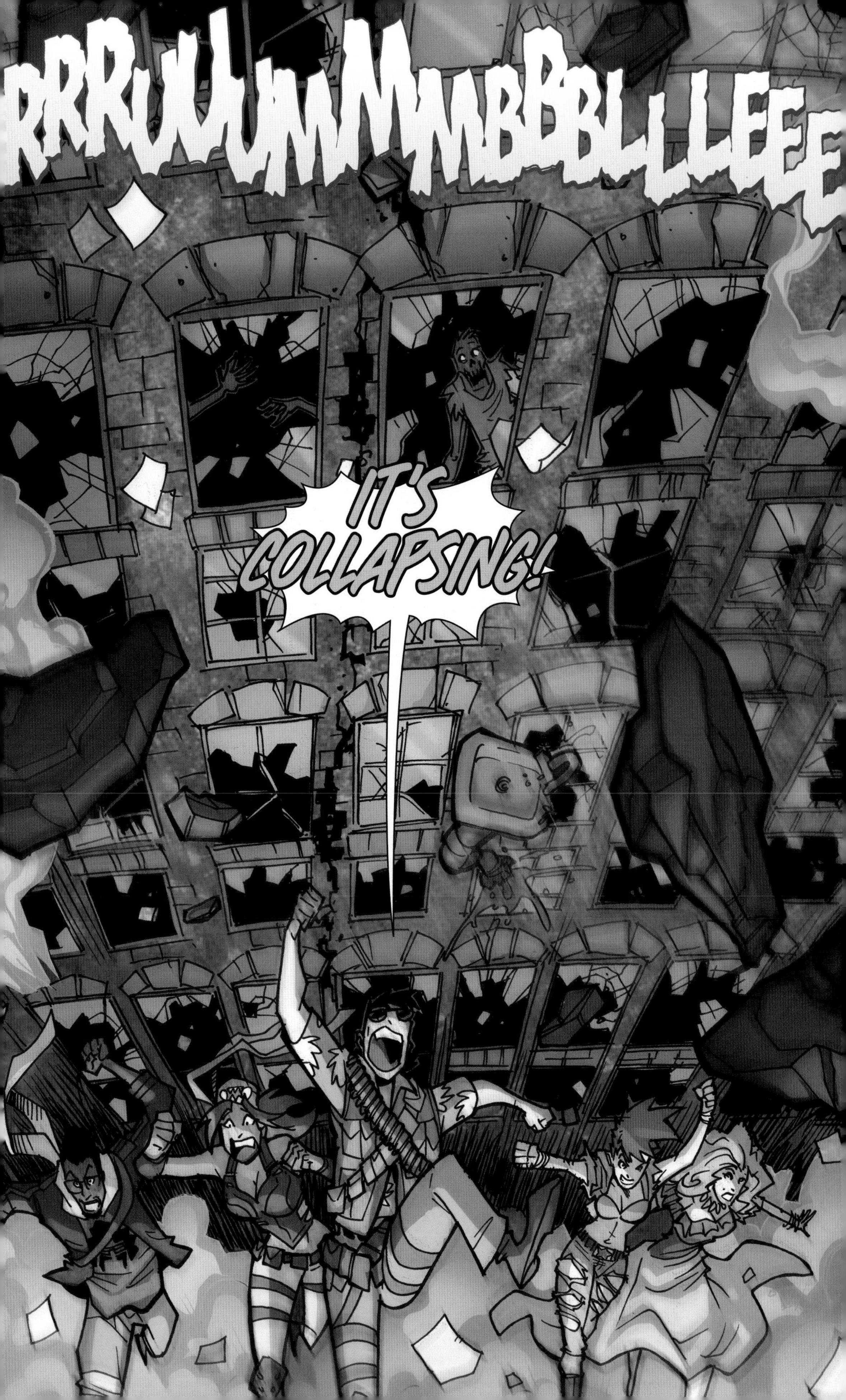
RRRUUUMMMBBBLLLEEE
IT'S COLLAPSING!

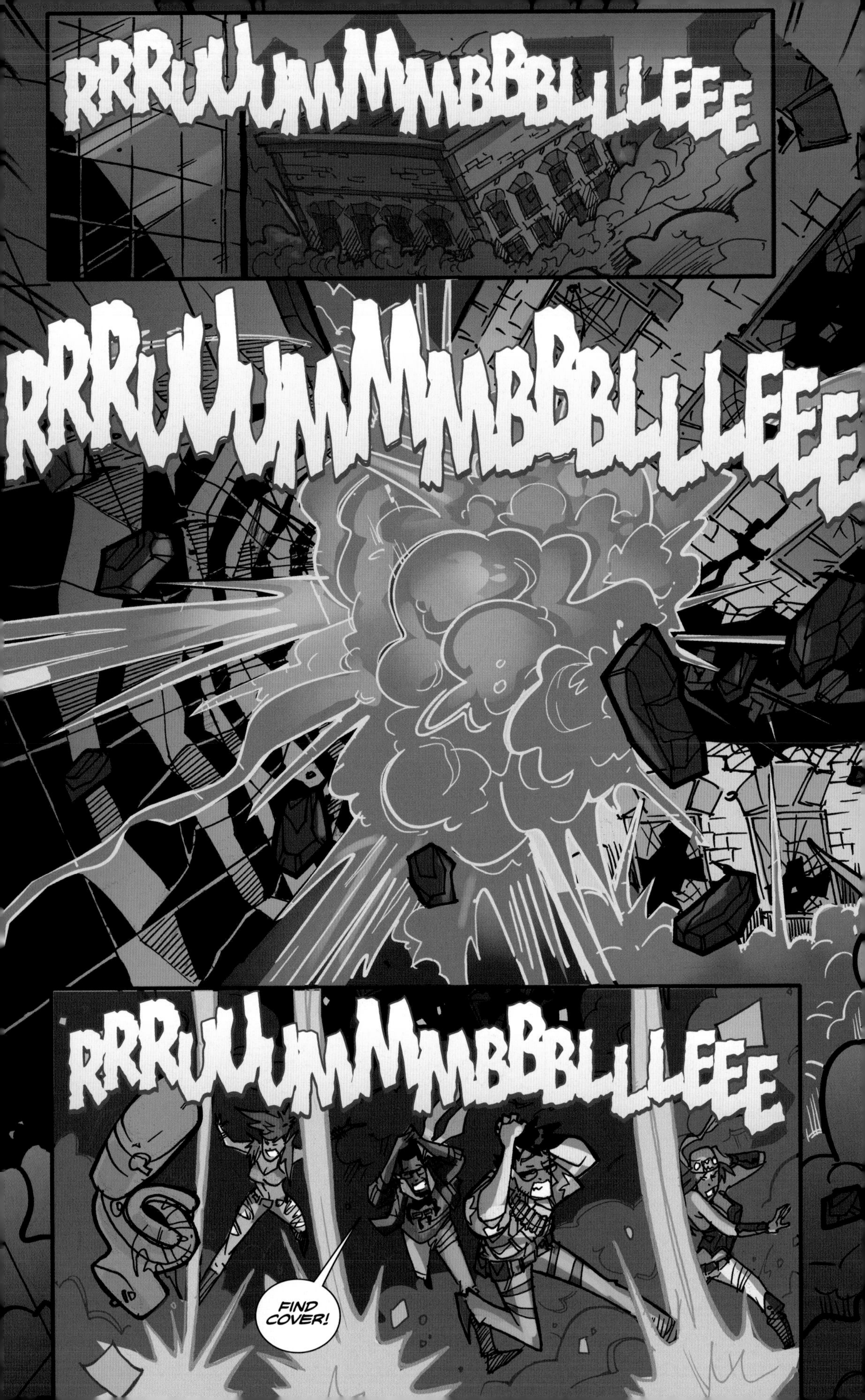
RRRUUUMMMBBBLLLEEE
RRRUUUMMMBBBLLLEEE
RRRUUUMMMBBBLLLEEE
FIND COVER!

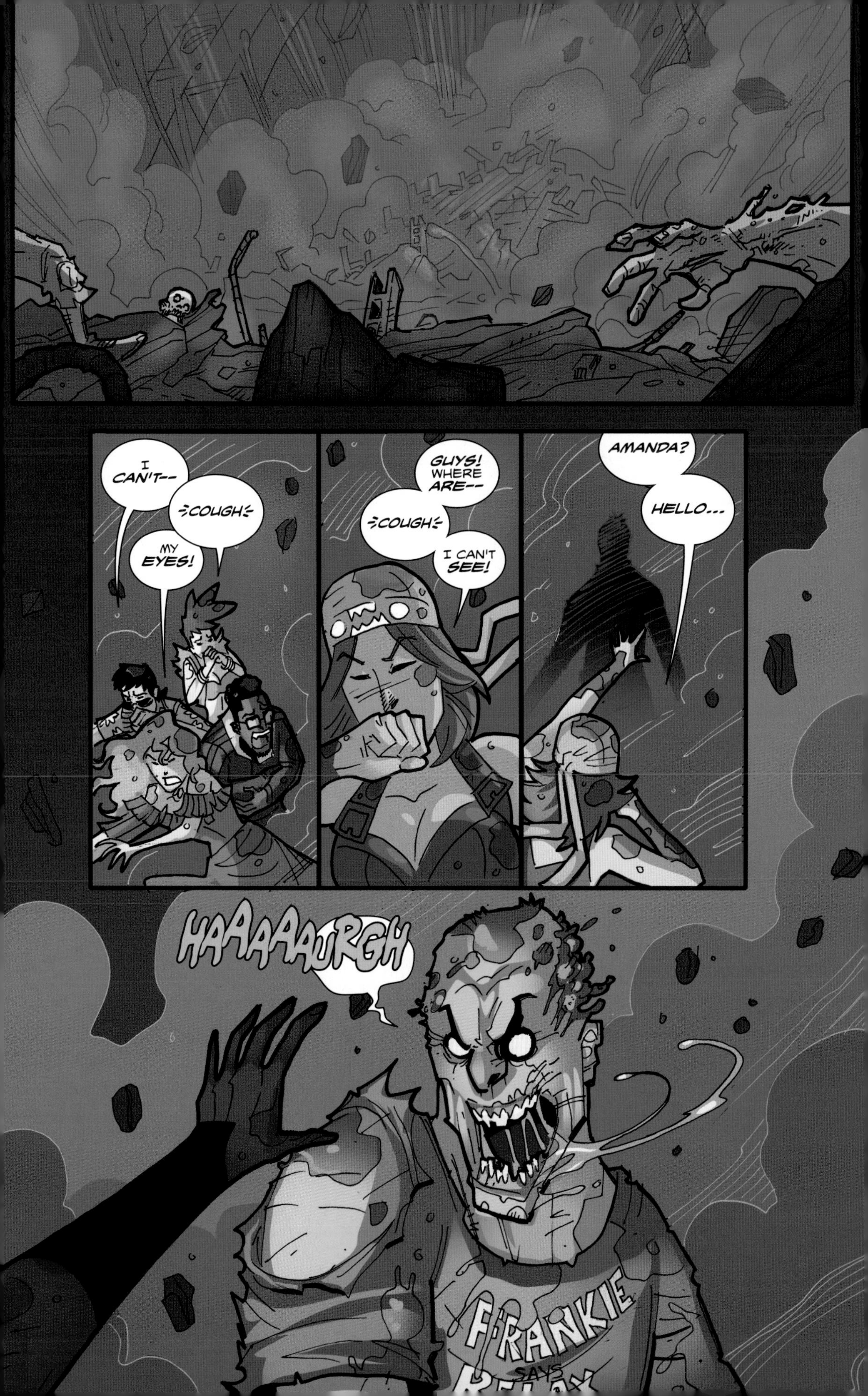
I CAN'T--
COUGH
MY EYES!
GUYS! WHERE ARE--
COUGH
I CAN'T SEE!
AMANDA?
HELLO...
HAAAAAURGH
FRANKIE SAYS

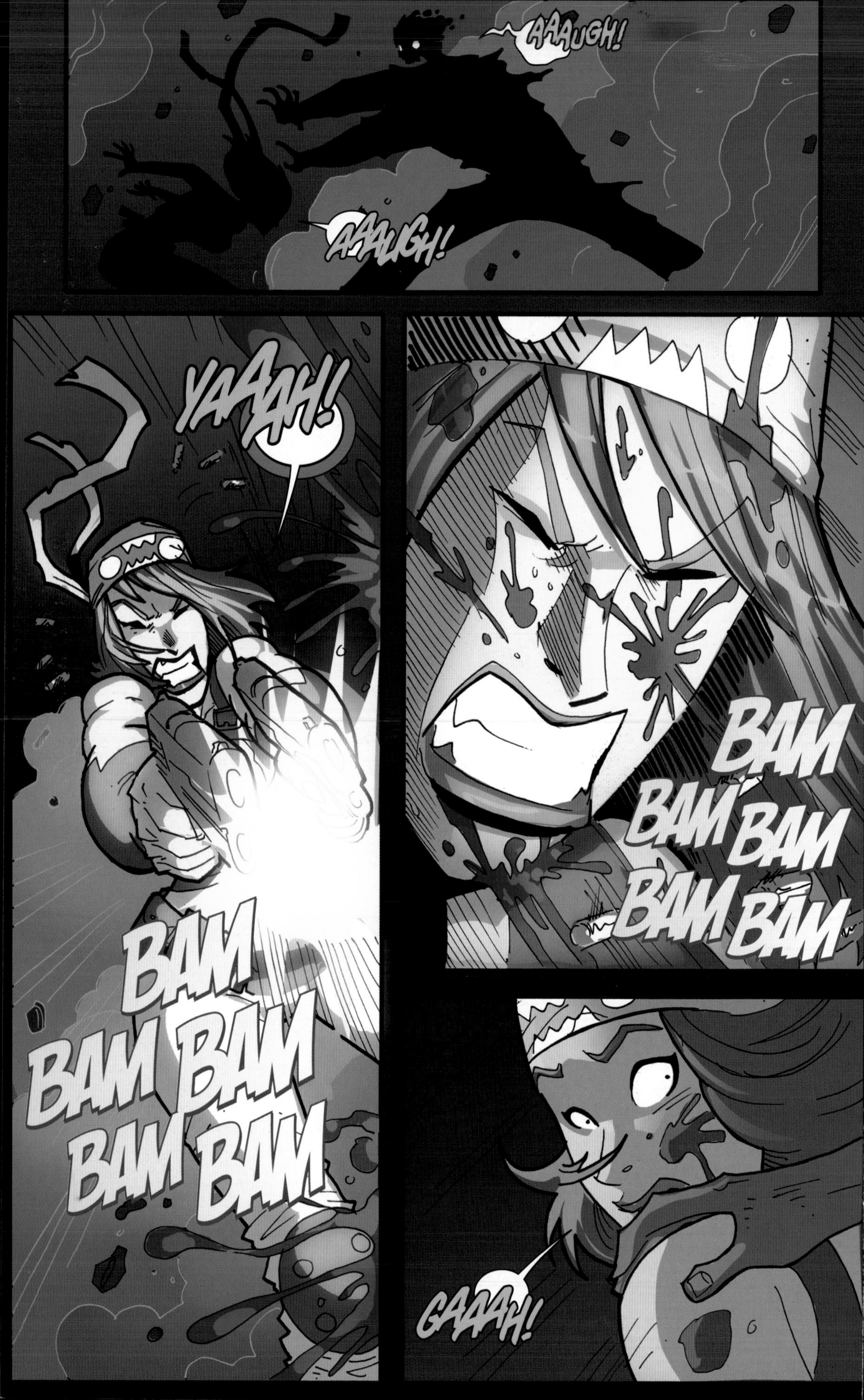
AAAUGH!
AAAUGH!
YAAAAH!
BAM
BAM BAM
BAM BAM
BAM
BAM BAM
BAM BAM
GAAAH!

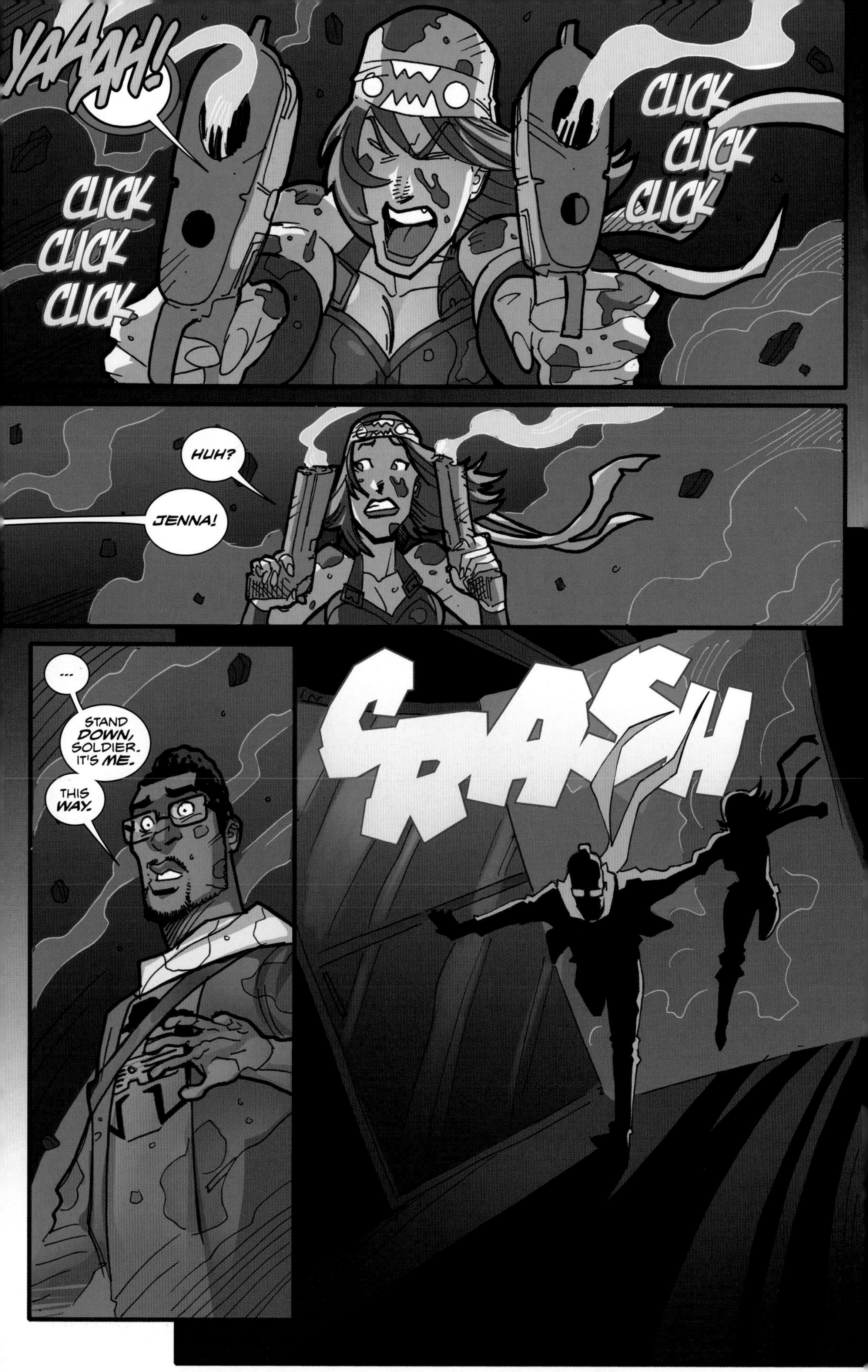
YAAAH!
CLICK CLICK CLICK
CLICK CLICK CLICK
HUH?
JENNA!
...
STAND DOWN, SOLDIER. IT'S ME.
THIS WAY.
CRASH

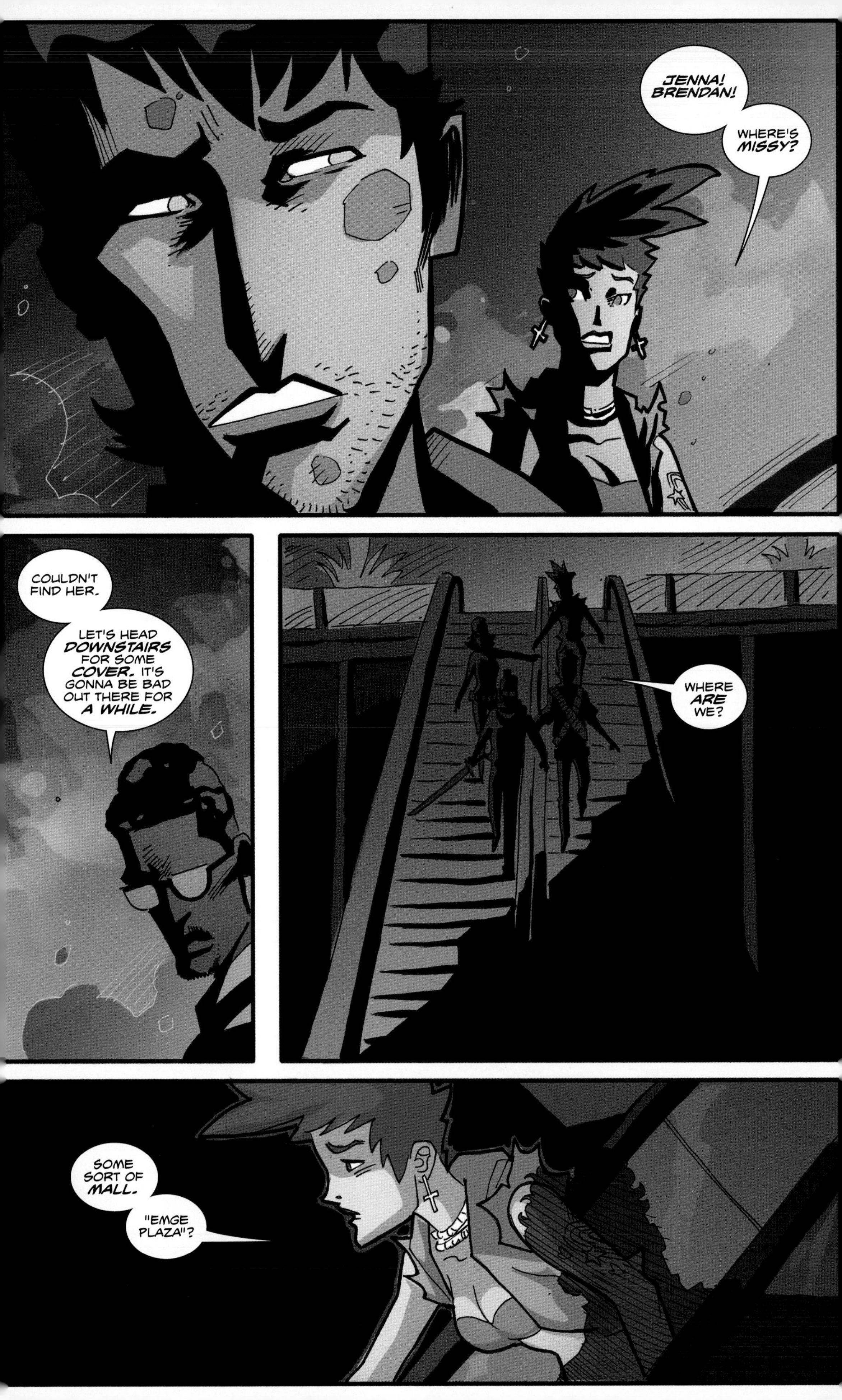
JENNA! BRENDAN!
WHERE'S MISSY?
COULDN'T FIND HER.
LET'S HEAD DOWNSTAIRS FOR SOME COVER. IT'S GONNA BE BAD OUT THERE FOR A WHILE.
WHERE ARE WE?
SOME SORT OF MALL.
"EMGE PLAZA"?

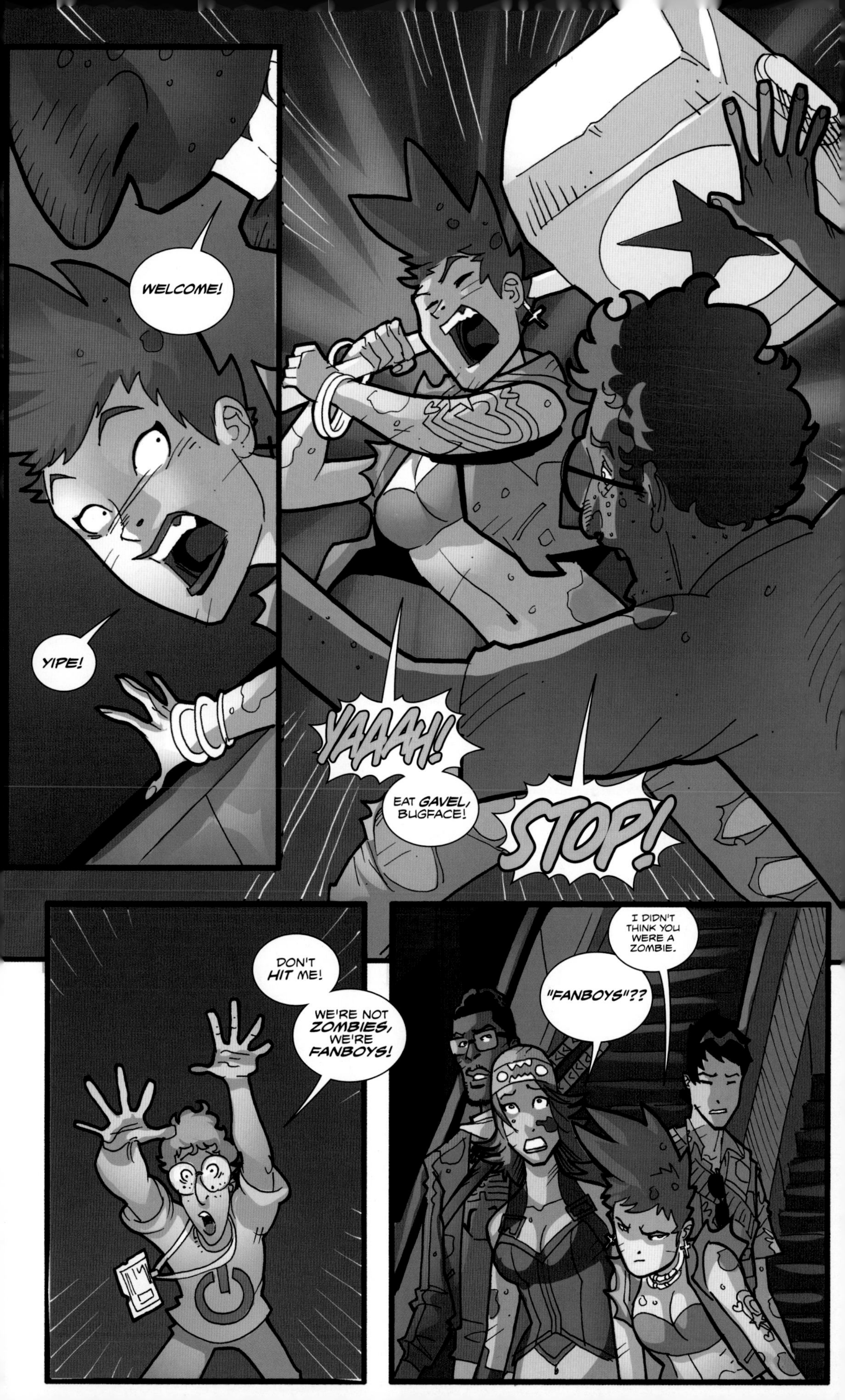
WELCOME!
YIPE!
YAAAH!
EAT GAVEL, BUGFACE!
STOP!
DON'T HIT ME!
WE'RE NOT ZOMBIES, WE'RE FANBOYS!
I DIDN'T THINK YOU WERE A ZOMBIE.
"FANBOYS"??

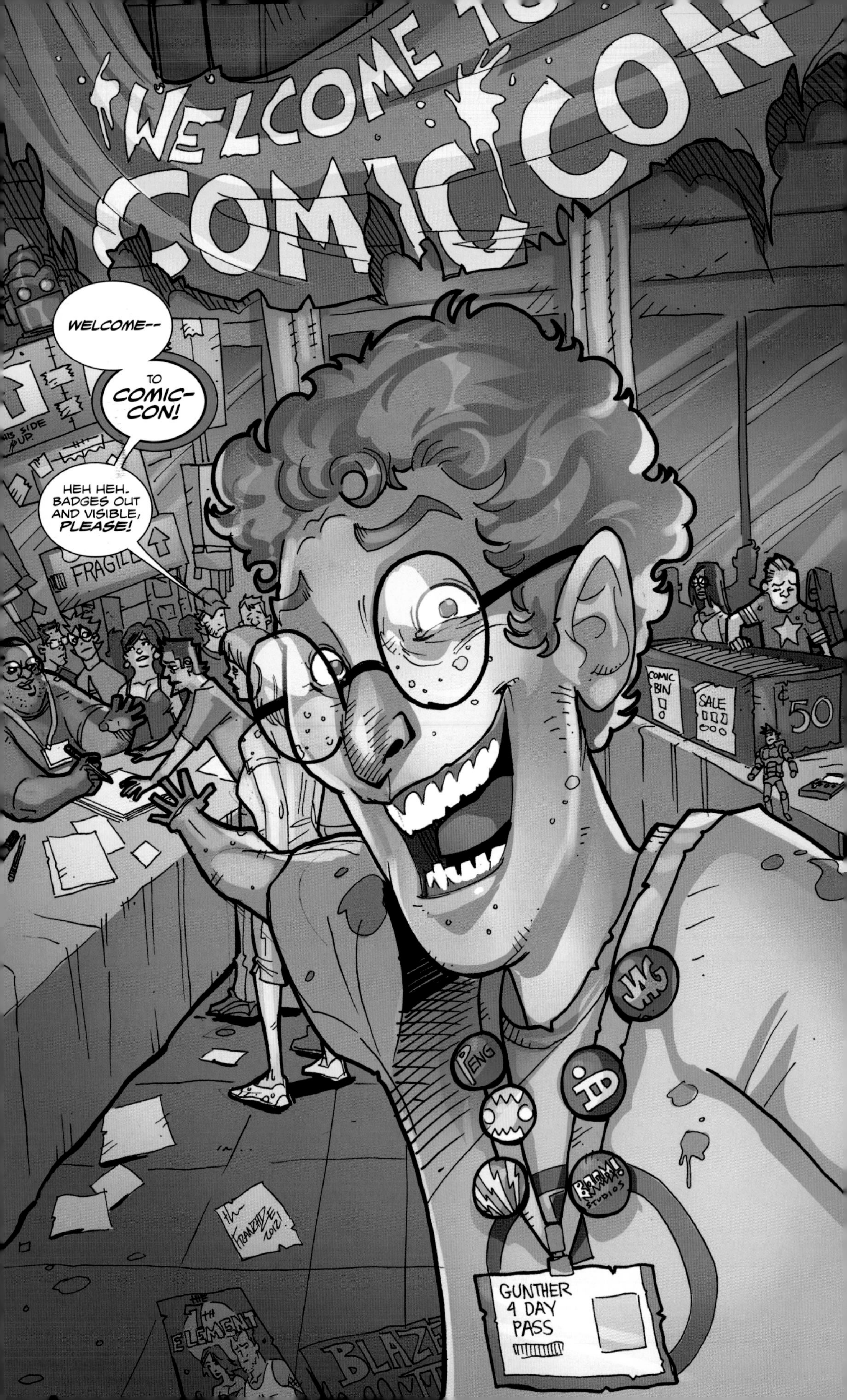
WELCOME TO
COMIC CON
WELCOME--
TO COMIC-CON!
HEH HEH. BADGES OUT AND VISIBLE, PLEASE!
COMIC BIN
SALE
¢50
GUNTHER
4 DAY
PASS
BLAZE

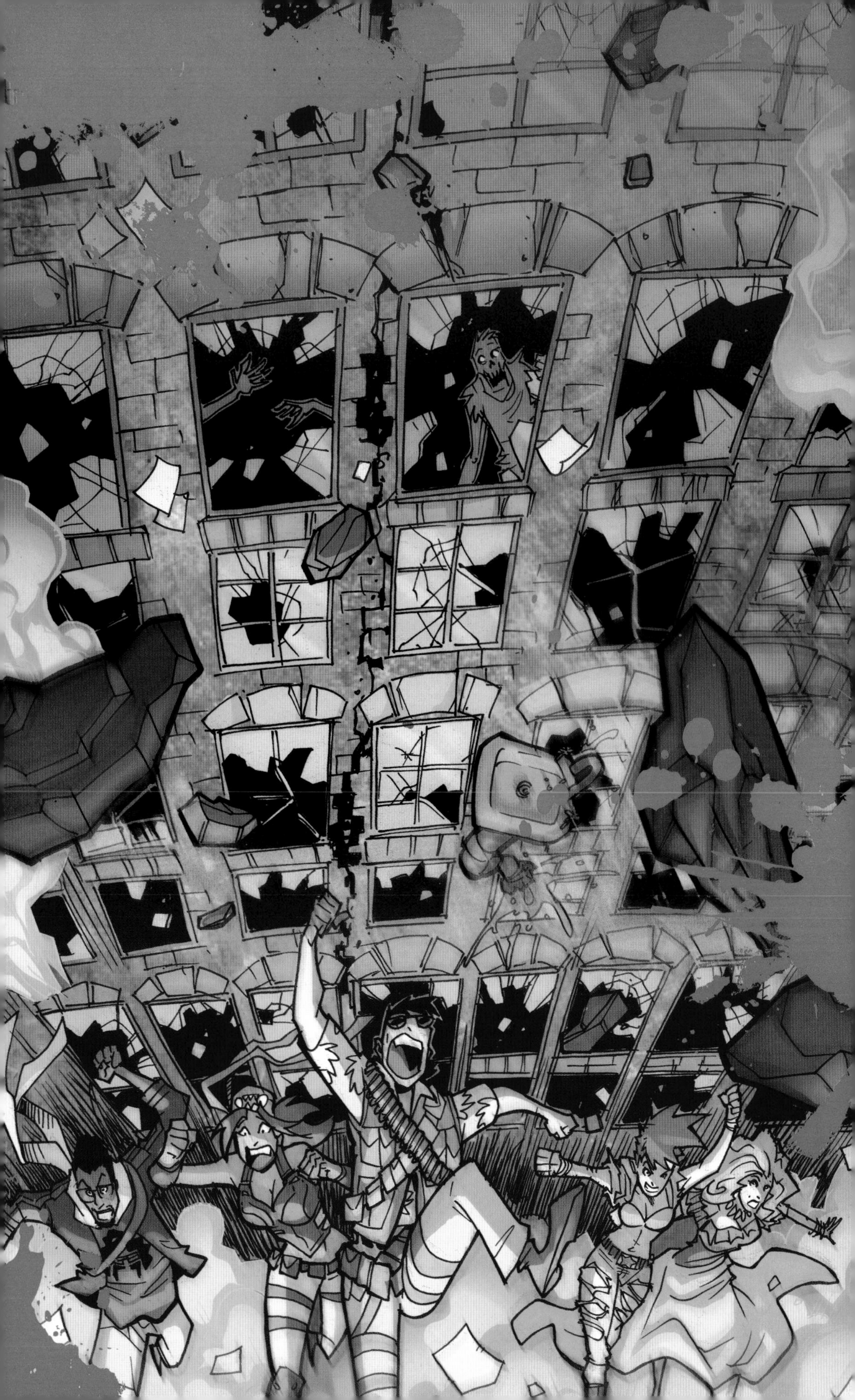

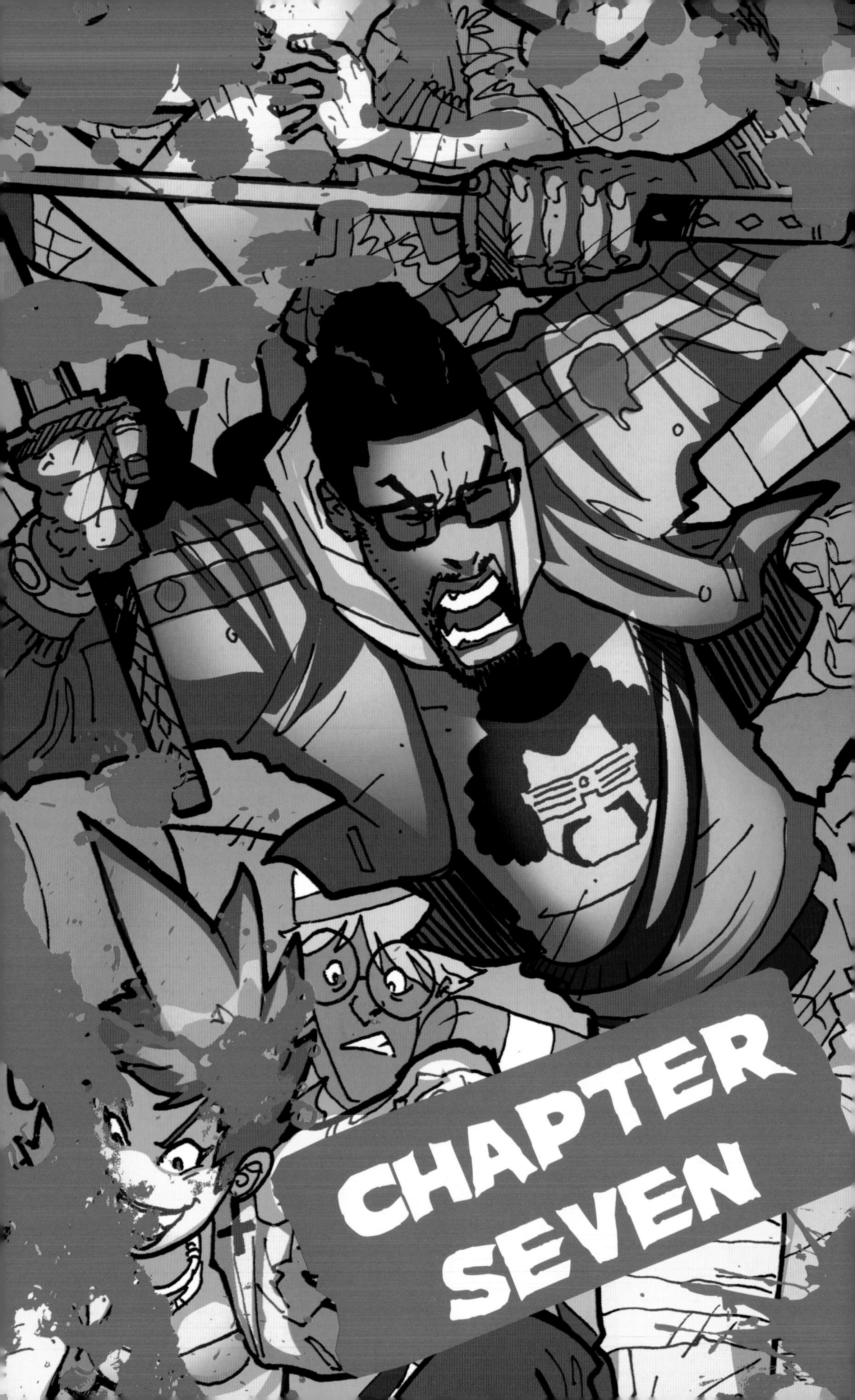
CHAPTER SEVEN

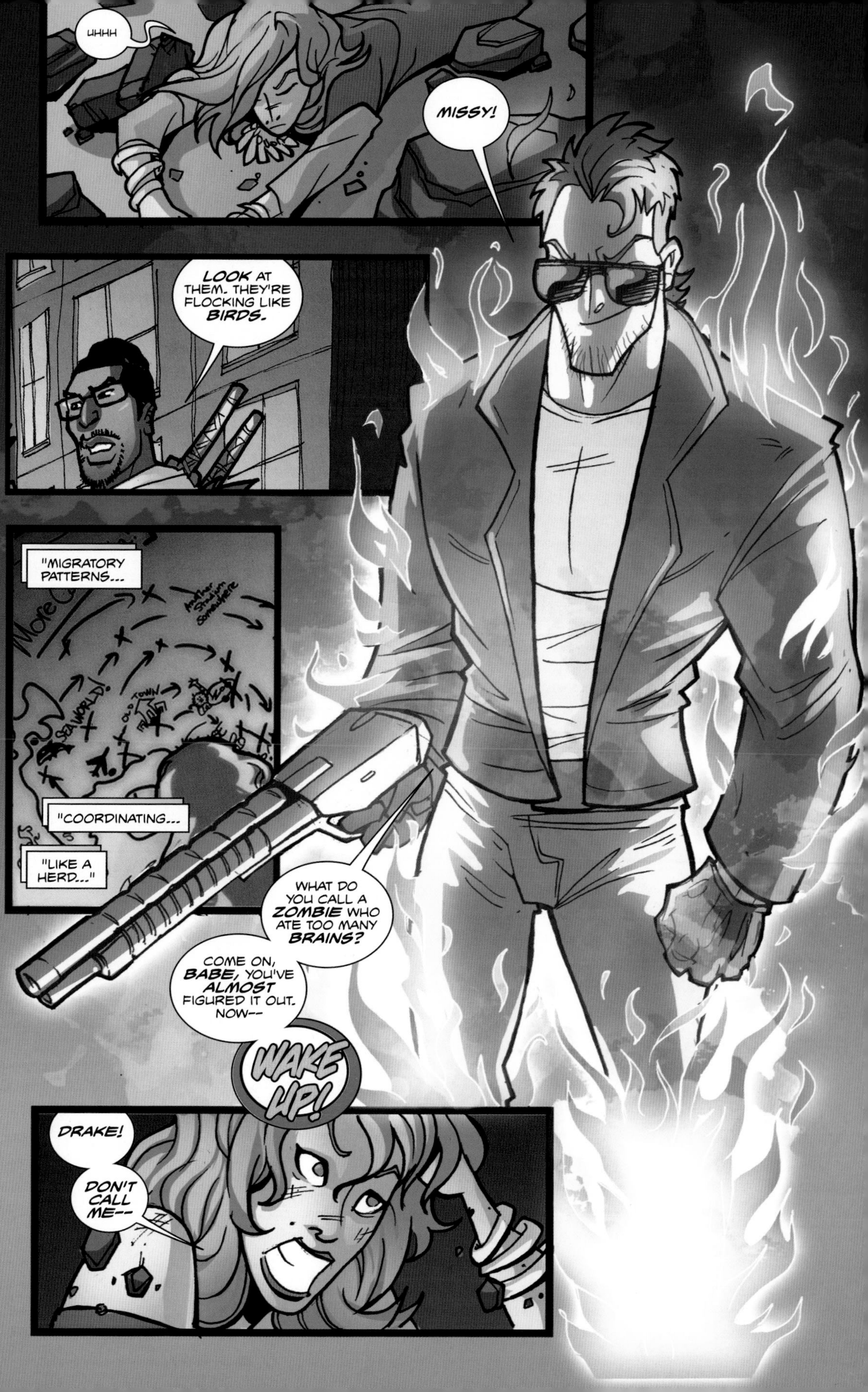
UHHH
MISSY!
LOOK AT THEM. THEY'RE FLOCKING LIKE BIRDS.
"MIGRATORY PATTERNS...
Another Stadium Somewhere
SEAWORLD!
OLD TOWN
"COORDINATING...
"LIKE A HERD..."
WHAT DO YOU CALL A ZOMBIE WHO ATE TOO MANY BRAINS?
COME ON, BABE, YOU'VE ALMOST FIGURED IT OUT. NOW--
WAKE UP!
DRAKE!
DON'T CALL ME--

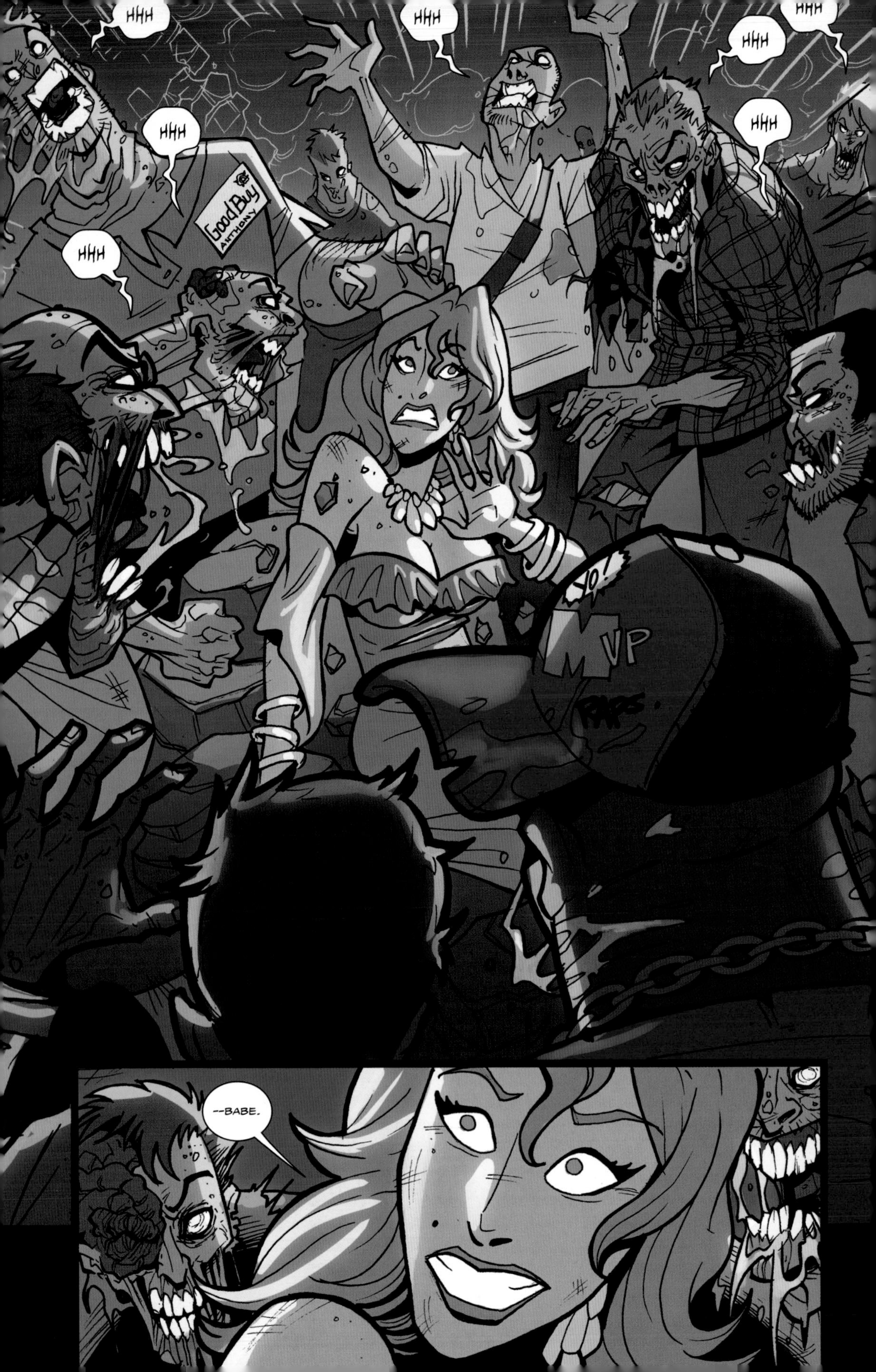
HHH
HHH
HHH
HHH
HHH
HHH
HHH
Good Buy
ANTHONY
YO!
MVP
--BABE.

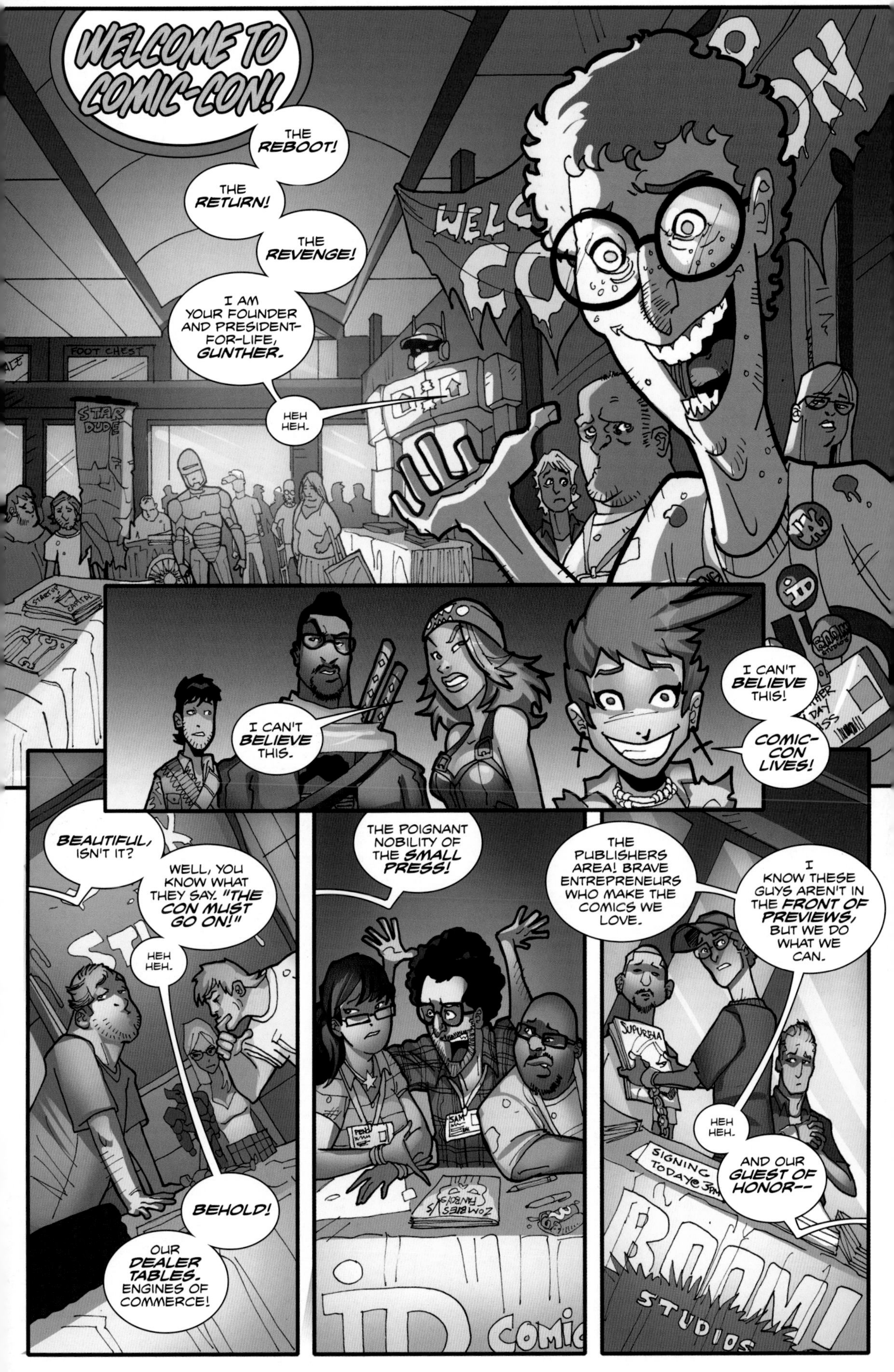
WELCOME TO COMIC-CON!
THE REBOOT!
THE RETURN!
THE REVENGE!
I AM YOUR FOUNDER AND PRESIDENT-FOR-LIFE, GUNTHER.
HEH HEH.
STAR DUDE
FOOT CHEST
I CAN'T BELIEVE THIS.
I CAN'T BELIEVE THIS!
COMIC-CON LIVES!
BEAUTIFUL, ISN'T IT?
WELL, YOU KNOW WHAT THEY SAY. "THE CON MUST GO ON!"
HEH HEH.
BEHOLD!
OUR DEALER TABLES. ENGINES OF COMMERCE!
THE POIGNANT NOBILITY OF THE SMALL PRESS!
ZOMBIES VS FANBOYS
SAM
THE PUBLISHERS AREA! BRAVE ENTREPRENEURS WHO MAKE THE COMICS WE LOVE.
I KNOW THESE GUYS AREN'T IN THE FRONT OF PREVIEWS, BUT WE DO WHAT WE CAN.
SUPURBIA
HEH HEH.
SIGNING TODAY@ 3PM
AND OUR GUEST OF HONOR--
BOOM! STUDIOS

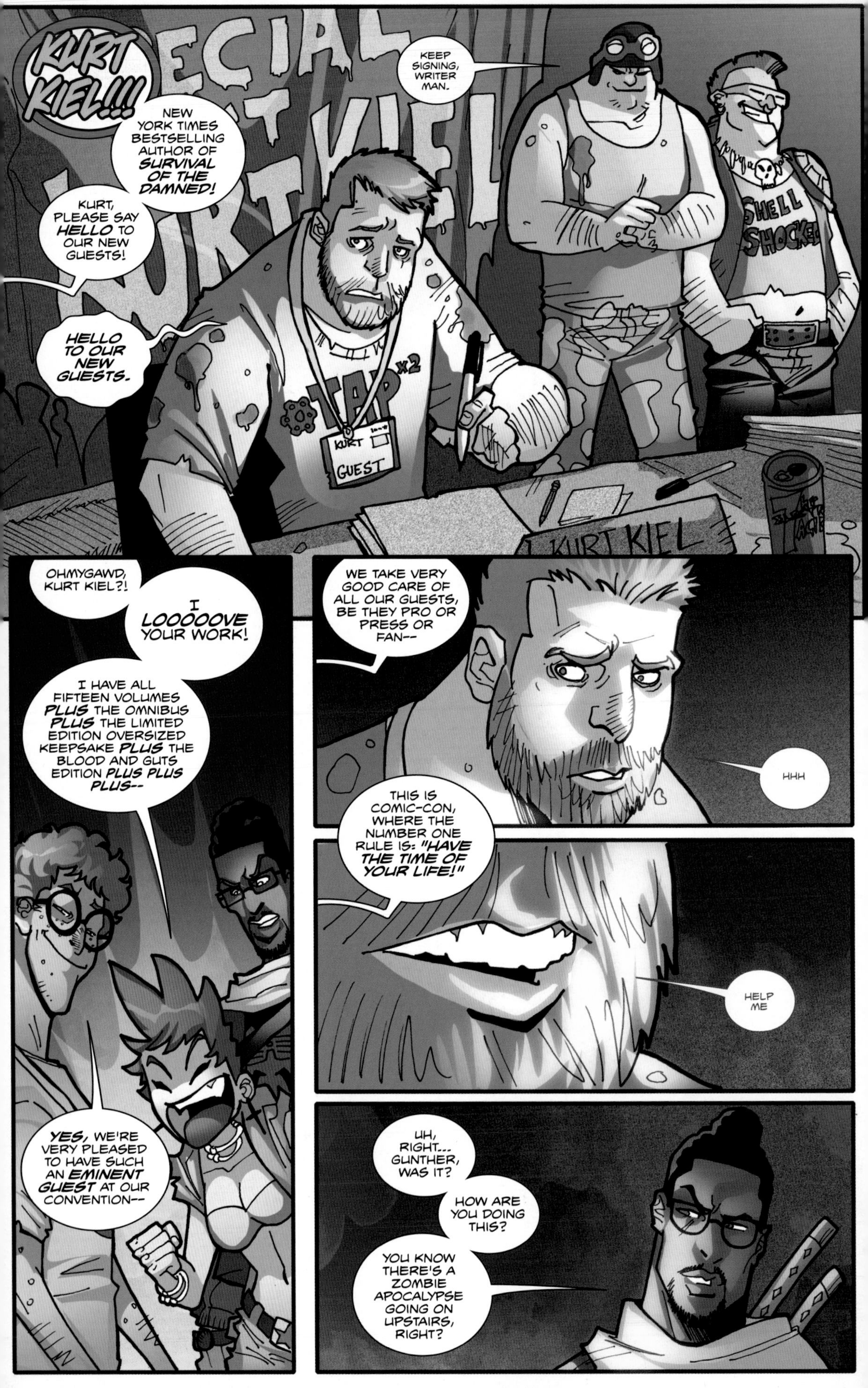

KURT KIEL!!!
NEW YORK TIMES BESTSELLING AUTHOR OF SURVIVAL OF THE DAMNED!
KURT, PLEASE SAY HELLO TO OUR NEW GUESTS!
HELLO TO OUR NEW GUESTS.
KEEP SIGNING, WRITER MAN.
SHELL SHOCKED
KURT
GUEST
KURT KIEL
OHMYGAWD, KURT KIEL?!
I LOOOOOVE YOUR WORK!
I HAVE ALL FIFTEEN VOLUMES PLUS THE OMNIBUS PLUS THE LIMITED EDITION OVERSIZED KEEPSAKE PLUS THE BLOOD AND GUTS EDITION PLUS PLUS PLUS--
YES, WE'RE VERY PLEASED TO HAVE SUCH AN EMINENT GUEST AT OUR CONVENTION--
WE TAKE VERY GOOD CARE OF ALL OUR GUESTS, BE THEY PRO OR PRESS OR FAN--
HHH
THIS IS COMIC-CON, WHERE THE NUMBER ONE RULE IS: "HAVE THE TIME OF YOUR LIFE!"
HELP ME
UH, RIGHT... GUNTHER, WAS IT?
HOW ARE YOU DOING THIS?
YOU KNOW THERE'S A ZOMBIE APOCALYPSE GOING ON UPSTAIRS, RIGHT?

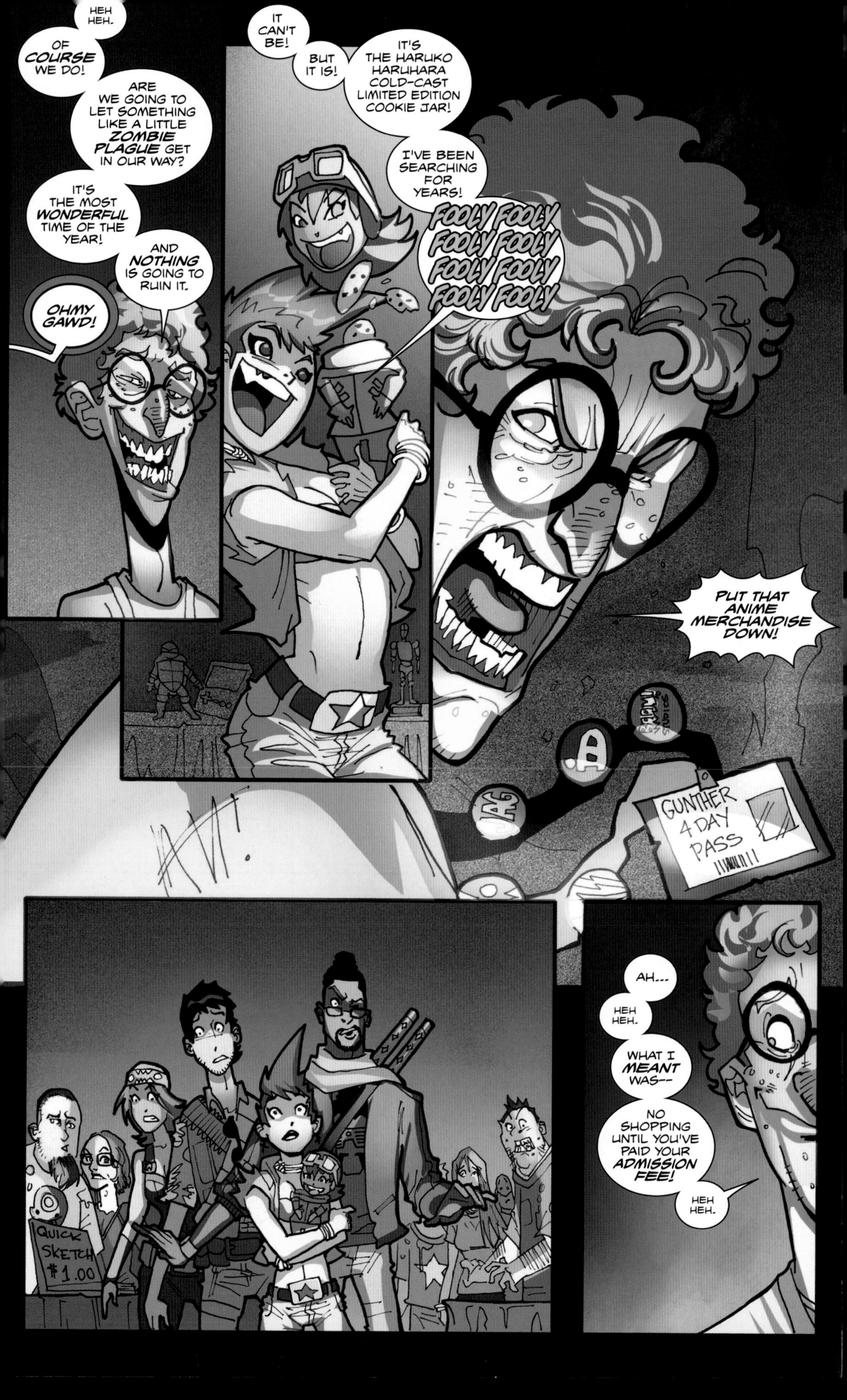
HEH HEH.
OF COURSE WE DO!
ARE WE GOING TO LET SOMETHING LIKE A LITTLE ZOMBIE PLAGUE GET IN OUR WAY?
IT'S THE MOST WONDERFUL TIME OF THE YEAR!
AND NOTHING IS GOING TO RUIN IT.
OHMY GAWD!
IT CAN'T BE!
BUT IT IS!
IT'S THE HARUKO HARUHARA COLD-CAST LIMITED EDITION COOKIE JAR!
I'VE BEEN SEARCHING FOR YEARS!
FOOLY FOOLY FOOLY FOOLY FOOLY FOOLY FOOLY FOOLY
PUT THAT ANIME MERCHANDISE DOWN!
GUNTHER 4 DAY PASS
QUICK SKETCH $1.00
AH...
HEH HEH.
WHAT I MEANT WAS--
NO SHOPPING UNTIL YOU'VE PAID YOUR ADMISSION FEE!
HEH HEH.

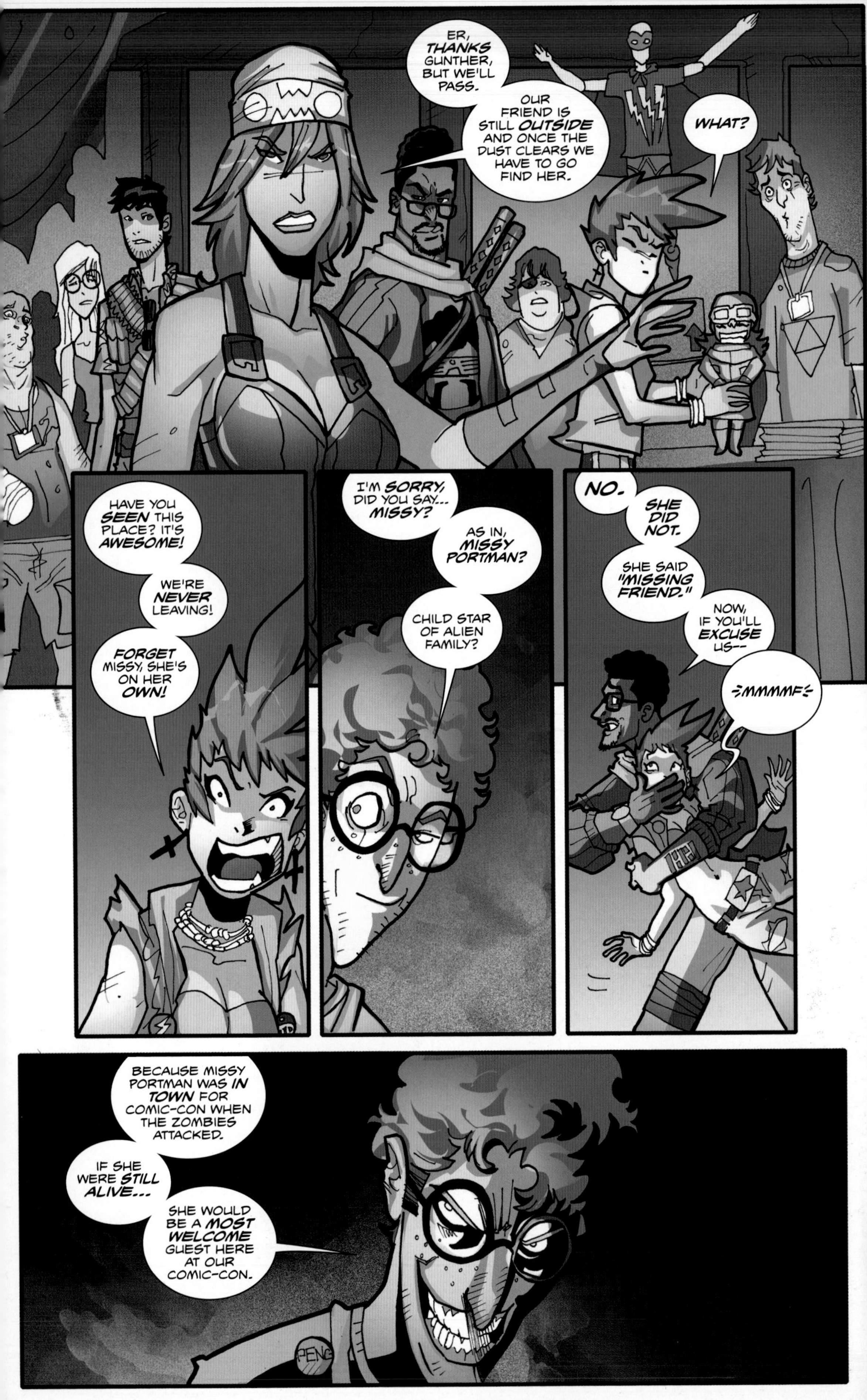
ER, THANKS GUNTHER, BUT WE'LL PASS.
OUR FRIEND IS STILL OUTSIDE AND ONCE THE DUST CLEARS WE HAVE TO GO FIND HER.
WHAT?
HAVE YOU SEEN THIS PLACE? IT'S AWESOME!
WE'RE NEVER LEAVING!
FORGET MISSY, SHE'S ON HER OWN!
I'M SORRY, DID YOU SAY... MISSY?
AS IN, MISSY PORTMAN?
CHILD STAR OF ALIEN FAMILY?
NO.
SHE DID NOT.
SHE SAID "MISSING FRIEND."
NOW, IF YOU'LL EXCUSE US--
-MMMMF-
BECAUSE MISSY PORTMAN WAS IN TOWN FOR COMIC-CON WHEN THE ZOMBIES ATTACKED.
IF SHE WERE STILL ALIVE...
SHE WOULD BE A MOST WELCOME GUEST HERE AT OUR COMIC-CON.
PENG

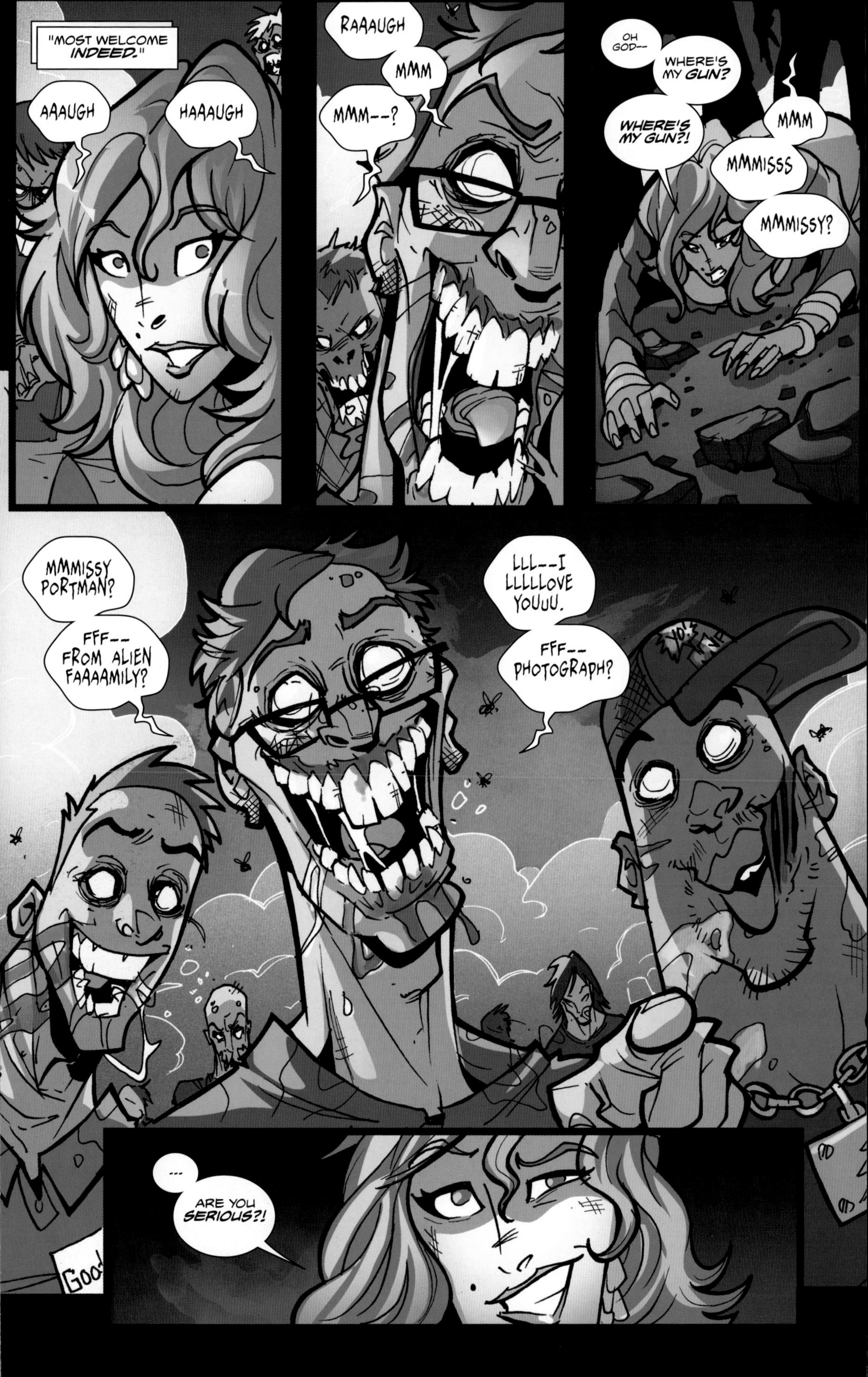
"MOST WELCOME INDEED."
AAAUGH
HAAAUGH
RAAAUGH
MMM
MMM--?
OH GOD--
WHERE'S MY GUN?
WHERE'S MY GUN?!
MMM
MMMISSS
MMMISSY?
MMMISSY PORTMAN?
FFF-- FROM ALIEN FAAAAMILY?
LLL--I LLLLLOVE YOUUU.
FFF-- PHOTOGRAPH?
...
ARE YOU SERIOUS?!

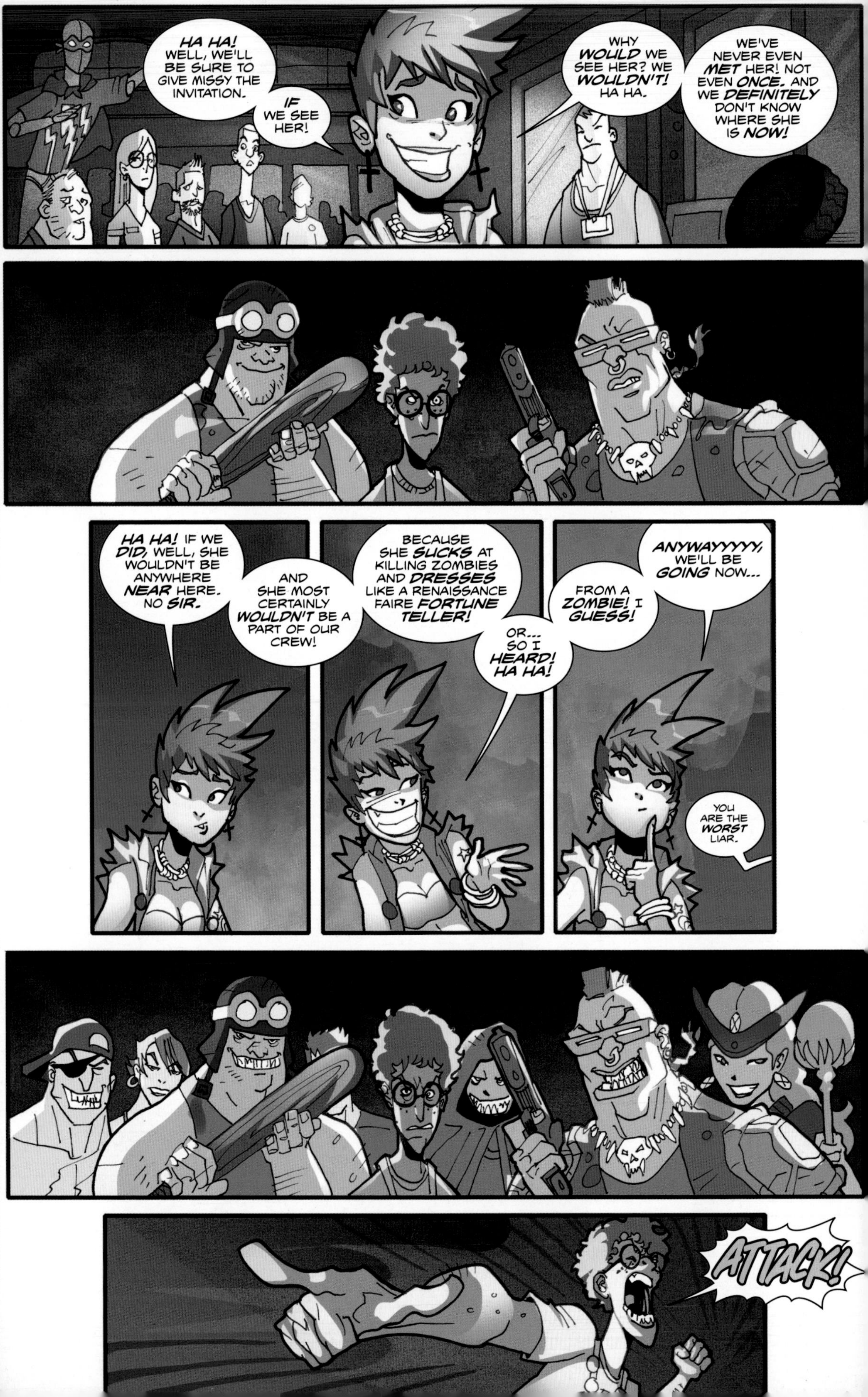
HA HA! WELL, WE'LL BE SURE TO GIVE MISSY THE INVITATION.
IF WE SEE HER!
WHY WOULD WE SEE HER? WE WOULDN'T! HA HA.
WE'VE NEVER EVEN MET HER! NOT EVEN ONCE. AND WE DEFINITELY DON'T KNOW WHERE SHE IS NOW!
HA HA! IF WE DID, WELL, SHE WOULDN'T BE ANYWHERE NEAR HERE. NO SIR.
AND SHE MOST CERTAINLY WOULDN'T BE A PART OF OUR CREW!
BECAUSE SHE SUCKS AT KILLING ZOMBIES AND DRESSES LIKE A RENAISSANCE FAIRE FORTUNE TELLER!
OR... SO I HEARD! HA HA!
FROM A ZOMBIE! I GUESS!
ANYWAYYYYY, WE'LL BE GOING NOW...
YOU ARE THE WORST LIAR.
ATTACK!

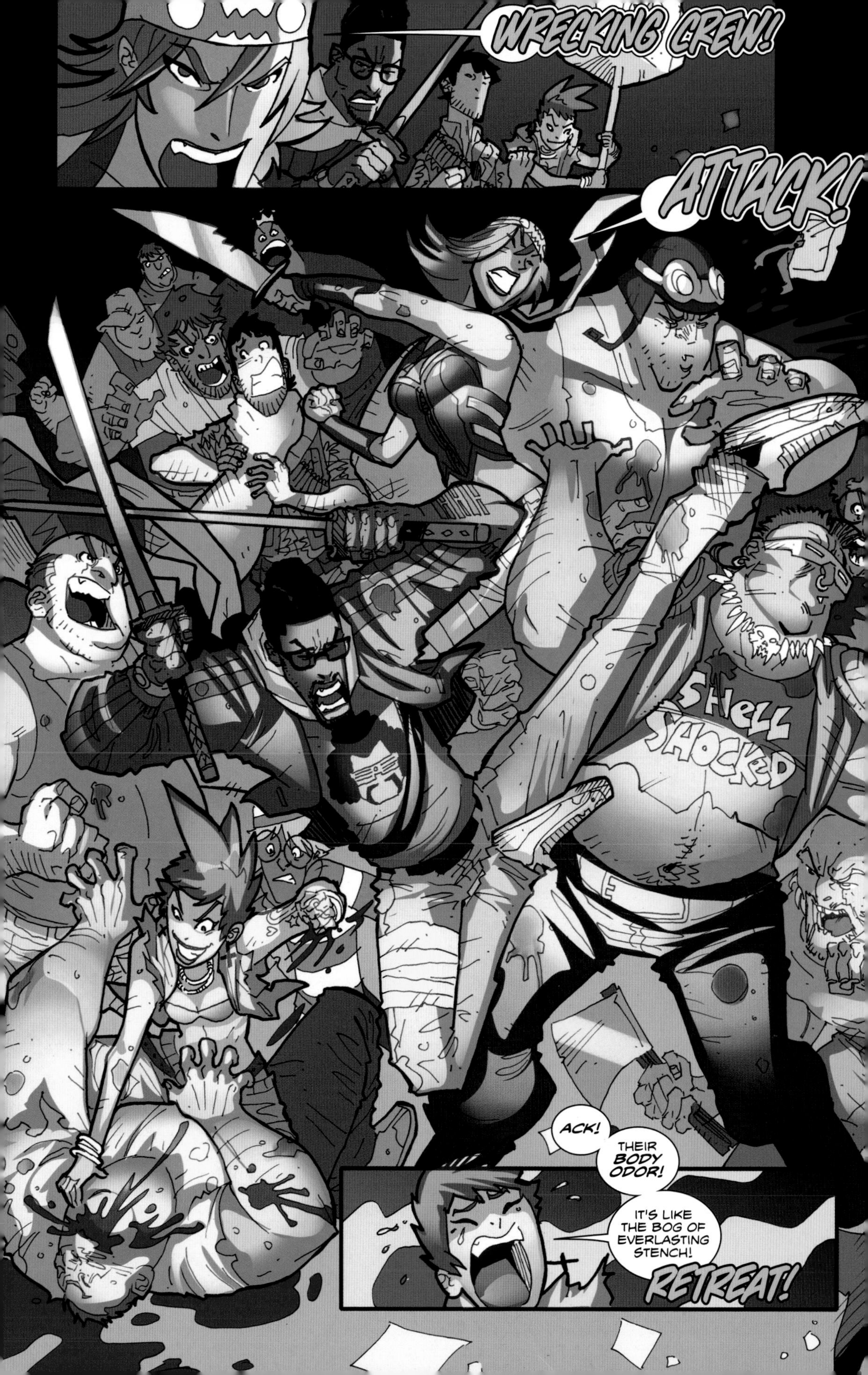
WRECKING CREW!
ATTACK!
SHELL SHOCKED
ACK!
THEIR BODY ODOR!
IT'S LIKE THE BOG OF EVERLASTING STENCH!
RETREAT!

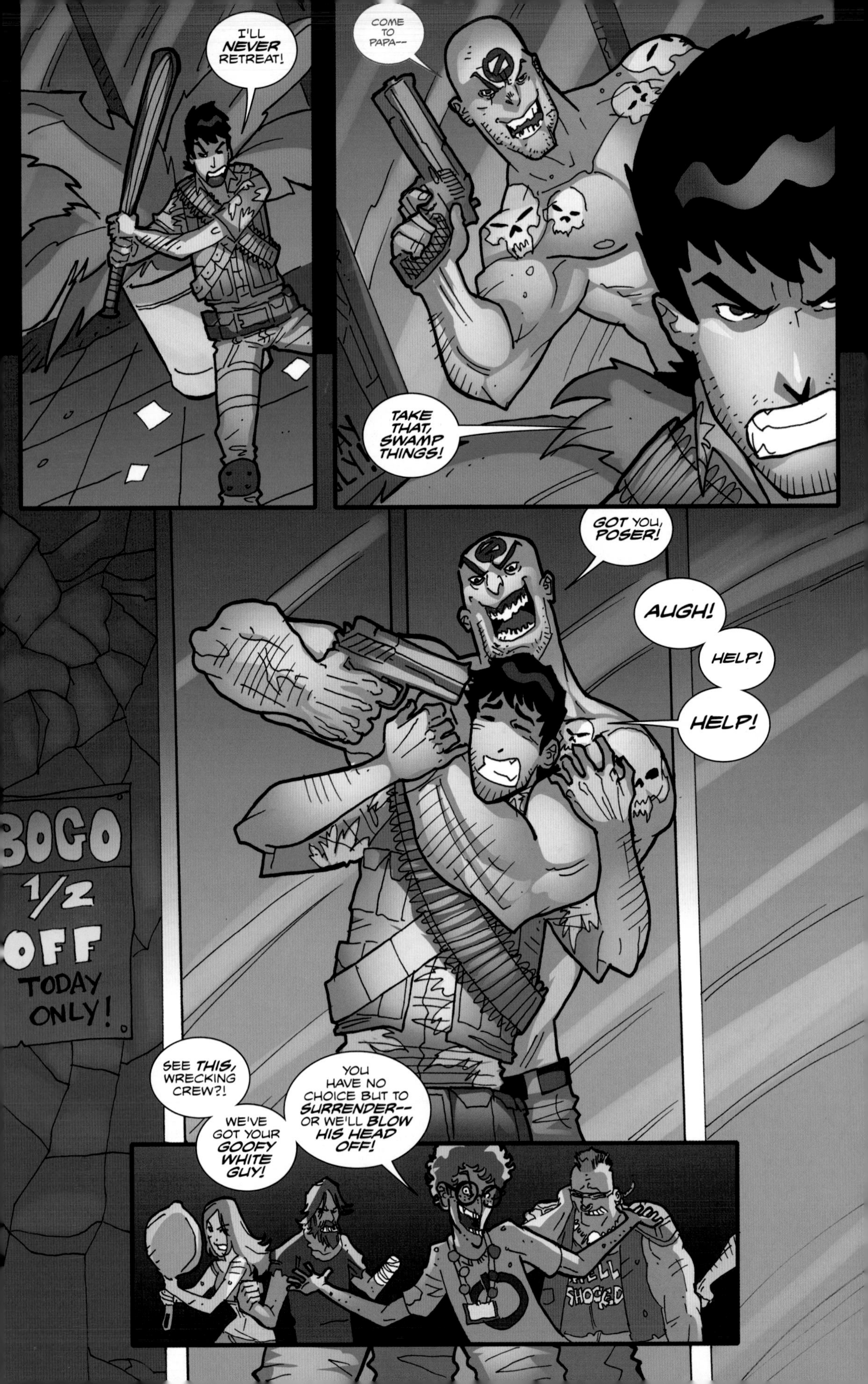

I'LL NEVER RETREAT!
COME TO PAPA--
TAKE THAT, SWAMP THINGS!
GOT YOU, POSER!
AUGH!
HELP!
HELP!
BOGO 1/2 OFF TODAY ONLY!
SEE THIS, WRECKING CREW?!
WE'VE GOT YOUR GOOFY WHITE GUY!
YOU HAVE NO CHOICE BUT TO SURRENDER-- OR WE'LL BLOW HIS HEAD OFF!

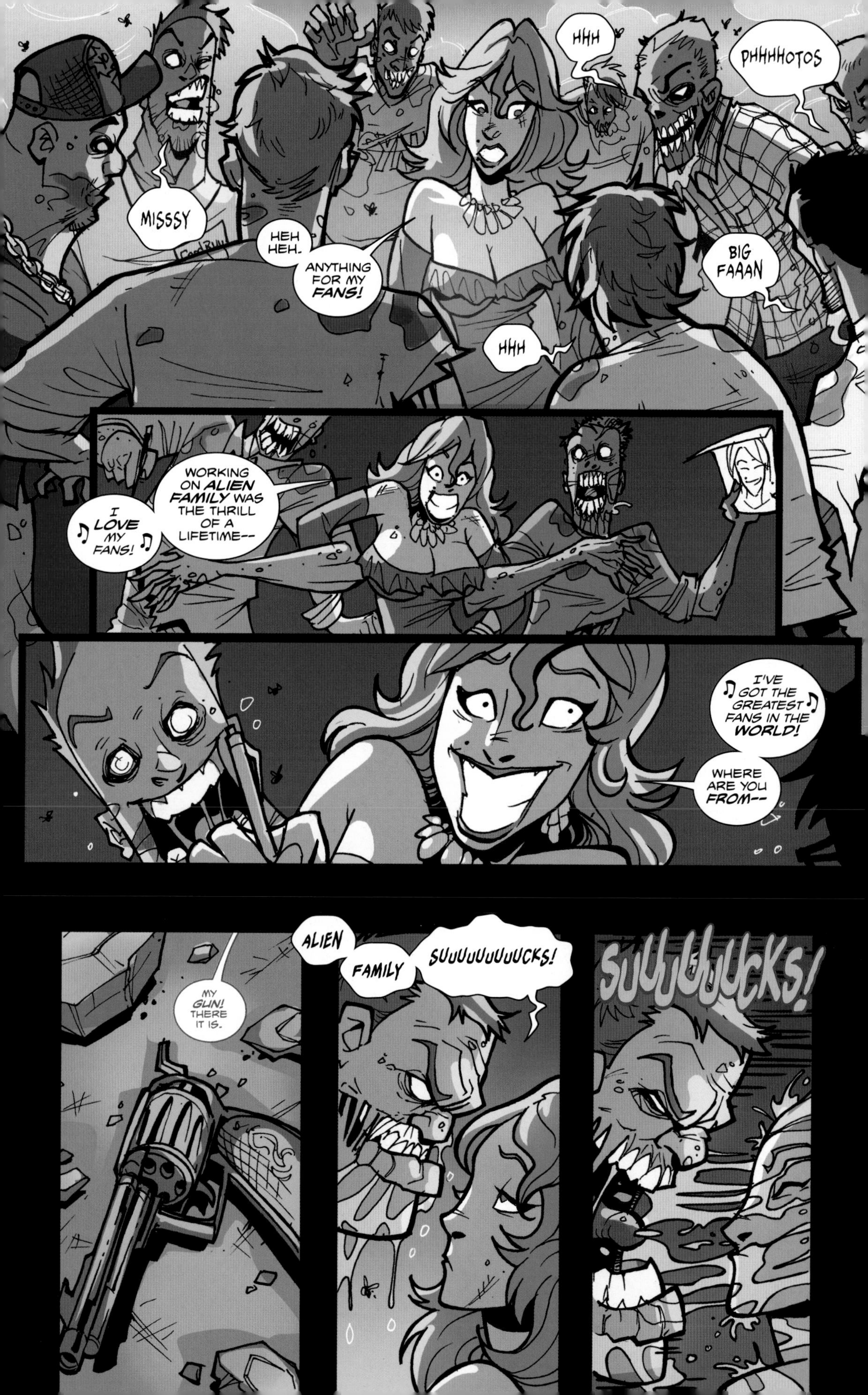
HHH
PHHHHOTOS
MISSSY
HEH HEH.
ANYTHING FOR MY FANS!
BIG FAAAN
HHH
WORKING ON ALIEN FAMILY WAS THE THRILL OF A LIFETIME--
♫ I LOVE MY FANS! ♫
♫ I'VE GOT THE GREATEST FANS IN THE WORLD! ♫
WHERE ARE YOU FROM--
MY GUN! THERE IT IS.
ALIEN
FAMILY
SUUUUUUUUUCKS!
SUUUUUUCKS!

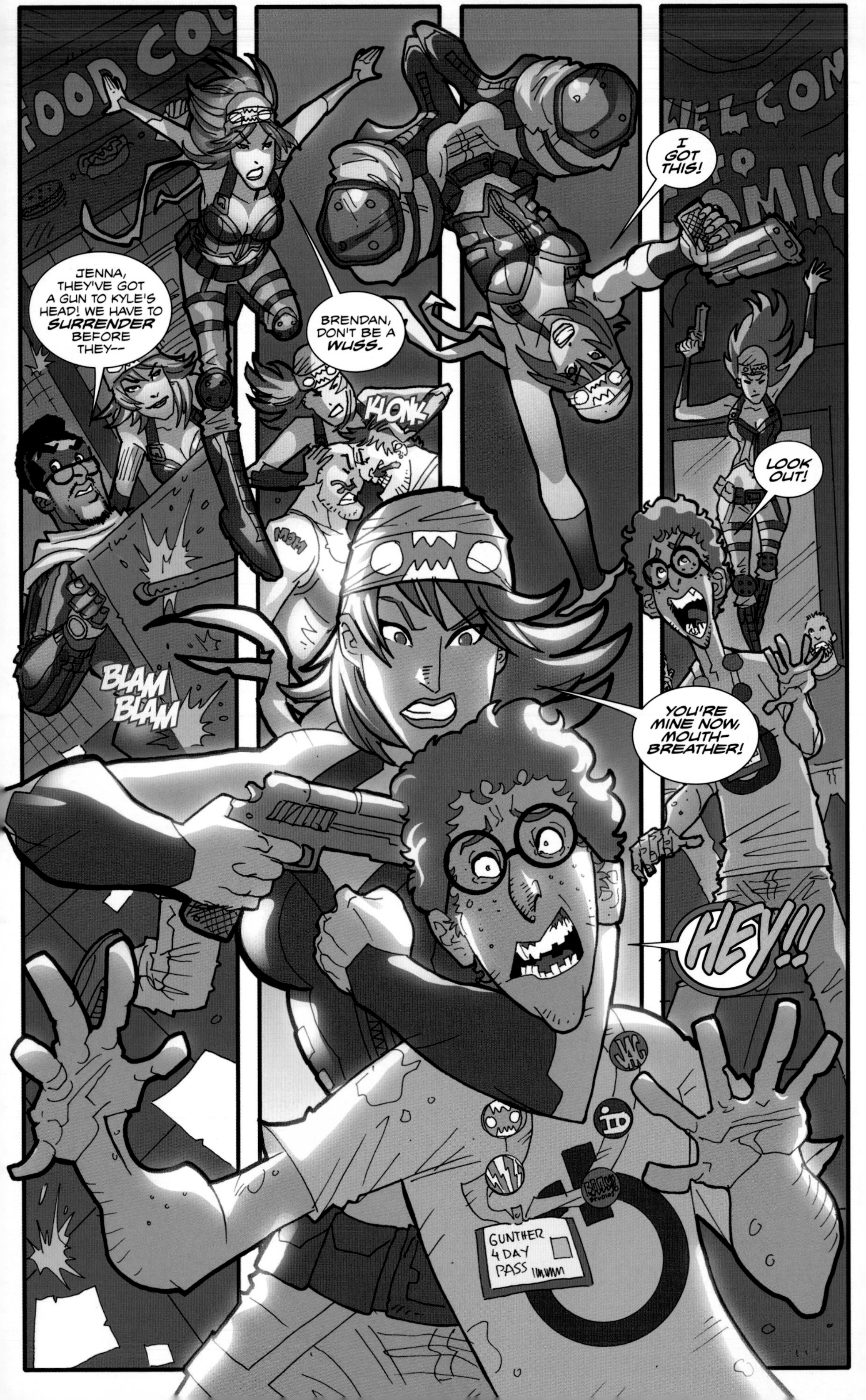

JENNA, THEY'VE GOT A GUN TO KYLE'S HEAD! WE HAVE TO SURRENDER BEFORE THEY--
BRENDAN, DON'T BE A WUSS.
KLONK
I GOT THIS!
LOOK OUT!
BLAM BLAM
YOU'RE MINE NOW, MOUTH-BREATHER!
HEY!!
GUNTHER 4 DAY PASS

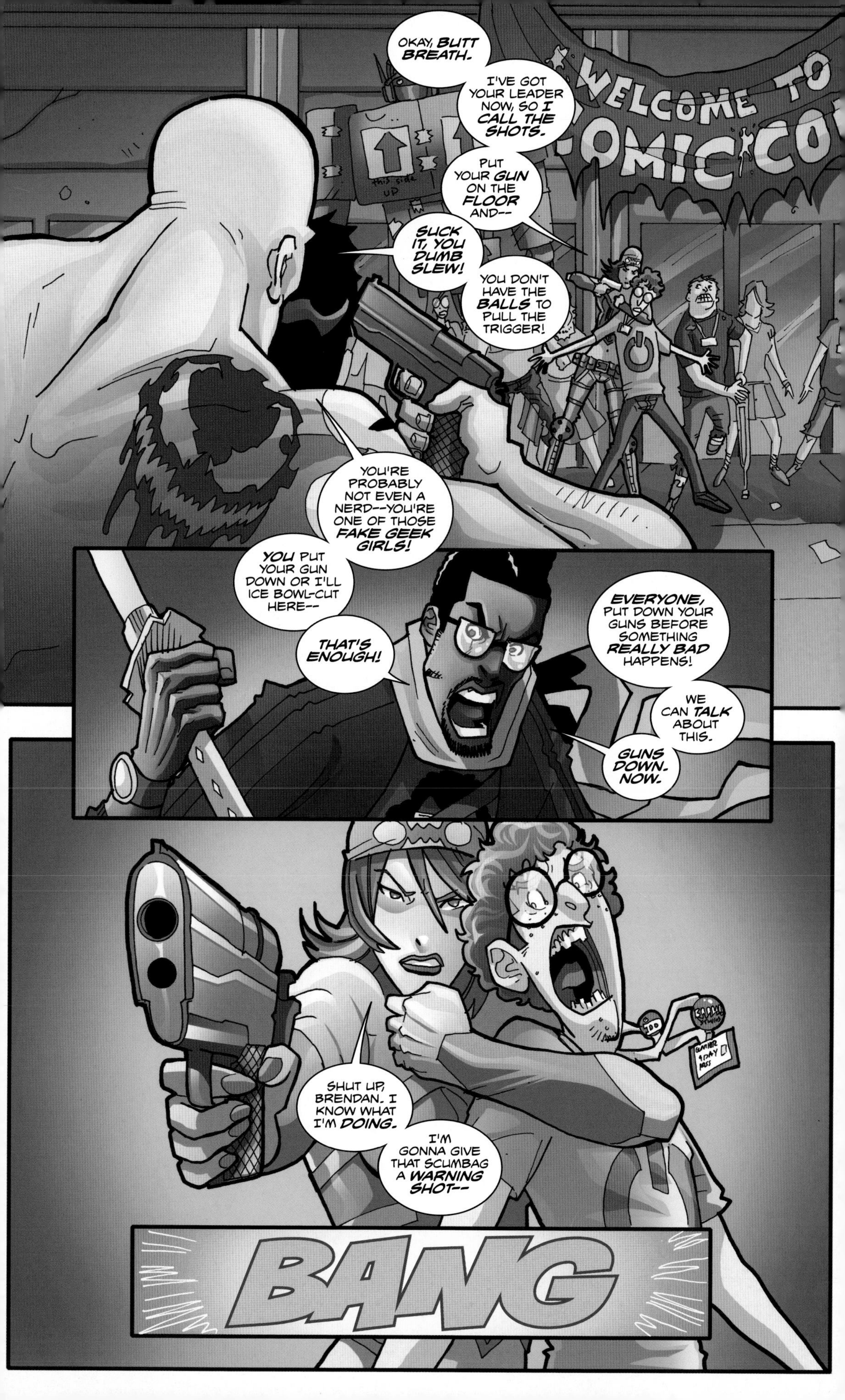

WELCOME TO COMIC-CON
OKAY, BUTT BREATH.
I'VE GOT YOUR LEADER NOW, SO I CALL THE SHOTS.
PUT YOUR GUN ON THE FLOOR AND--
SUCK IT, YOU DUMB SLEW!
YOU DON'T HAVE THE BALLS TO PULL THE TRIGGER!
YOU'RE PROBABLY NOT EVEN A NERD--YOU'RE ONE OF THOSE FAKE GEEK GIRLS!
YOU PUT YOUR GUN DOWN OR I'LL ICE BOWL-CUT HERE--
THAT'S ENOUGH!
EVERYONE, PUT DOWN YOUR GUNS BEFORE SOMETHING REALLY BAD HAPPENS!
WE CAN TALK ABOUT THIS.
GUNS DOWN. NOW.
SHUT UP, BRENDAN. I KNOW WHAT I'M DOING.
I'M GONNA GIVE THAT SCUMBAG A WARNING SHOT--
BANG

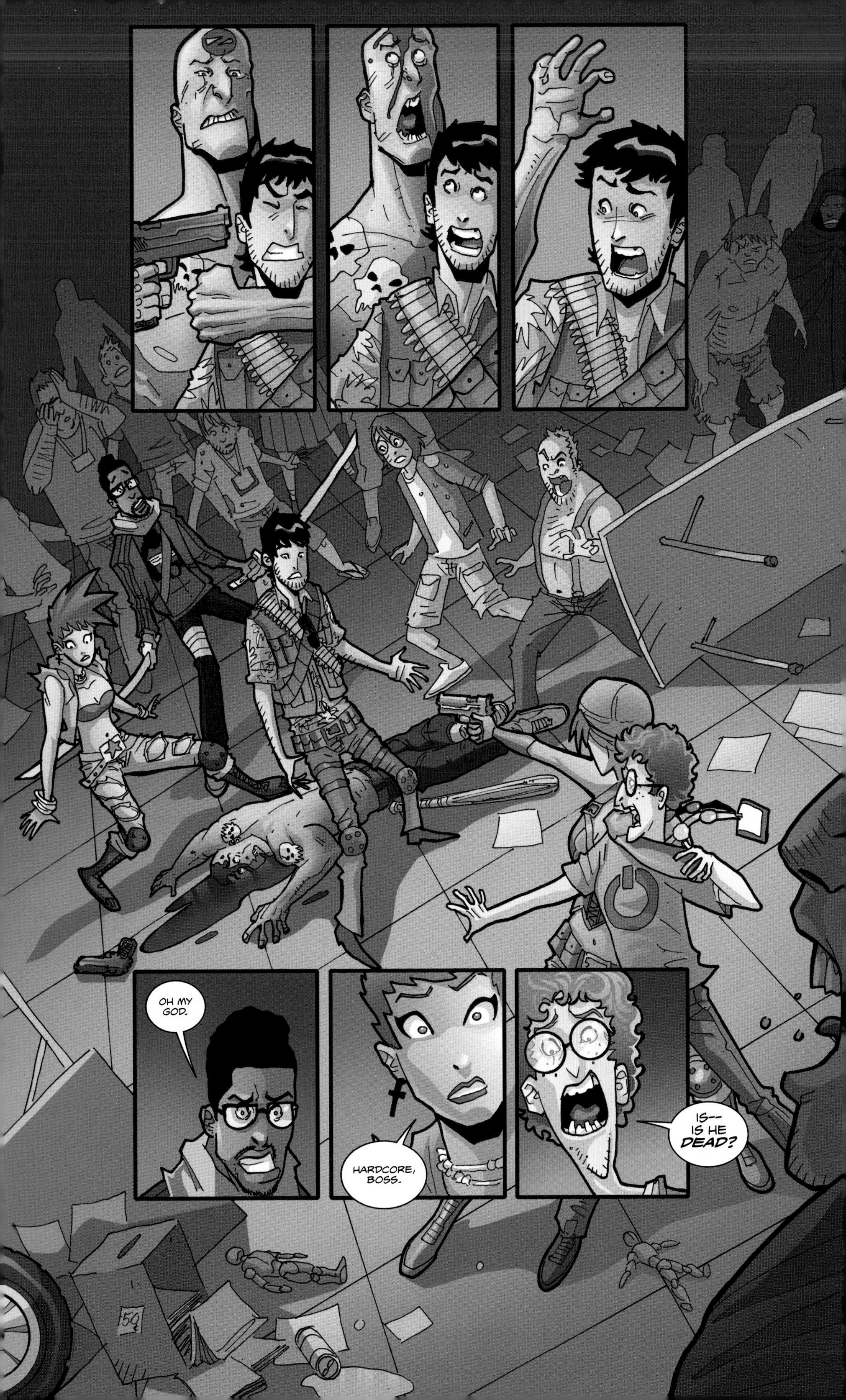
OH MY GOD.
HARDCORE, BOSS.
IS--
IS HE DEAD?

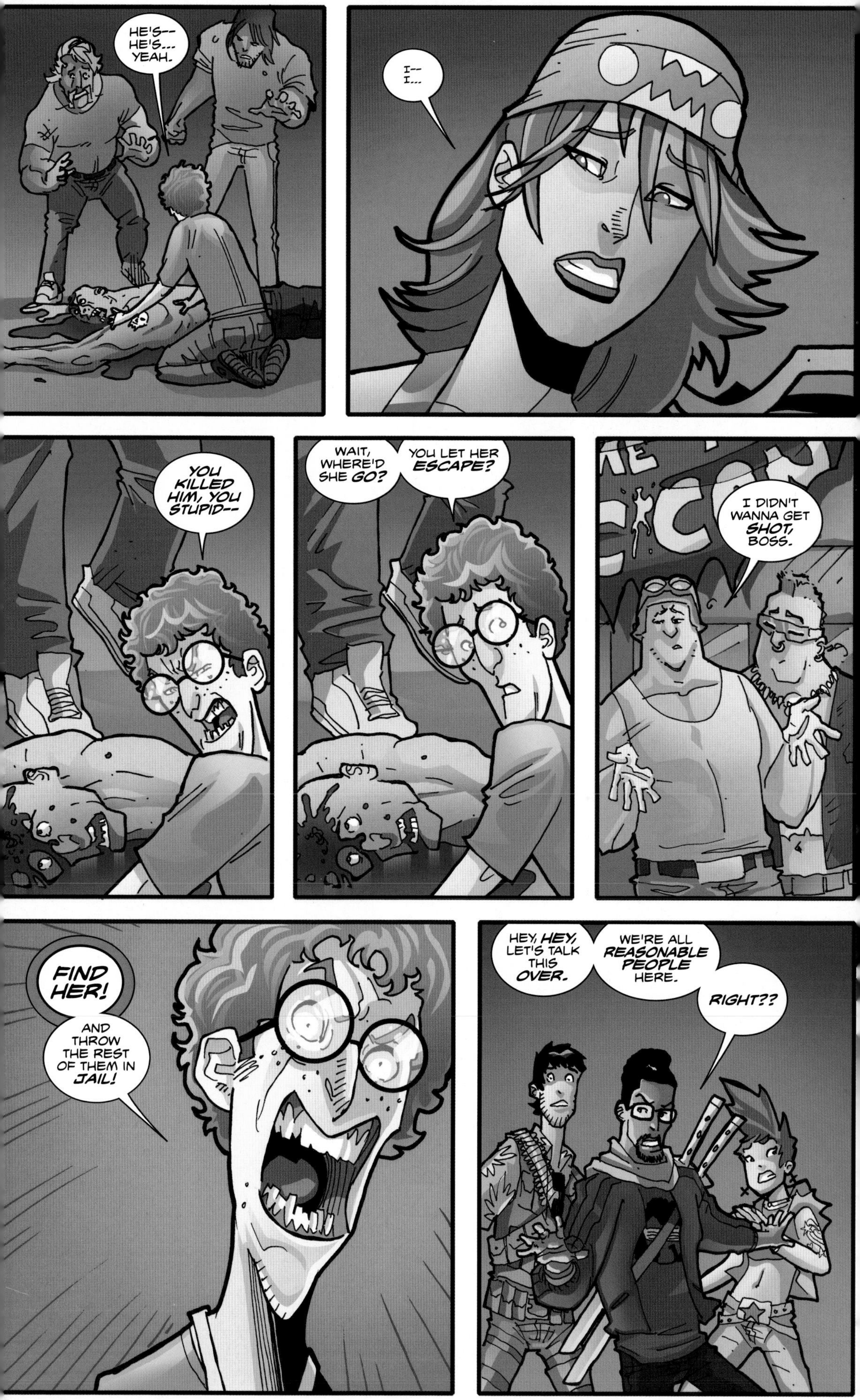
HE'S-- HE'S... YEAH.
I-- I...
YOU KILLED HIM, YOU STUPID--
WAIT, WHERE'D SHE GO?
YOU LET HER ESCAPE?
I DIDN'T WANNA GET SHOT, BOSS.
FIND HER!
AND THROW THE REST OF THEM IN JAIL!
HEY, HEY, LET'S TALK THIS OVER.
WE'RE ALL REASONABLE PEOPLE HERE.
RIGHT??

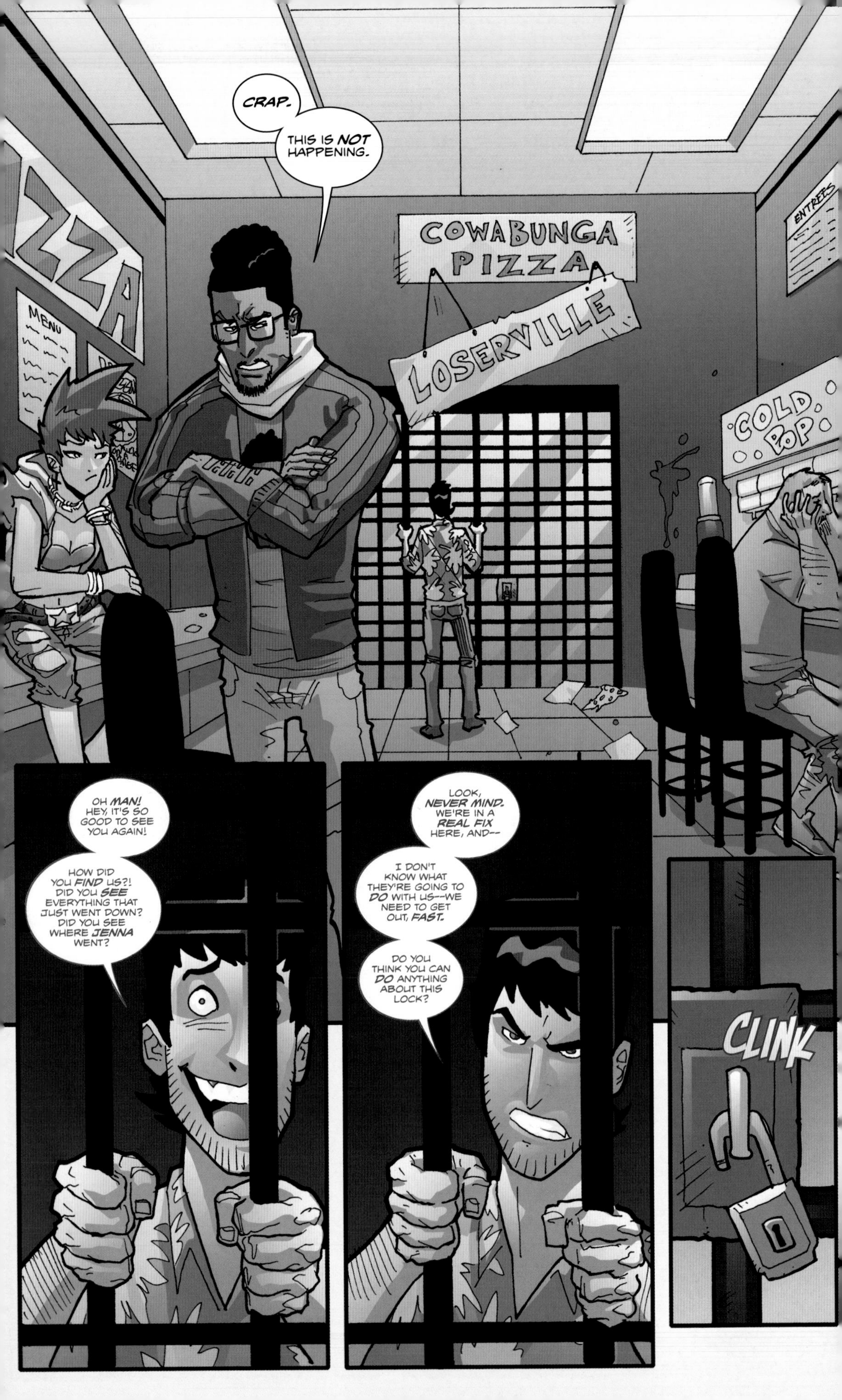

CRAP.
THIS IS NOT HAPPENING.
COWABUNGA PIZZA
LOSERVILLE
MENU
ENTREES
COLD POP
OH MAN! HEY, IT'S SO GOOD TO SEE YOU AGAIN!
HOW DID YOU FIND US?! DID YOU SEE EVERYTHING THAT JUST WENT DOWN? DID YOU SEE WHERE JENNA WENT?
LOOK, NEVER MIND. WE'RE IN A REAL FIX HERE, AND--
I DON'T KNOW WHAT THEY'RE GOING TO DO WITH US--WE NEED TO GET OUT, FAST.
DO YOU THINK YOU CAN DO ANYTHING ABOUT THIS LOCK?
CLINK

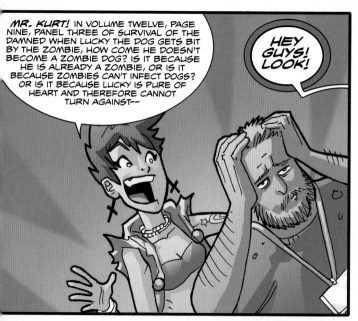

MR. KURT! IN VOLUME TWELVE, PAGE NINE, PANEL THREE OF SURVIVAL OF THE DAMNED WHEN LUCKY THE DOG GETS BIT BY THE ZOMBIE, HOW COME HE DOESN'T BECOME A ZOMBIE, OR IS IT BECAUSE HE IS ALREADY A ZOMBIE, OR IS IT BECAUSE ZOMBIES CAN'T INFECT DOGS? OR IS IT BECAUSE LUCKY IS PURE OF HEART AND THEREFORE CANNOT TURN AGAINST--

HEY GUYS! LOOK!

THE DOOR IS OPEN! WE'RE FREE!

I--UH. I PICKED THE LOCK MYSELF!

HA! YOU?!

WHO ARE YOU, JAMES BOND?!

I DON'T BELIEVE IT.

EAT SOME!

I DON'T EITHER, BUT I'M NOT SURE IT MAKES A DIFFERENCE.

WHO KNOWS WHAT THESE GROATY DERPS HAVE IN STORE FOR US.

LET'S GET THE HELL OUT OF HERE.

YOU'RE ESCAPING?

TAKE ME WITH YOU!

PLEASE!

WHAT ARE YOU GONNA DO OUT THERE, MISTER COMIC BOOK WRITER? WRITE US A KILLER THOUGHT BALLOON?

CAN YOU SHOOT? FIGHT? DRIVE?

WE HAVEN'T HAD GOOD LUCK WITH STRANGERS TODAY.

HOW DO I KNOW WE CAN TRUST YOU?

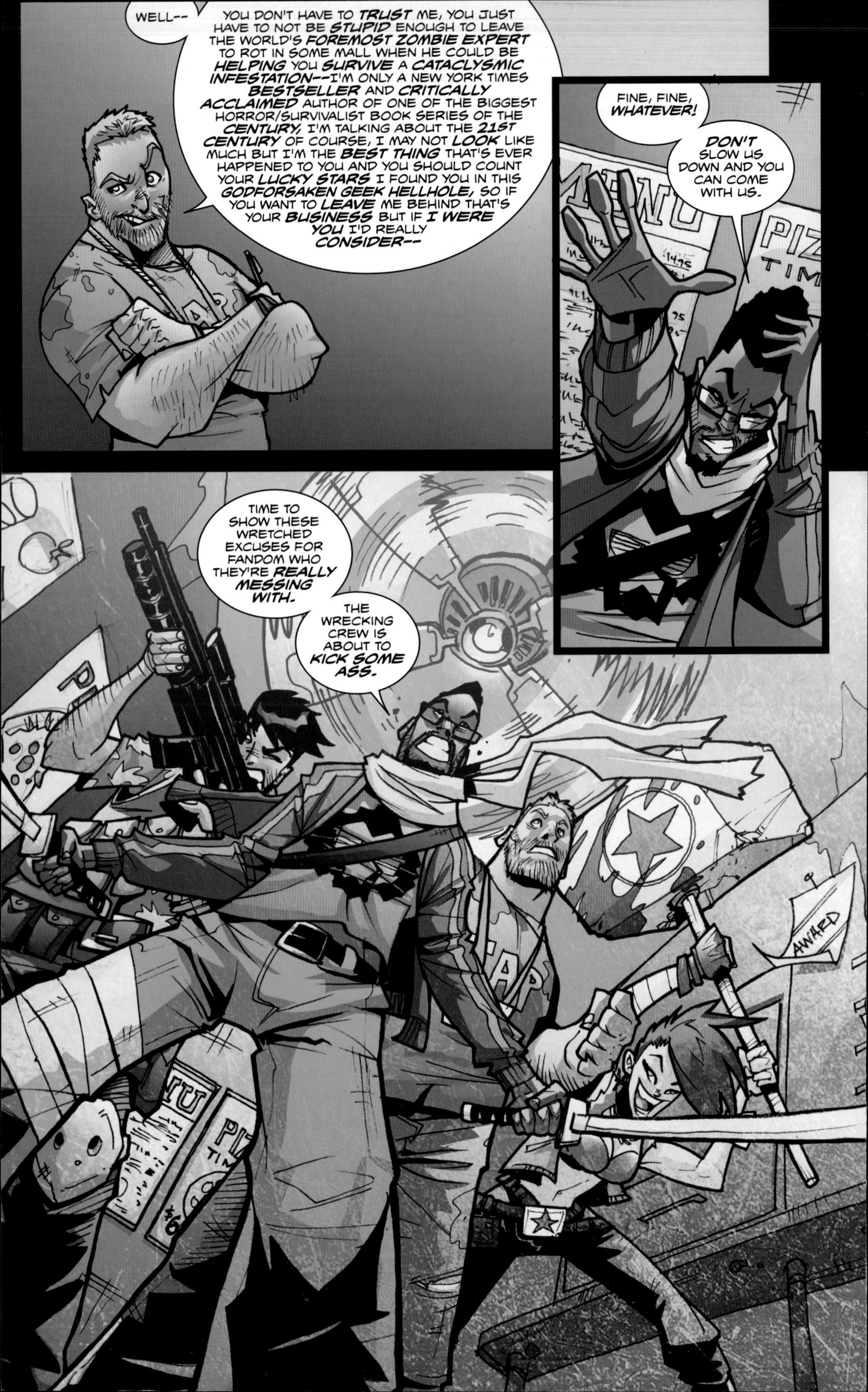
WELL--
YOU DON'T HAVE TO TRUST ME, YOU JUST HAVE TO NOT BE STUPID ENOUGH TO LEAVE THE WORLD'S FOREMOST ZOMBIE EXPERT TO ROT IN SOME MALL WHEN HE COULD BE HELPING YOU SURVIVE A CATACLYSMIC INFESTATION--I'M ONLY A NEW YORK TIMES BESTSELLER AND CRITICALLY ACCLAIMED AUTHOR OF ONE OF THE BIGGEST HORROR/SURVIVALIST BOOK SERIES OF THE CENTURY, I'M TALKING ABOUT THE 21ST CENTURY OF COURSE, I MAY NOT LOOK LIKE MUCH BUT I'M THE BEST THING THAT'S EVER HAPPENED TO YOU AND YOU SHOULD COUNT YOUR LUCKY STARS I FOUND YOU IN THIS GODFORSAKEN GEEK HELLHOLE, SO IF YOU WANT TO LEAVE ME BEHIND THAT'S YOUR BUSINESS BUT IF I WERE YOU I'D REALLY CONSIDER--
FINE, FINE, WHATEVER!
DON'T SLOW US DOWN AND YOU CAN COME WITH US.
TIME TO SHOW THESE WRETCHED EXCUSES FOR FANDOM WHO THEY'RE REALLY MESSING WITH.
THE WRECKING CREW IS ABOUT TO KICK SOME ASS.
AWARD

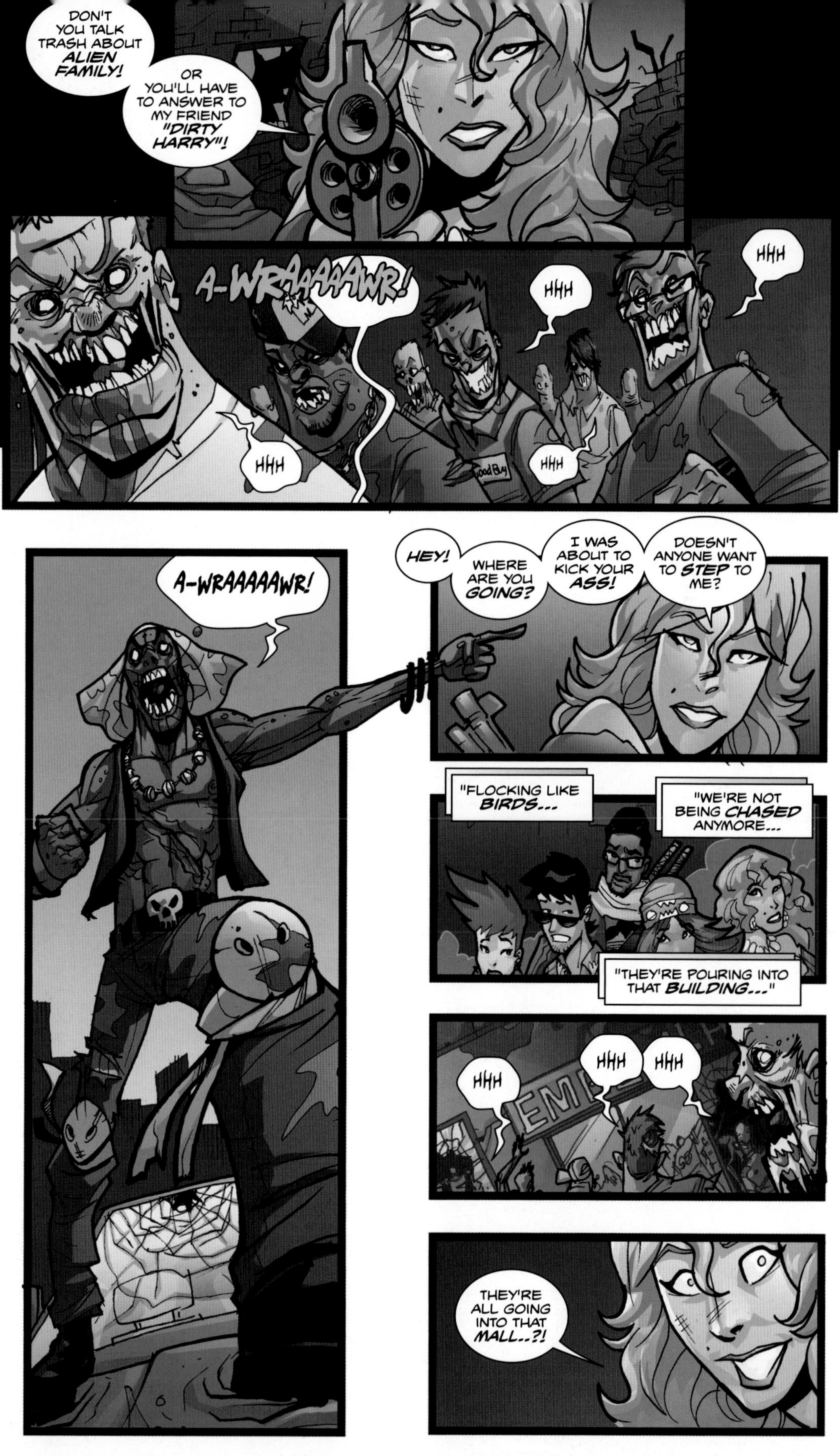
DON'T YOU TALK TRASH ABOUT ALIEN FAMILY!
OR YOU'LL HAVE TO ANSWER TO MY FRIEND "DIRTY HARRY"!
A-WRAAAAAWR!
HHH
HHH
HHH
HHH
A-WRAAAAAWR!
HEY!
WHERE ARE YOU GOING?
I WAS ABOUT TO KICK YOUR ASS!
DOESN'T ANYONE WANT TO STEP TO ME?
"FLOCKING LIKE BIRDS...
"WE'RE NOT BEING CHASED ANYMORE...
"THEY'RE POURING INTO THAT BUILDING..."
HHH
HHH
HHH
THEY'RE ALL GOING INTO THAT MALL..?!

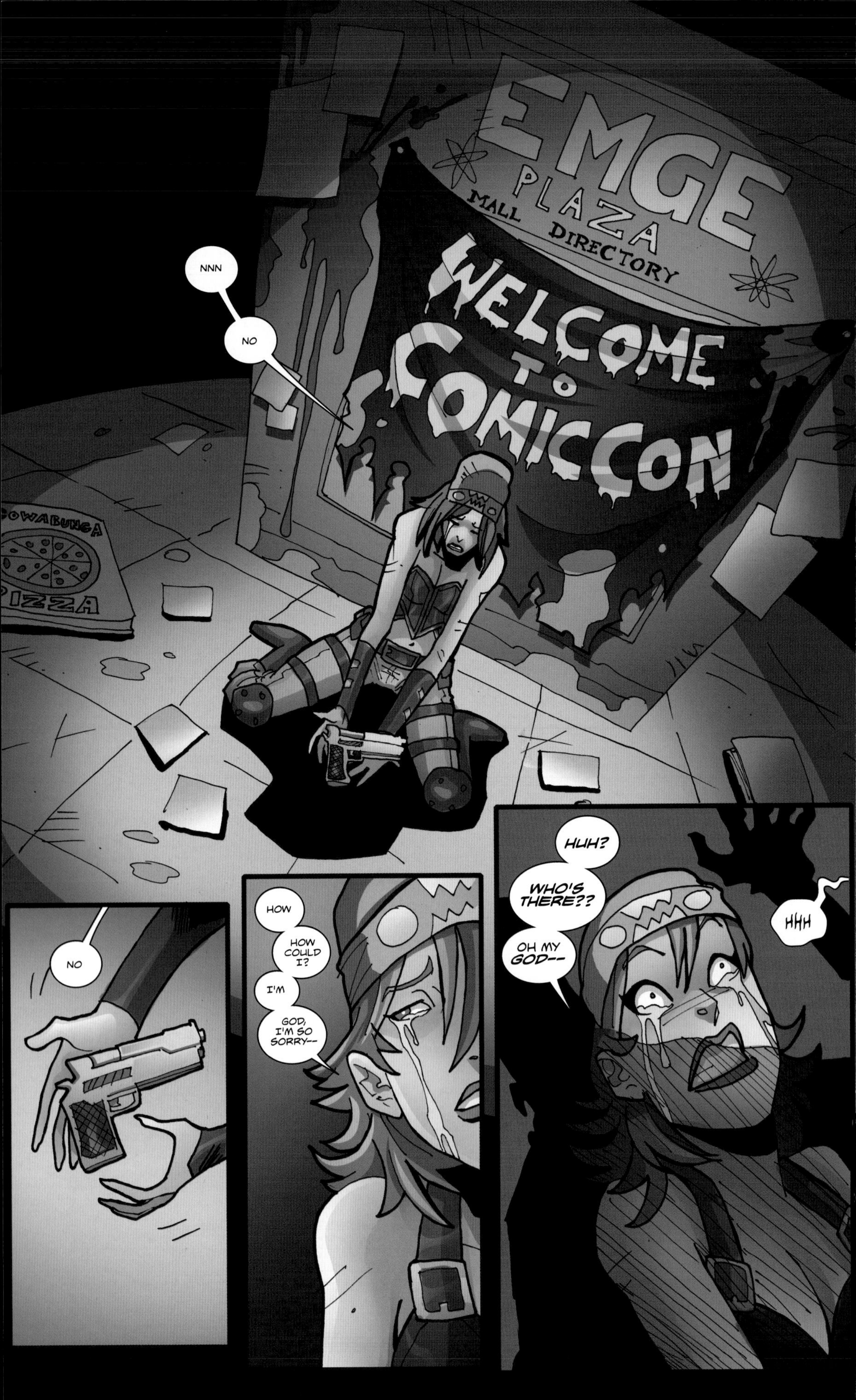
EMGE
PLAZA
MALL DIRECTORY
WELCOME TO COMICCON
COWABUNGA PIZZA
NNN
NO
NO
HOW
HOW COULD I?
I'M
GOD, I'M SO SORRY--
HUH?
WHO'S THERE??
OH MY GOD--
HHH

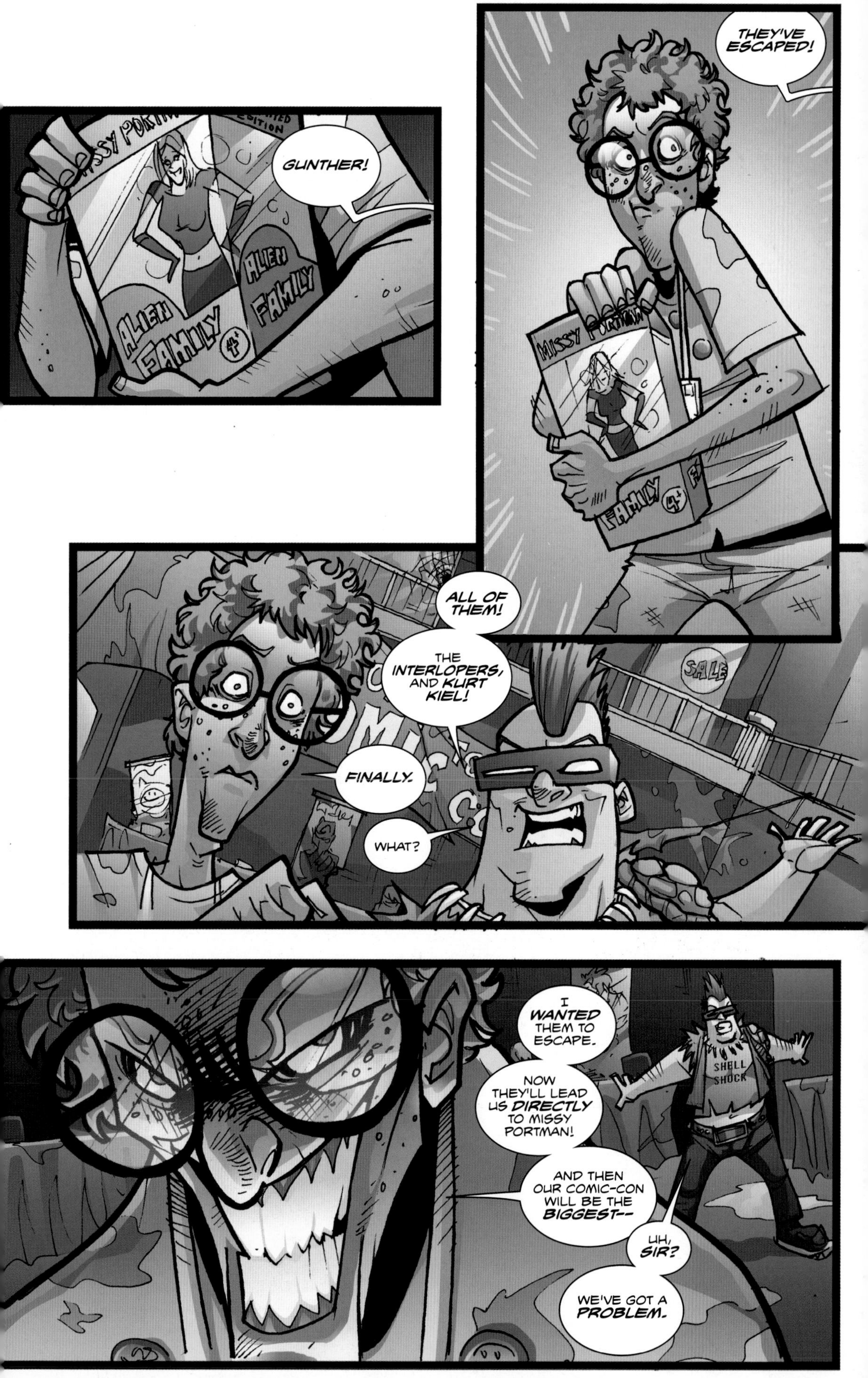
MISSY PORTMAN
LIMITED EDITION
ALIEN FAMILY
4+
GUNTHER!
THEY'VE ESCAPED!
ALL OF THEM!
THE INTERLOPERS, AND KURT KIEL!
FINALLY.
WHAT?
SALE
I WANTED THEM TO ESCAPE.
NOW THEY'LL LEAD US DIRECTLY TO MISSY PORTMAN!
AND THEN OUR COMIC-CON WILL BE THE BIGGEST--
SHELL SHOCK
UH, SIR?
WE'VE GOT A PROBLEM.

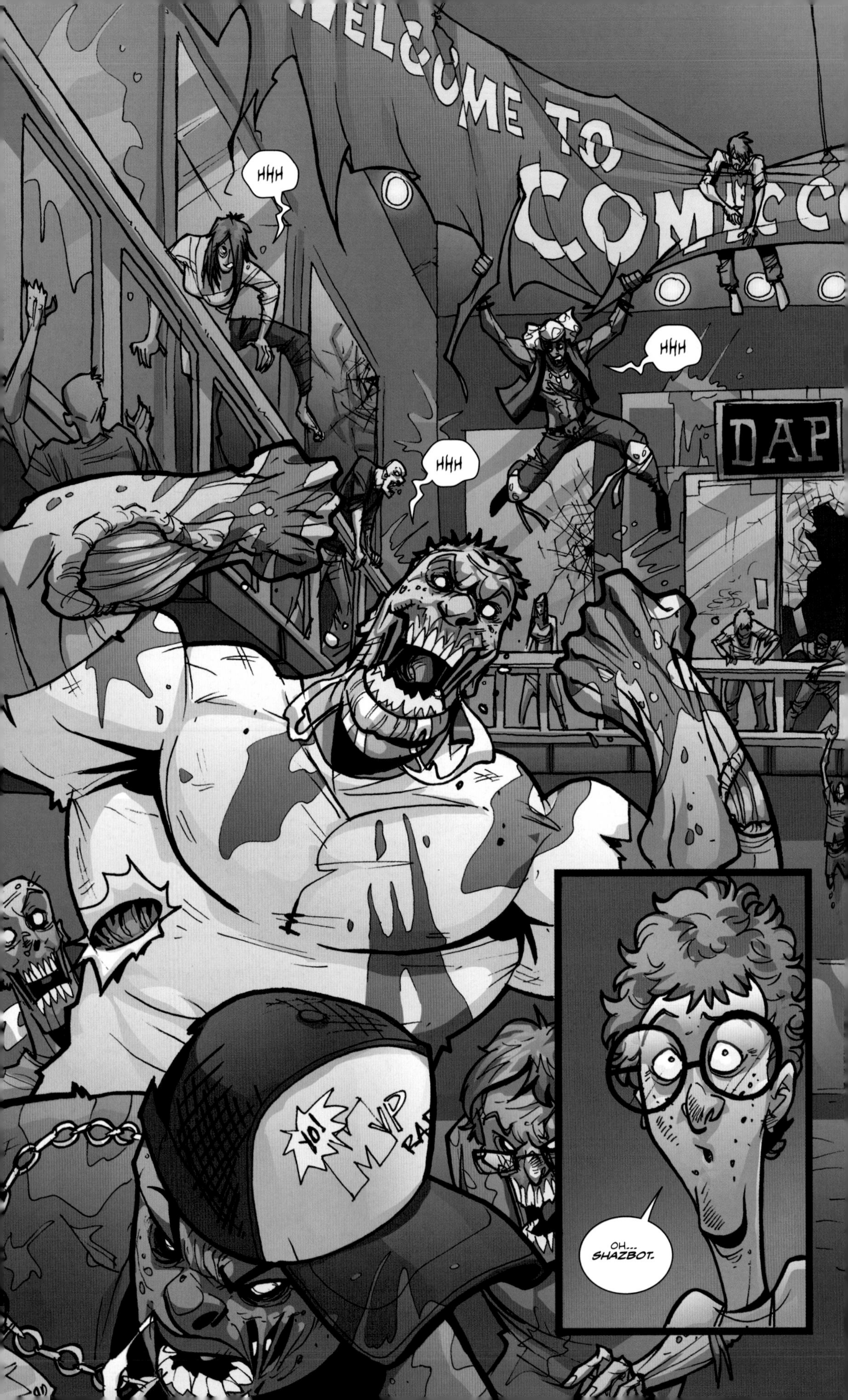
WELCOME TO
COMIC CO
HHH
HHH
DAP
HHH
YO!
OH... SHAZBOT.

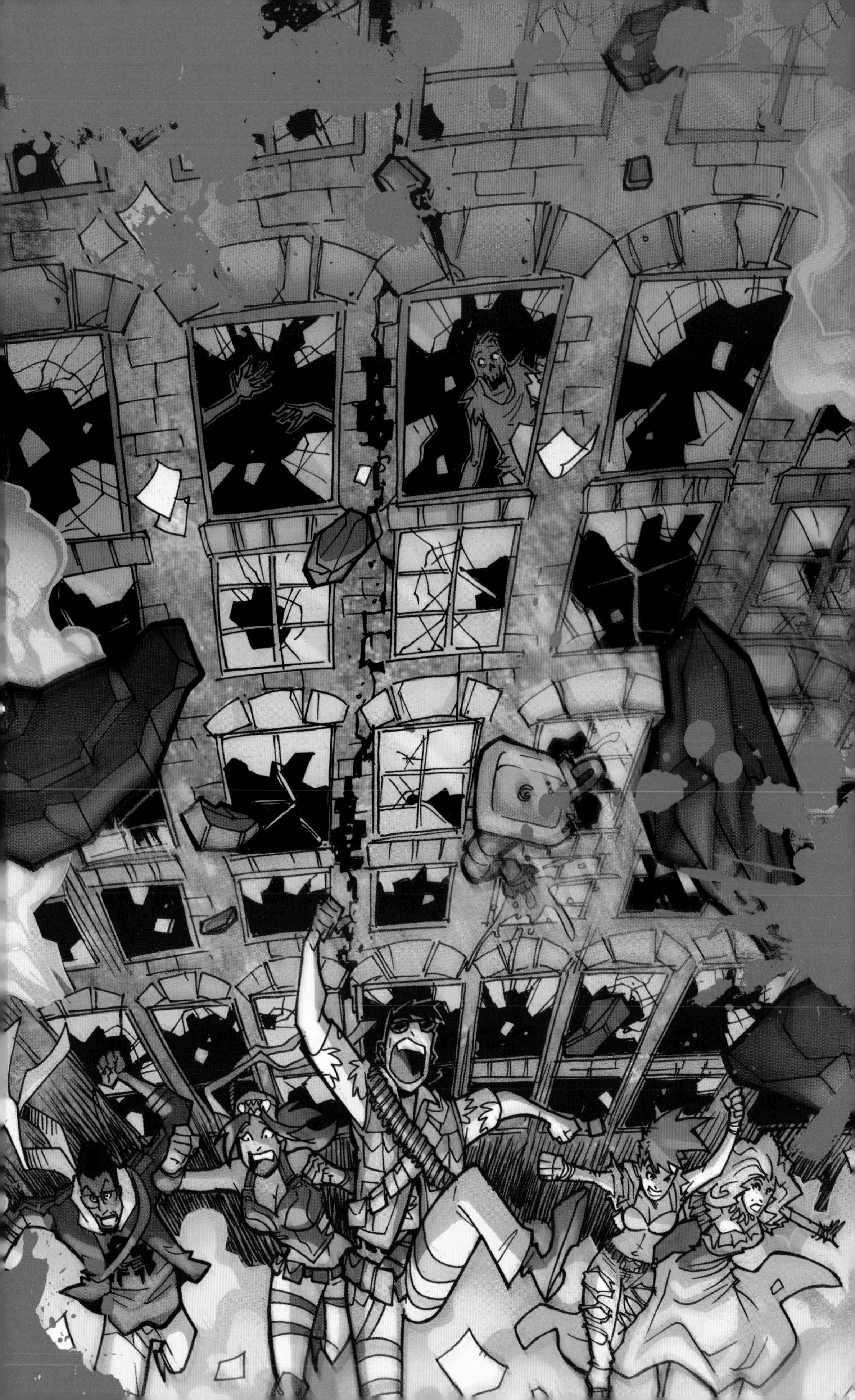

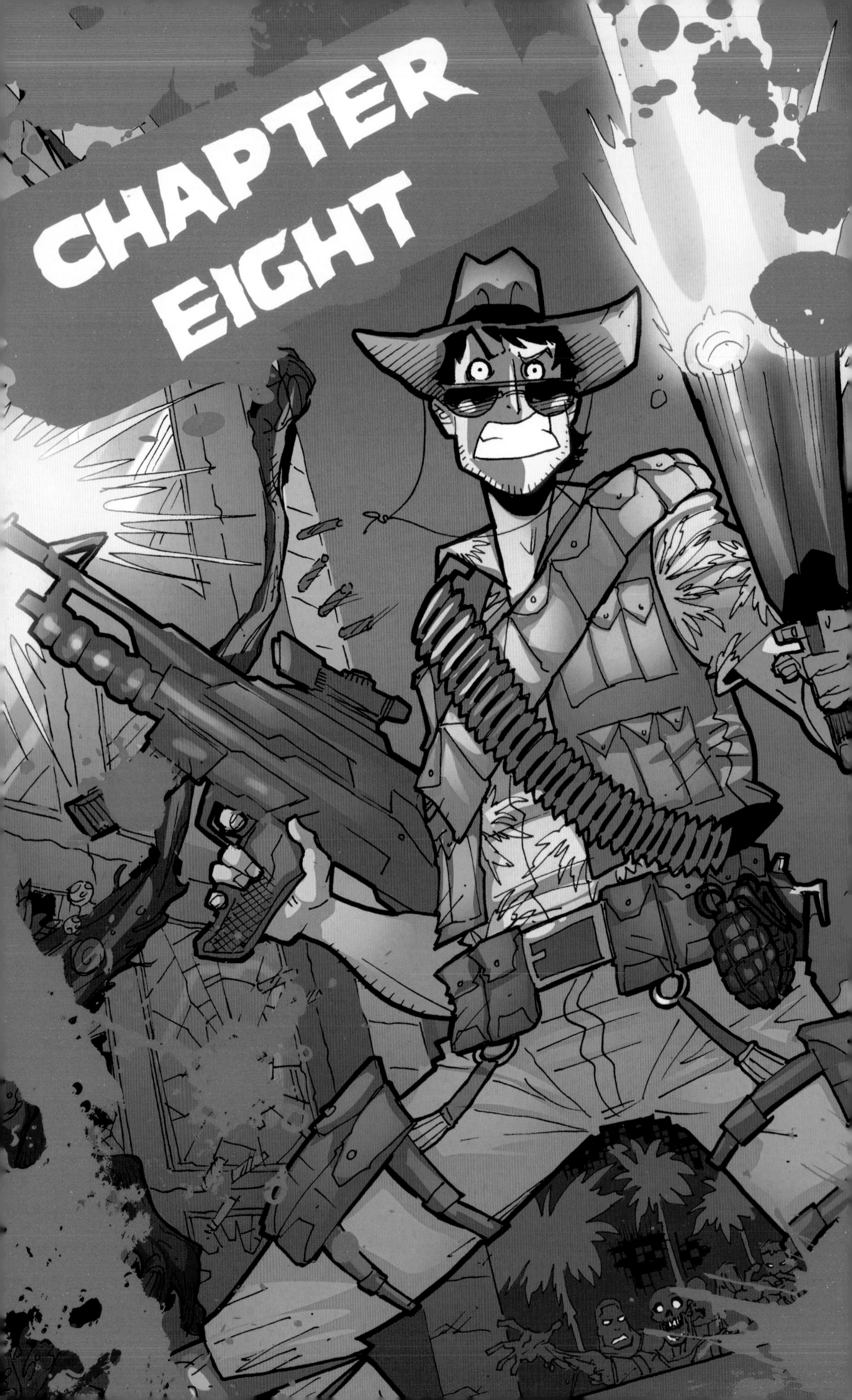
CHAPTER EIGHT

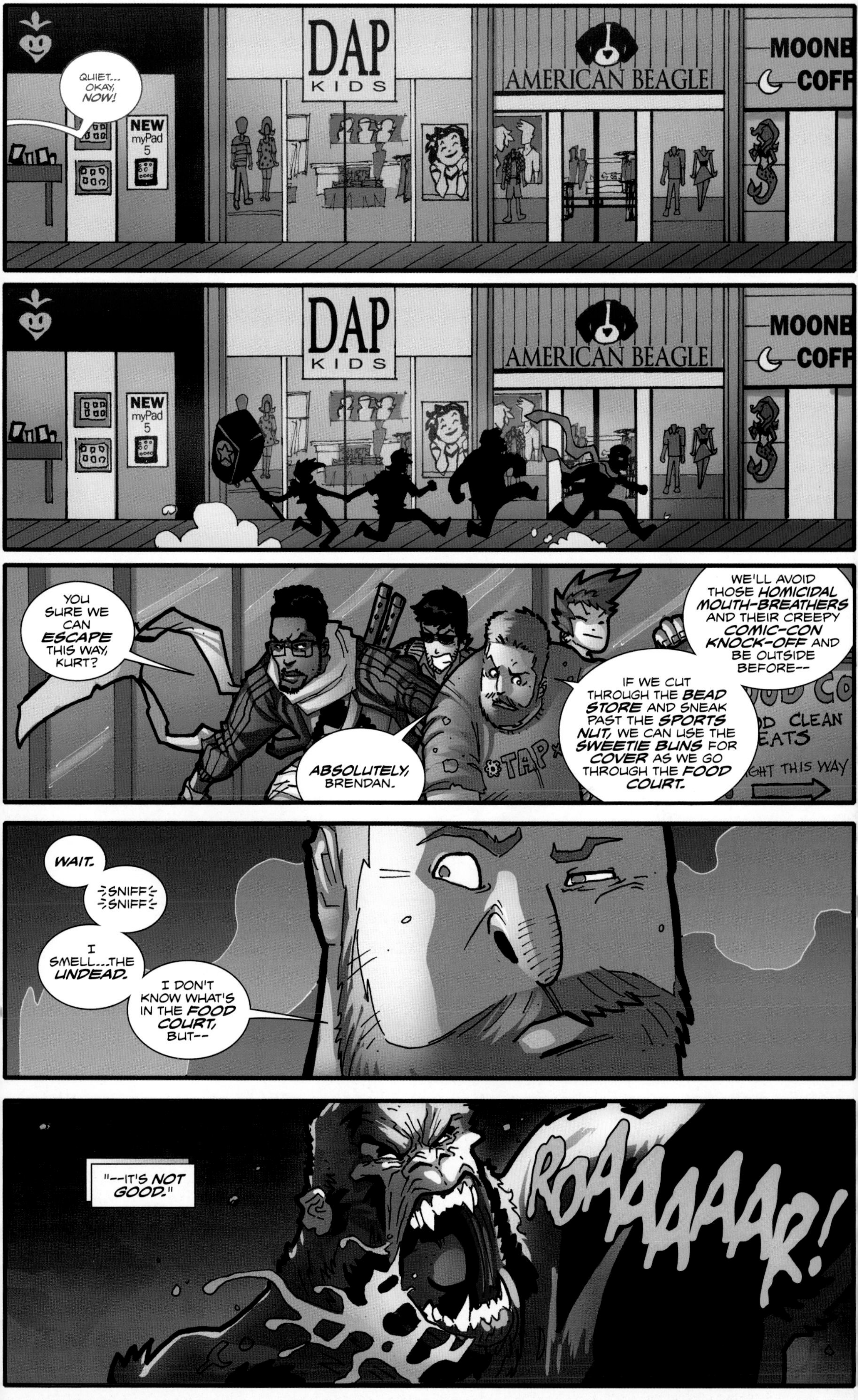
QUIET... OKAY, NOW!
DAP KIDS
AMERICAN BEAGLE
MOONB
COFF
NEW myPad 5
DAP KIDS
AMERICAN BEAGLE
MOONB
COFF
NEW myPad 5
YOU SURE WE CAN ESCAPE THIS WAY, KURT?
ABSOLUTELY, BRENDAN.
IF WE CUT THROUGH THE BEAD STORE AND SNEAK PAST THE SPORTS NUT, WE CAN USE THE SWEETIE BUNS FOR COVER AS WE GO THROUGH THE FOOD COURT.
WE'LL AVOID THOSE HOMICIDAL MOUTH-BREATHERS AND THEIR CREEPY COMIC-CON KNOCK-OFF AND BE OUTSIDE BEFORE--
TAP
OD CLEAN
EATS
GHT THIS WAY
WAIT.
SNIFF SNIFF
I SMELL...THE UNDEAD.
I DON'T KNOW WHAT'S IN THE FOOD COURT, BUT--
"--IT'S NOT GOOD."
ROAAAAAAR!

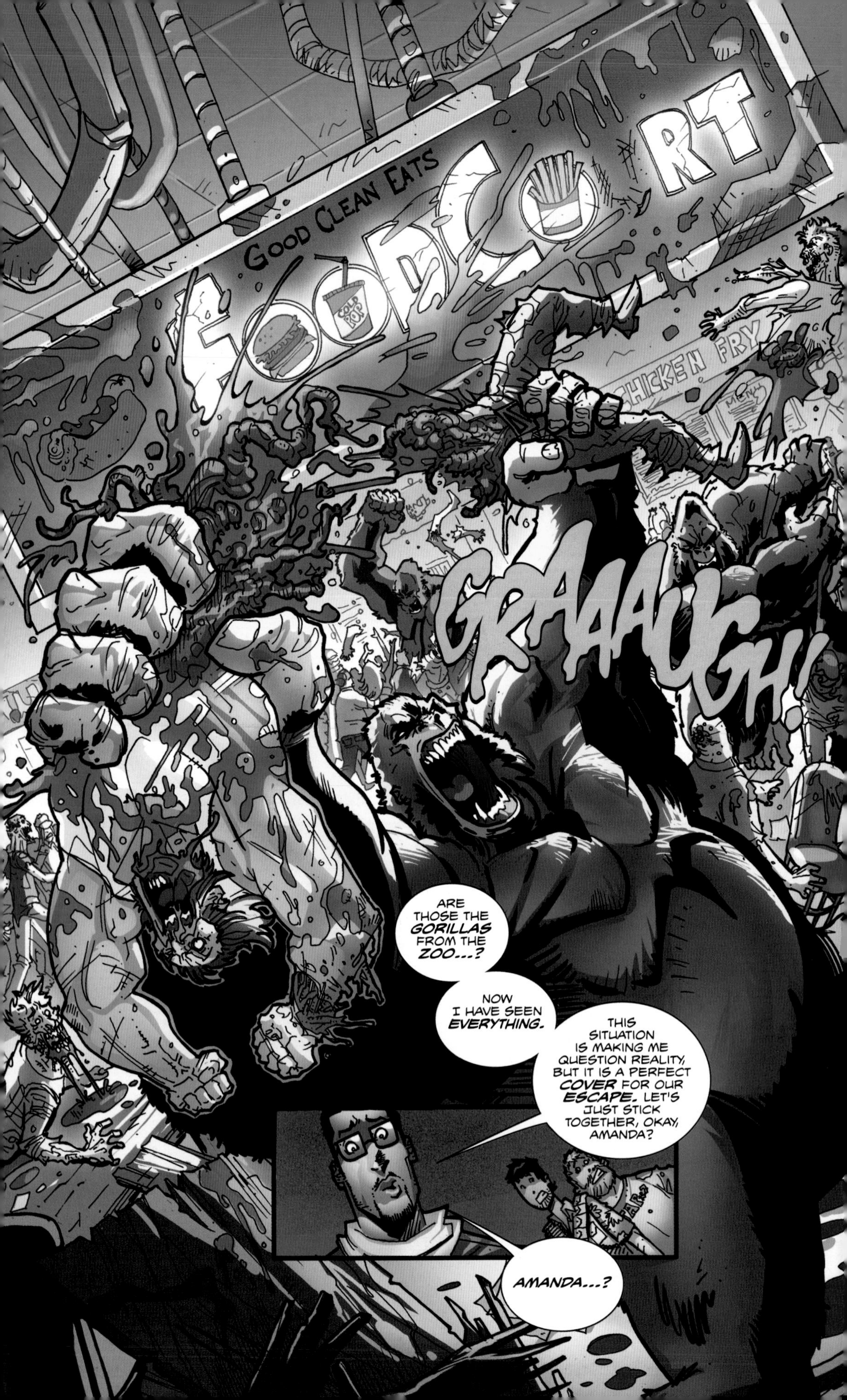
GOOD CLEAN EATS
FOOD COURT
COLD POP
CHICKEN FRY
GRAAAUGH!!
ARE THOSE THE GORILLAS FROM THE ZOO...?
NOW I HAVE SEEN EVERYTHING.
THIS SITUATION IS MAKING ME QUESTION REALITY, BUT IT IS A PERFECT COVER FOR OUR ESCAPE. LET'S JUST STICK TOGETHER, OKAY, AMANDA?
AMANDA...?

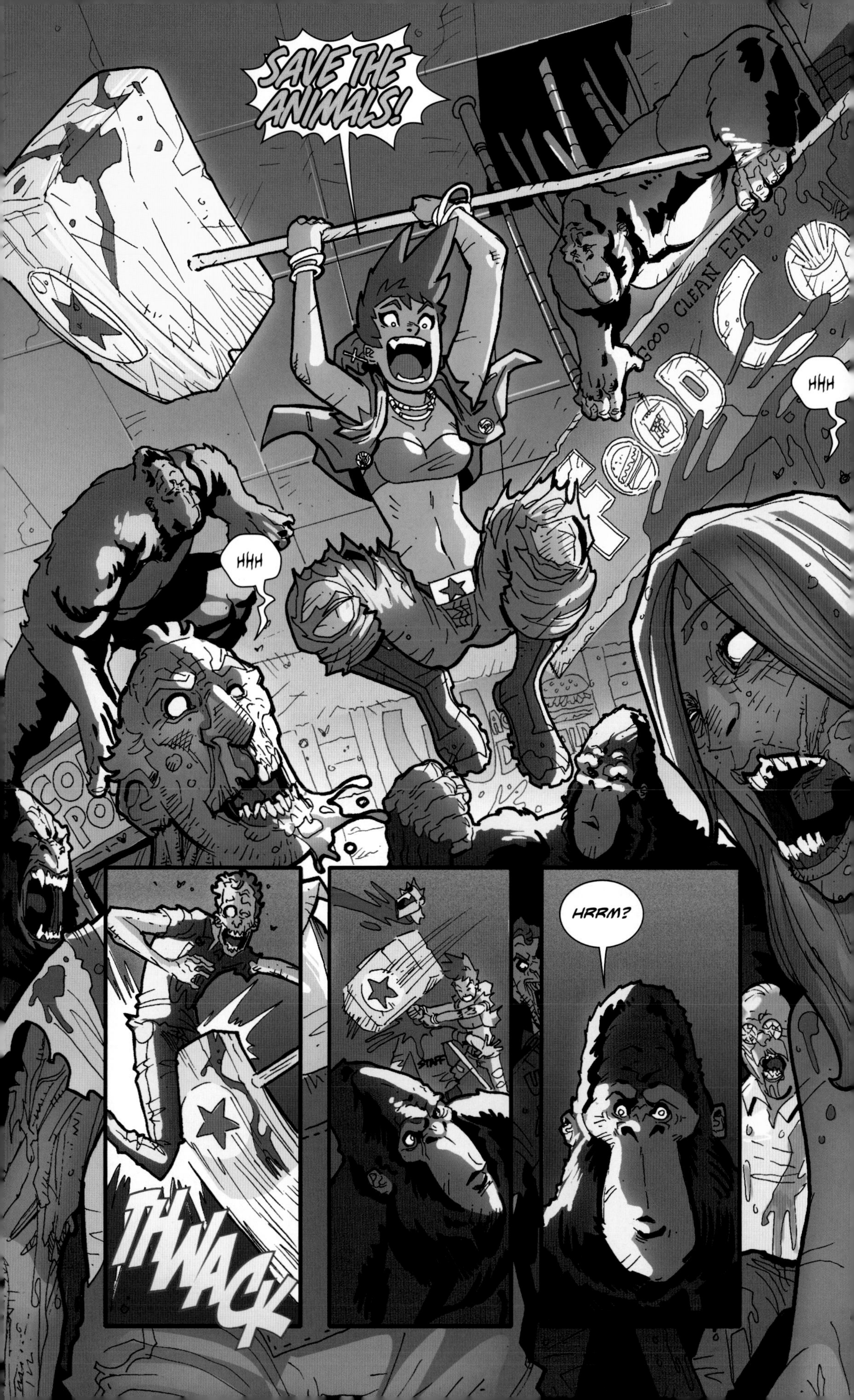
SAVE THE ANIMALS!
HHH
HHH
GOOD CLEAN EATS
FOOD
THWACK
STAFF
HRRM?

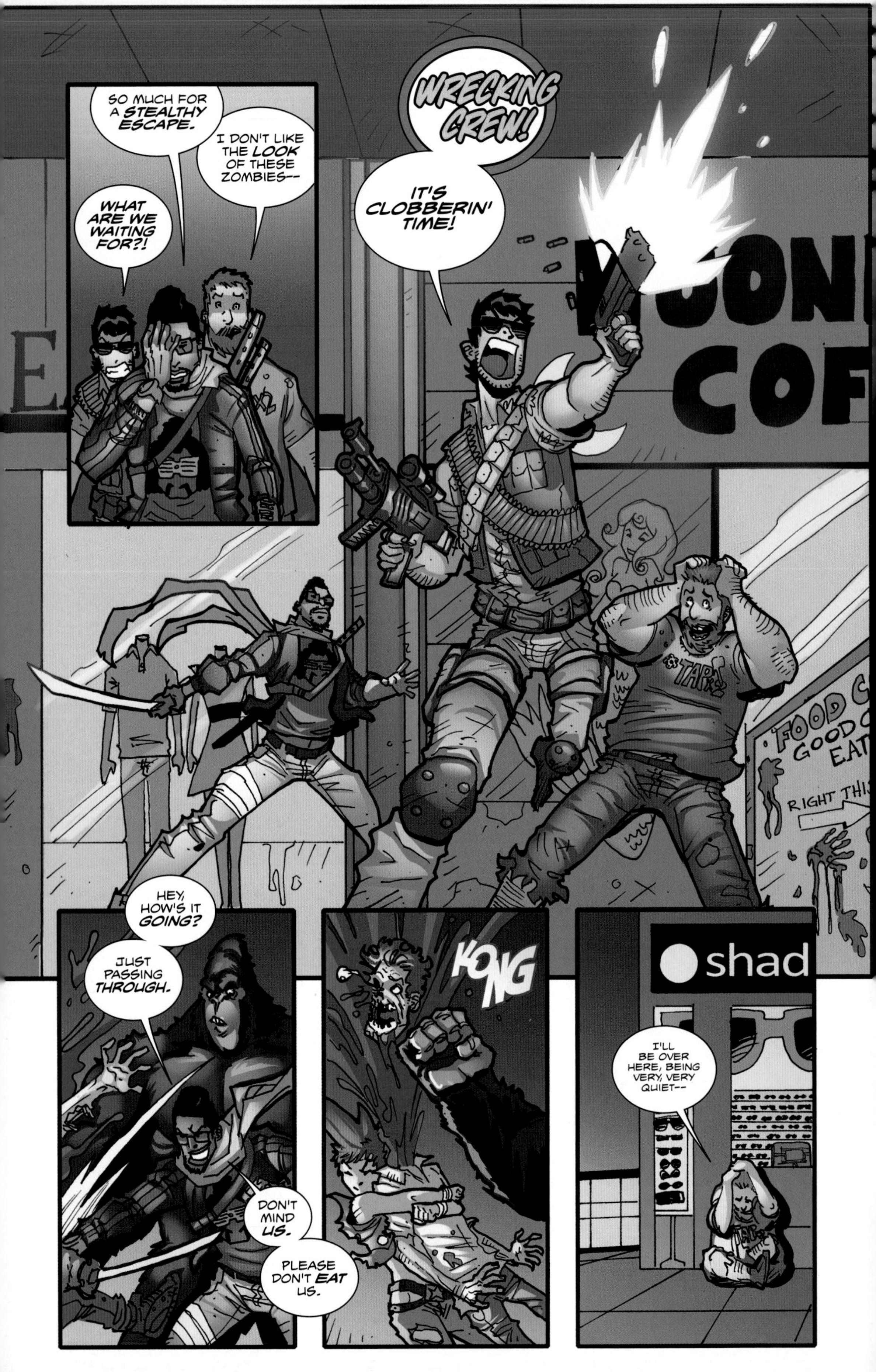
SO MUCH FOR A STEALTHY ESCAPE.
I DON'T LIKE THE LOOK OF THESE ZOMBIES--
WHAT ARE WE WAITING FOR?!
WRECKING CREW!
IT'S CLOBBERIN' TIME!
COF
FOOD C
GOOD
EAT
RIGHT THI
HEY, HOW'S IT GOING?
JUST PASSING THROUGH.
DON'T MIND US.
PLEASE DON'T EAT US.
KONG
shad
I'LL BE OVER HERE, BEING VERY, VERY QUIET--

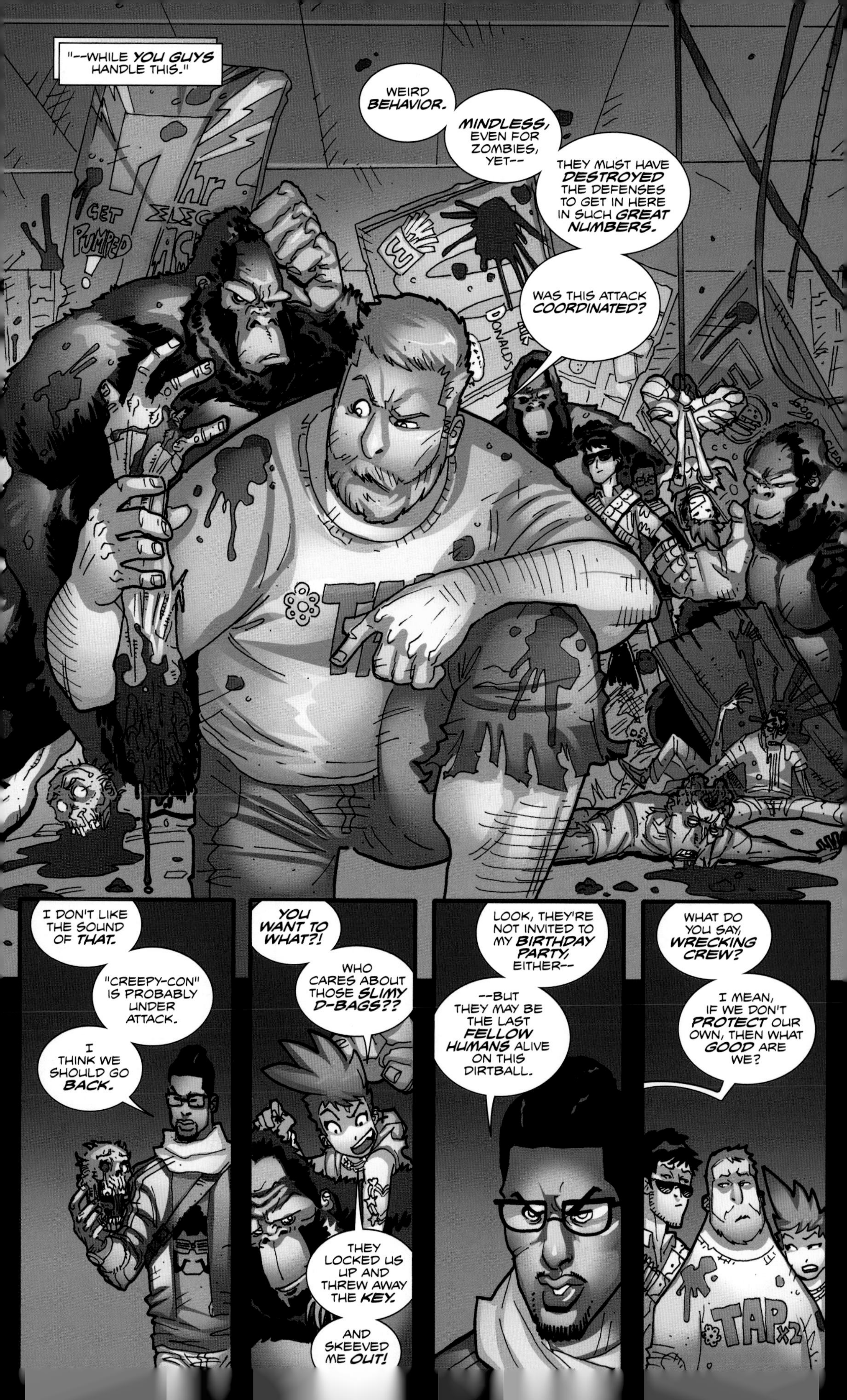
"--WHILE YOU GUYS HANDLE THIS."
WEIRD BEHAVIOR.
MINDLESS, EVEN FOR ZOMBIES, YET--
THEY MUST HAVE DESTROYED THE DEFENSES TO GET IN HERE IN SUCH GREAT NUMBERS.
WAS THIS ATTACK COORDINATED?
I DON'T LIKE THE SOUND OF THAT.
"CREEPY-CON" IS PROBABLY UNDER ATTACK.
I THINK WE SHOULD GO BACK.
YOU WANT TO WHAT?!
WHO CARES ABOUT THOSE SLIMY D-BAGS??
THEY LOCKED US UP AND THREW AWAY THE KEY.
AND SKEEVED ME OUT!
LOOK, THEY'RE NOT INVITED TO MY BIRTHDAY PARTY, EITHER--
--BUT THEY MAY BE THE LAST FELLOW HUMANS ALIVE ON THIS DIRTBALL.
WHAT DO YOU SAY, WRECKING CREW?
I MEAN, IF WE DON'T PROTECT OUR OWN, THEN WHAT GOOD ARE WE?
TAP x2

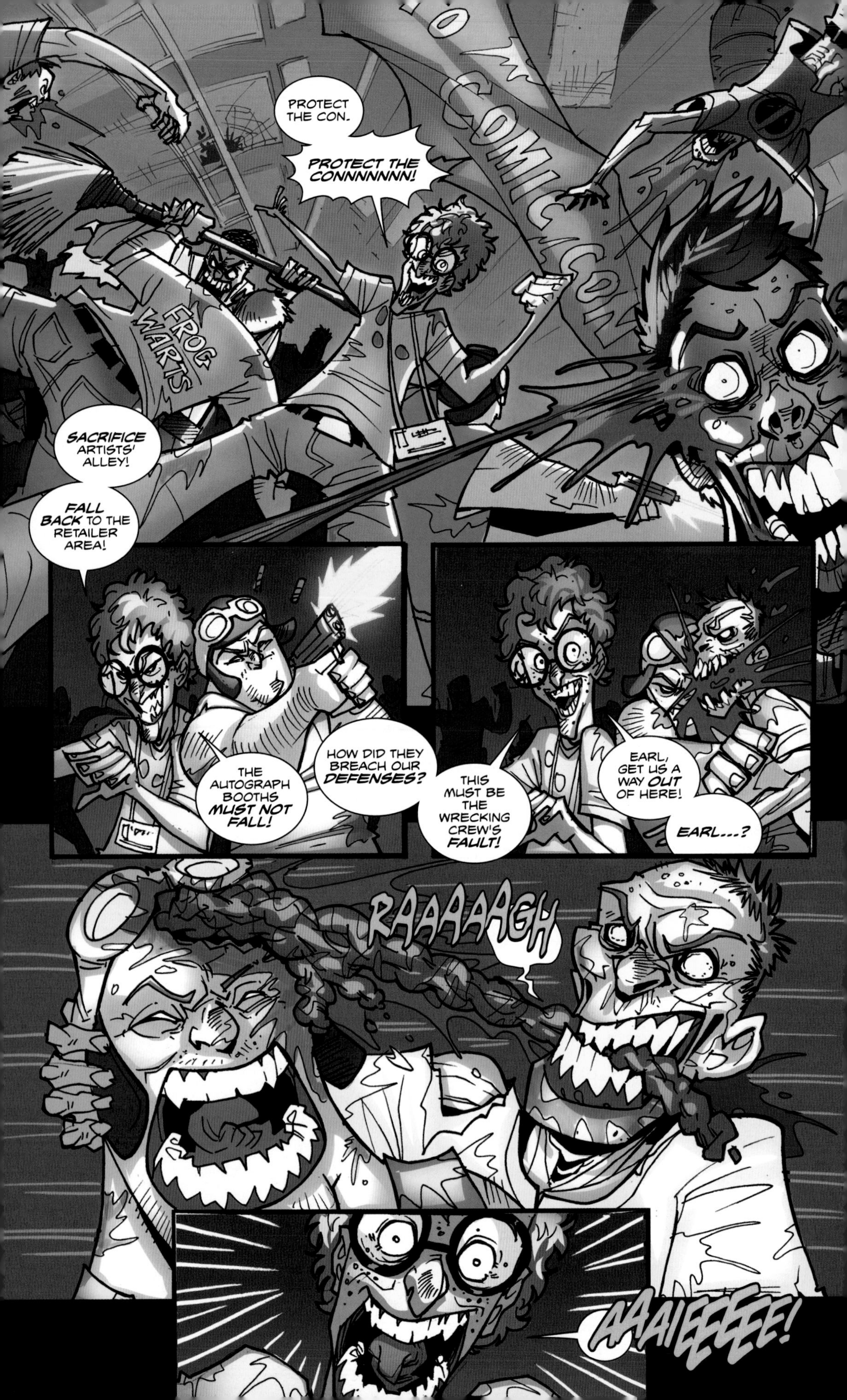
PROTECT THE CON.
PROTECT THE CONNNNNNN!
SACRIFICE ARTISTS' ALLEY!
FALL BACK TO THE RETAILER AREA!
THE AUTOGRAPH BOOTHS MUST NOT FALL!
HOW DID THEY BREACH OUR DEFENSES?
THIS MUST BE THE WRECKING CREW'S FAULT!
EARL, GET US A WAY OUT OF HERE!
EARL...?
RAAAAAGH
AAAIEEEEEE!

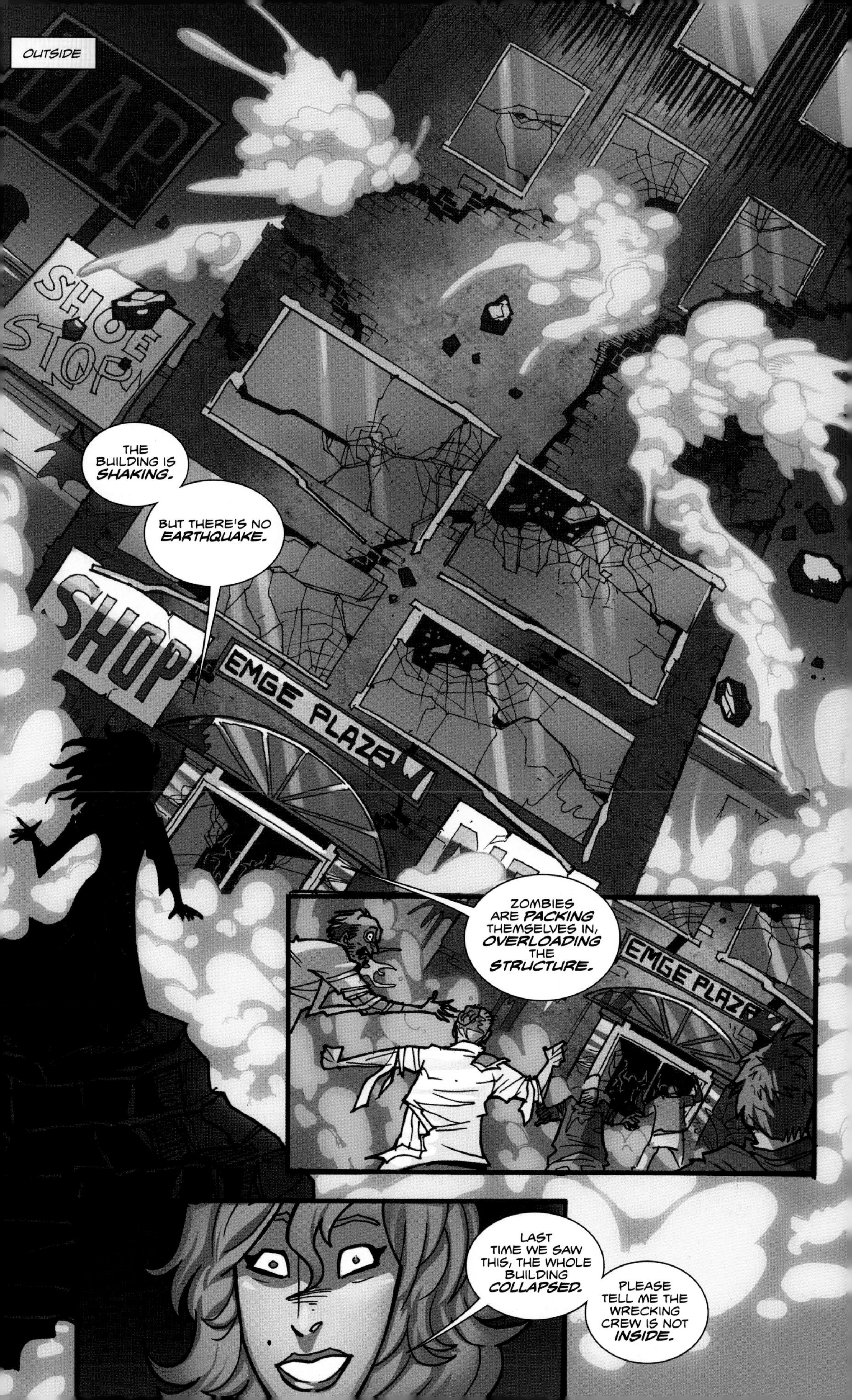
OUTSIDE
SHOE STOP
SHOP
EMGE PLAZE
THE BUILDING IS SHAKING.
BUT THERE'S NO EARTHQUAKE.
ZOMBIES ARE PACKING THEMSELVES IN, OVERLOADING THE STRUCTURE.
EMGE PLAZA
LAST TIME WE SAW THIS, THE WHOLE BUILDING COLLAPSED.
PLEASE TELL ME THE WRECKING CREW IS NOT INSIDE.

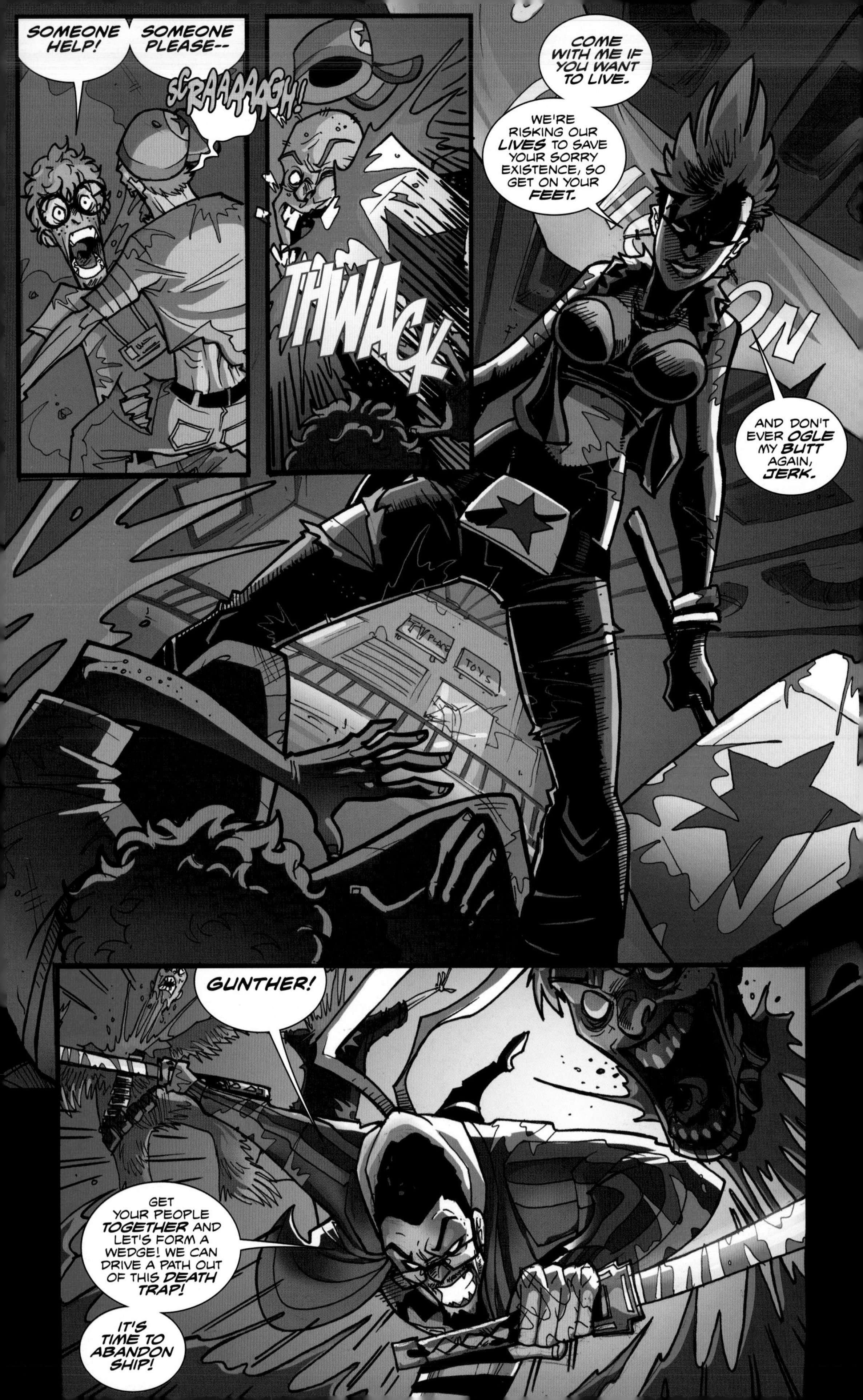
SOMEONE HELP!
SOMEONE PLEASE--
SCRAAAAAGH!
THWACK
COME WITH ME IF YOU WANT TO LIVE.
WE'RE RISKING OUR LIVES TO SAVE YOUR SORRY EXISTENCE, SO GET ON YOUR FEET.
AND DON'T EVER OGLE MY BUTT AGAIN, JERK.
TOYS
GUNTHER!
GET YOUR PEOPLE TOGETHER AND LET'S FORM A WEDGE! WE CAN DRIVE A PATH OUT OF THIS DEATH TRAP!
IT'S TIME TO ABANDON SHIP!

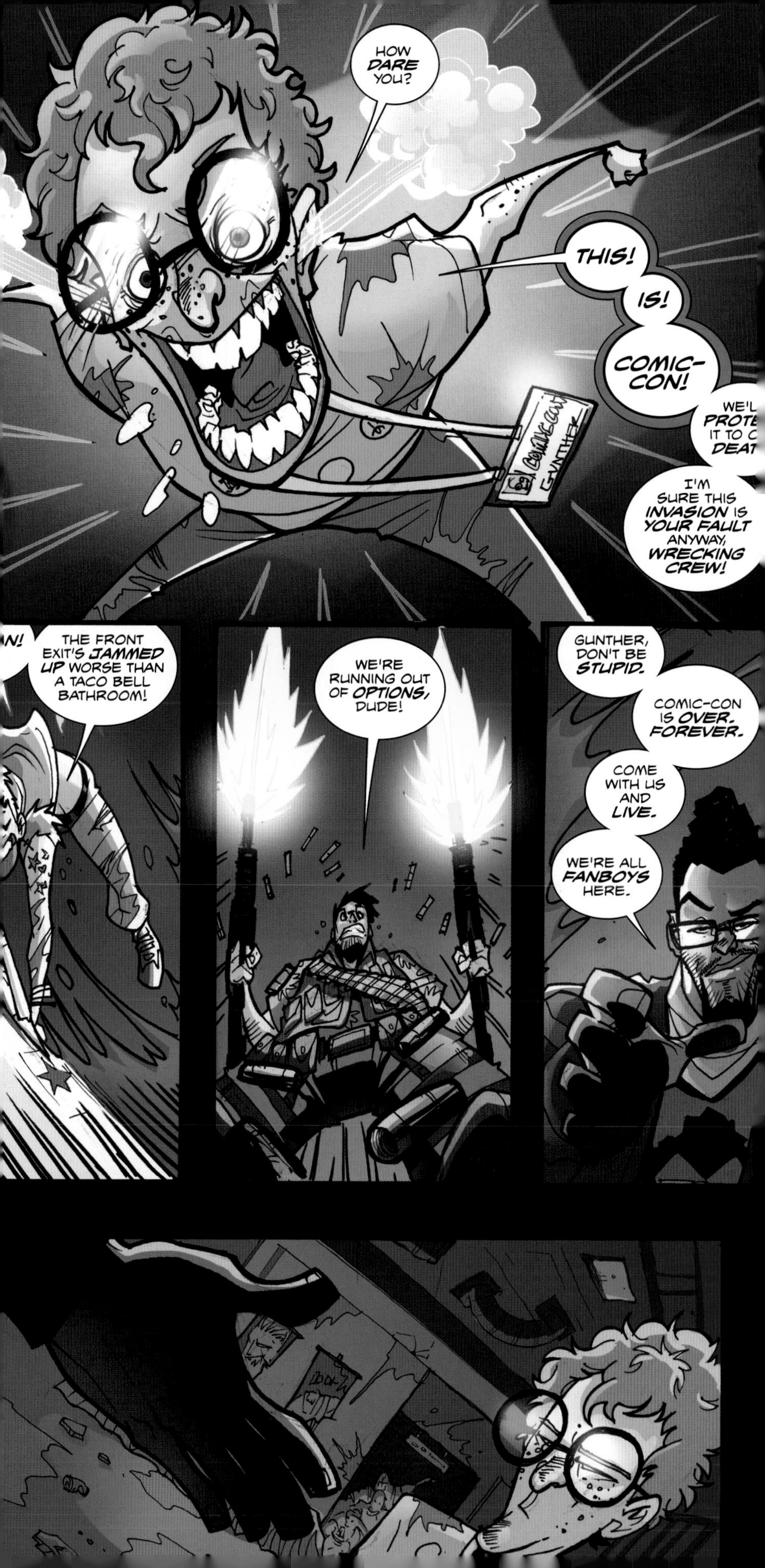
HOW DARE YOU?
THIS!
IS!
COMIC-CON!
WE'L PROTE IT TO O DEAT
I'M SURE THIS INVASION IS YOUR FAULT ANYWAY, WRECKING CREW!
N!
THE FRONT EXIT'S JAMMED UP WORSE THAN A TACO BELL BATHROOM!
WE'RE RUNNING OUT OF OPTIONS, DUDE!
GUNTHER, DON'T BE STUPID.
COMIC-CON IS OVER. FOREVER.
COME WITH US AND LIVE.
WE'RE ALL FANBOYS HERE.

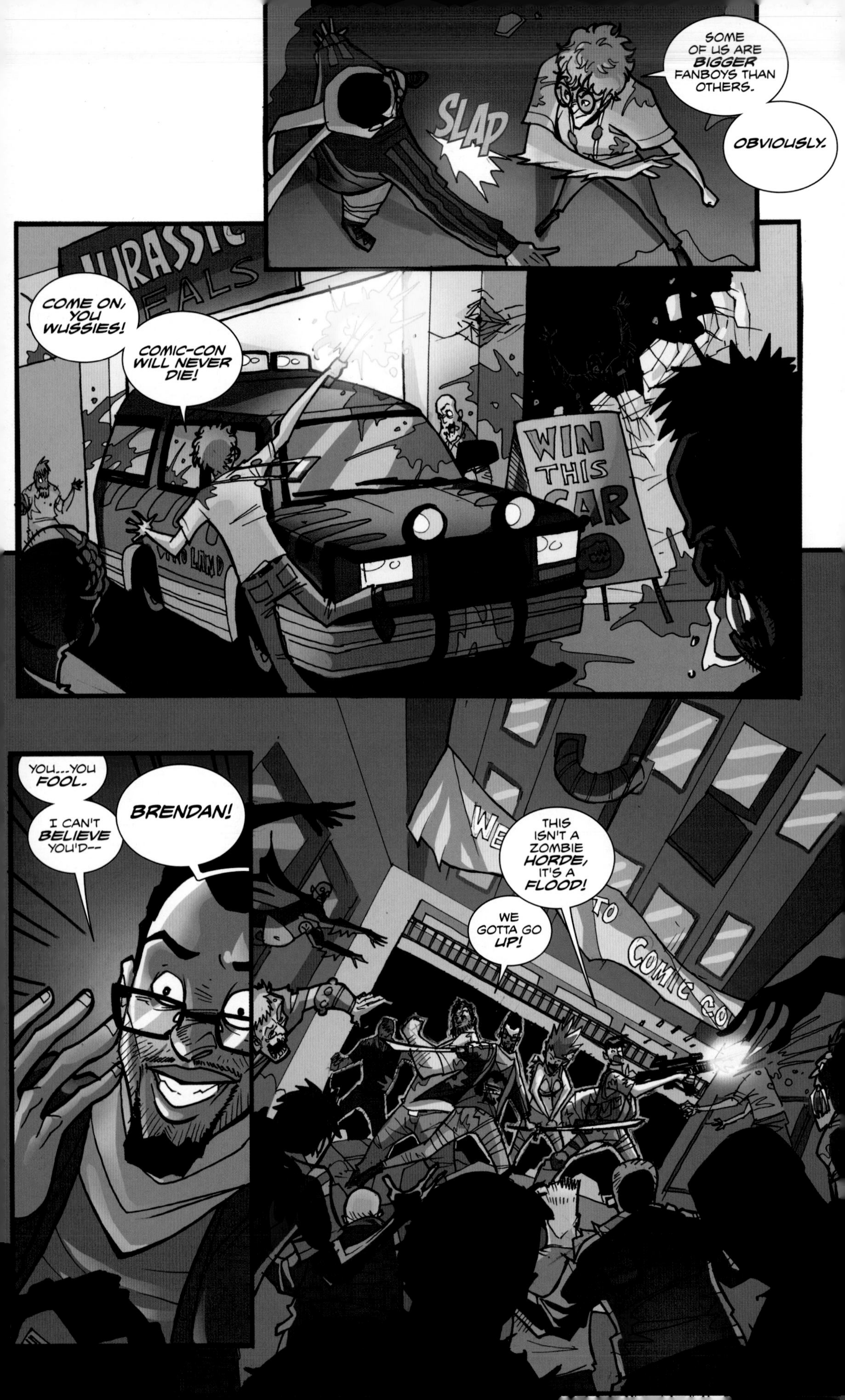
SOME OF US ARE BIGGER FANBOYS THAN OTHERS.
SLAP
OBVIOUSLY.
COME ON, YOU WUSSIES!
COMIC-CON WILL NEVER DIE!
WIN THIS CAR
YOU...YOU FOOL.
I CAN'T BELIEVE YOU'D--
BRENDAN!
THIS ISN'T A ZOMBIE HORDE, IT'S A FLOOD!
WE GOTTA GO UP!

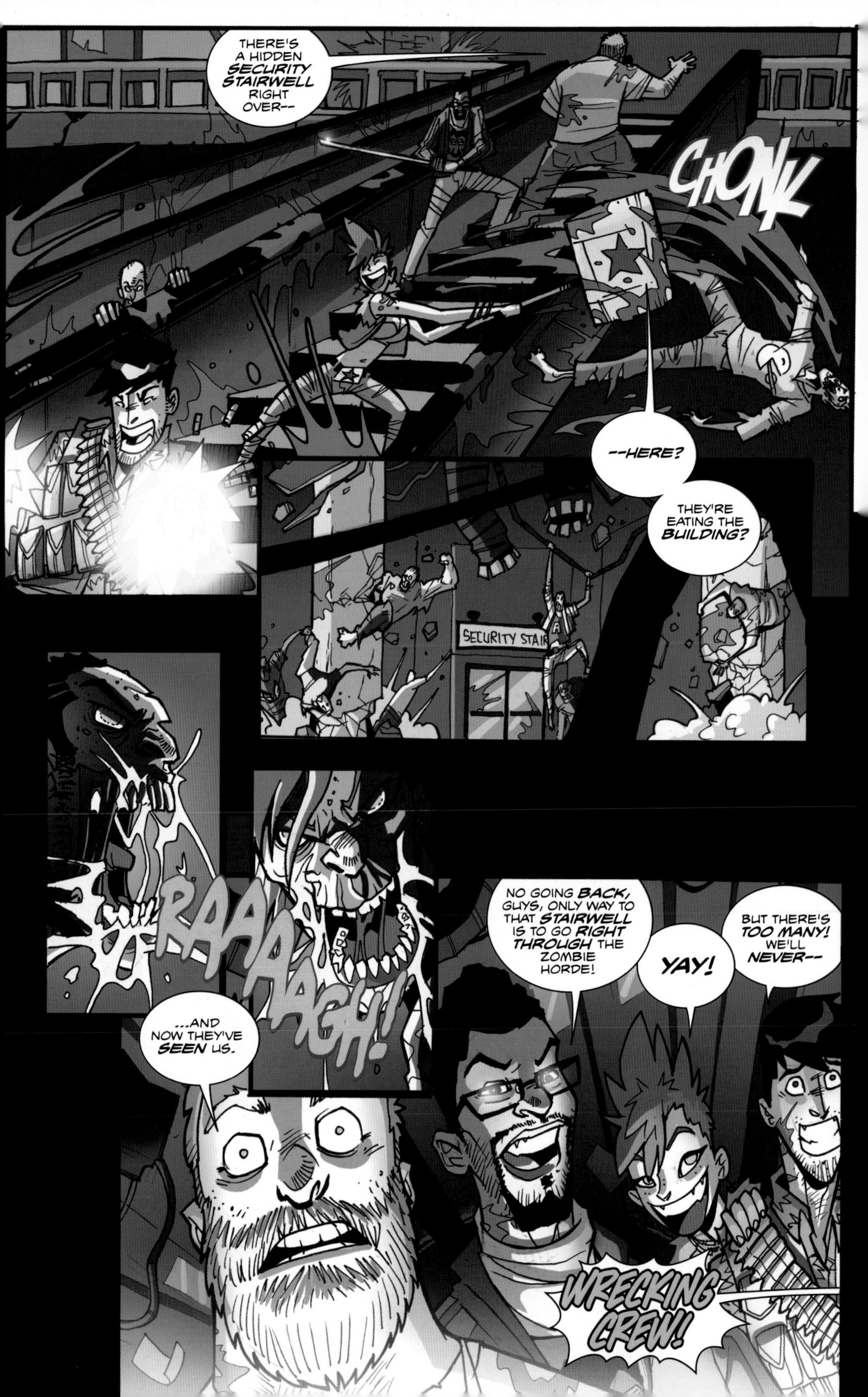
THERE'S A HIDDEN SECURITY STAIRWELL RIGHT OVER--
CHONK
--HERE?
THEY'RE EATING THE BUILDING?
SECURITY STAIR
RAAAAAGH!!
...AND NOW THEY'VE SEEN US.
NO GOING BACK, GUYS, ONLY WAY TO THAT STAIRWELL IS TO GO RIGHT THROUGH THE ZOMBIE HORDE!
YAY!
BUT THERE'S TOO MANY! WE'LL NEVER--
WRECKING CREW!

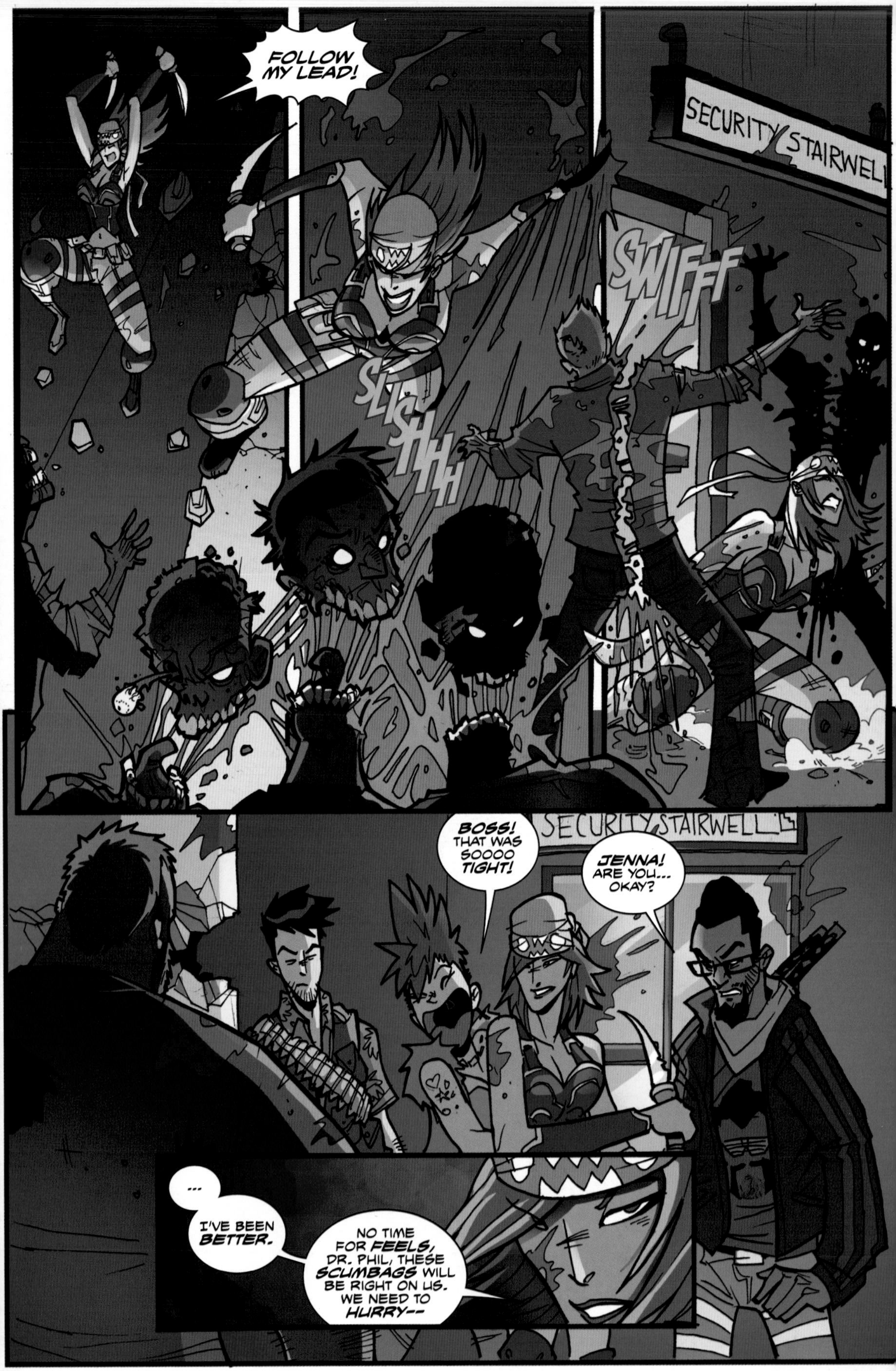
FOLLOW MY LEAD!
SECURITY STAIRWELL
SWIFFF
SLISHHH
SECURITY STAIRWELL
BOSS! THAT WAS SOOOO TIGHT!
JENNA! ARE YOU... OKAY?
...
I'VE BEEN BETTER.
NO TIME FOR FEELS, DR. PHIL, THESE SCUMBAGS WILL BE RIGHT ON US. WE NEED TO HURRY--

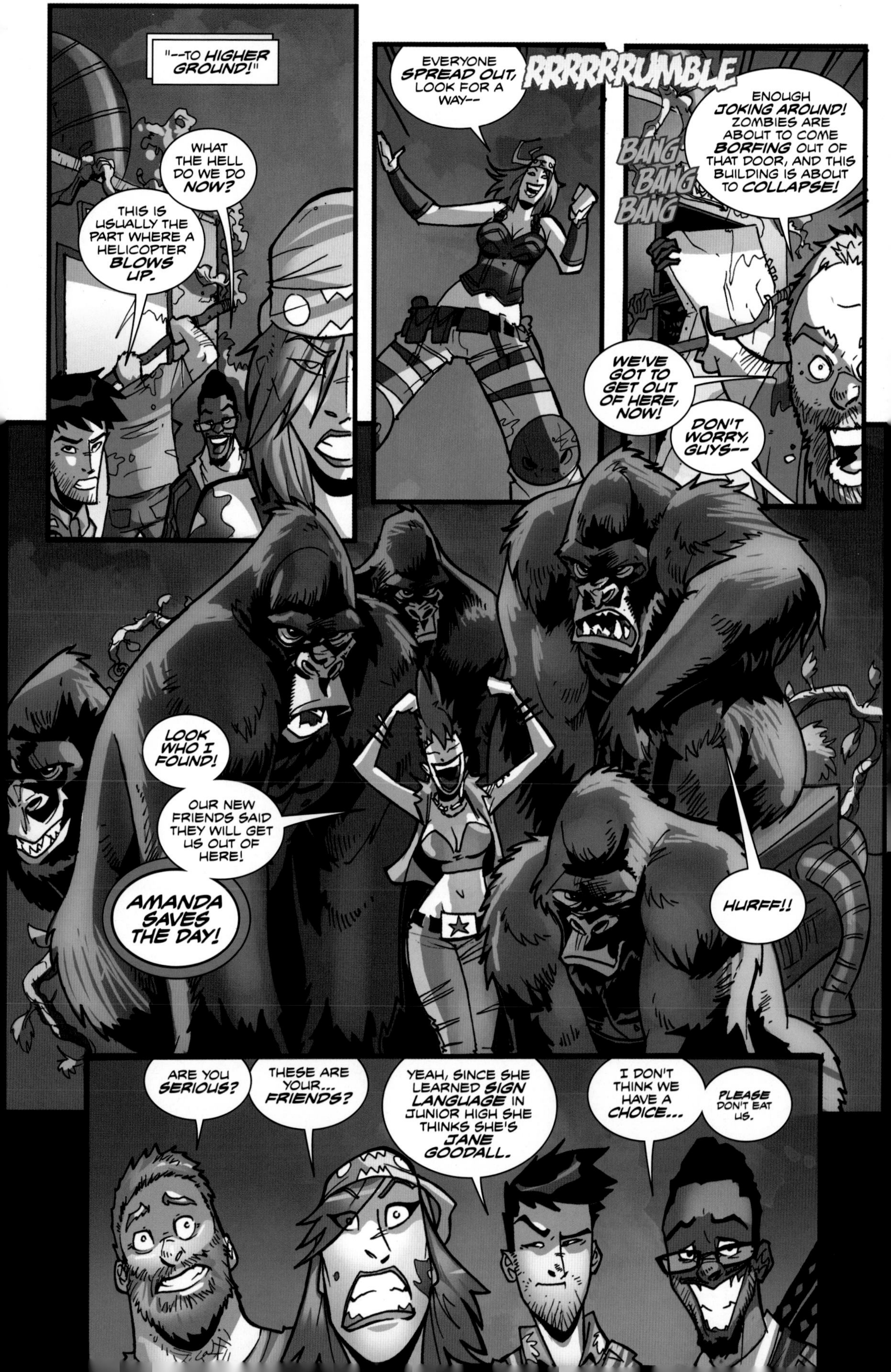
"--TO HIGHER GROUND!"
WHAT THE HELL DO WE DO NOW?
THIS IS USUALLY THE PART WHERE A HELICOPTER BLOWS UP.
EVERYONE SPREAD OUT, LOOK FOR A WAY--
RRRRRRUMBLE
BANG BANG BANG
ENOUGH JOKING AROUND! ZOMBIES ARE ABOUT TO COME BORFING OUT OF THAT DOOR, AND THIS BUILDING IS ABOUT TO COLLAPSE!
WE'VE GOT TO GET OUT OF HERE, NOW!
DON'T WORRY, GUYS--
LOOK WHO I FOUND!
OUR NEW FRIENDS SAID THEY WILL GET US OUT OF HERE!
AMANDA SAVES THE DAY!
HURFF!!
ARE YOU SERIOUS?
THESE ARE YOUR... FRIENDS?
YEAH, SINCE SHE LEARNED SIGN LANGUAGE IN JUNIOR HIGH SHE THINKS SHE'S JANE GOODALL.
I DON'T THINK WE HAVE A CHOICE...
PLEASE DON'T EAT US.

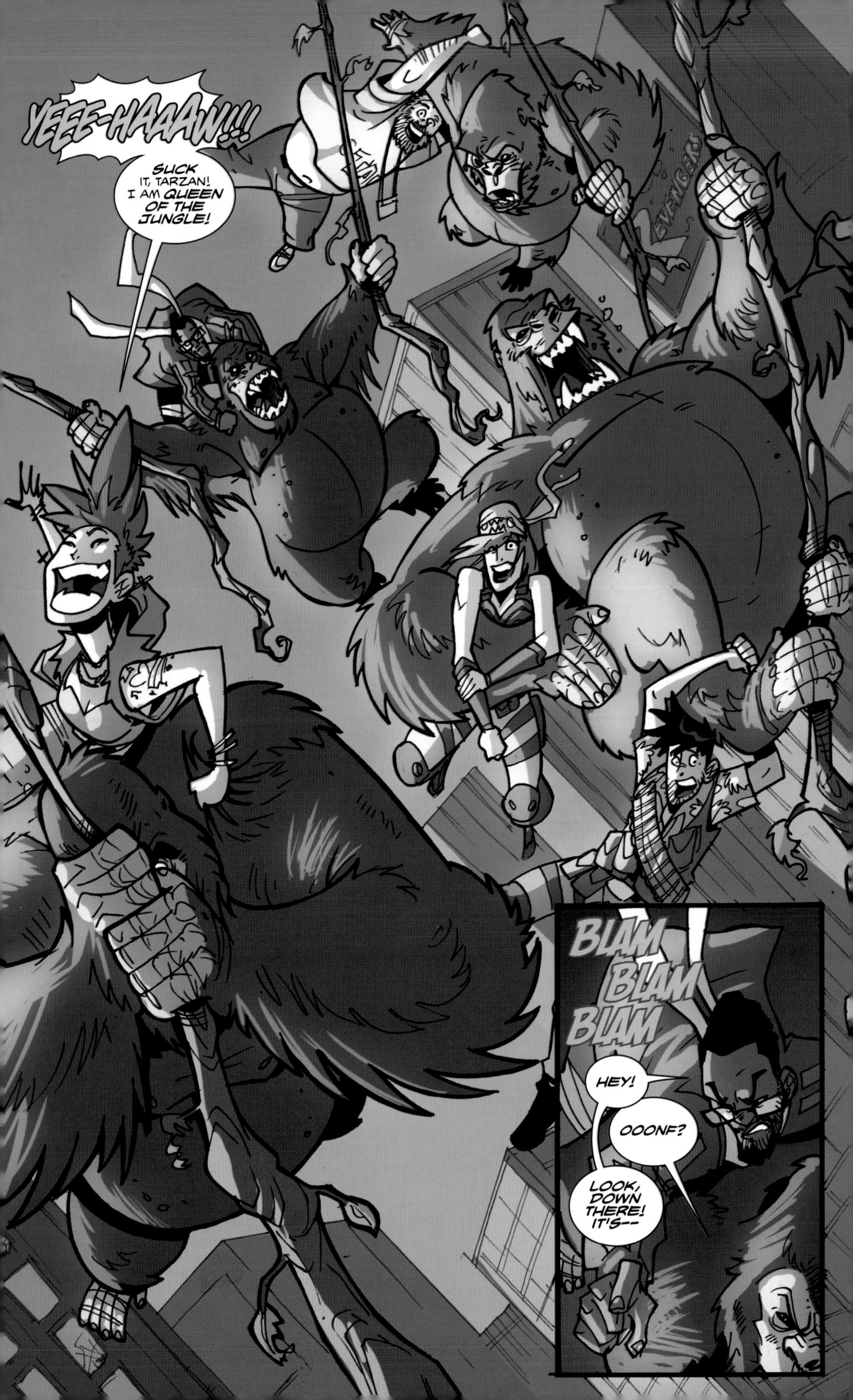
YEEE-HAAAW!!!
SUCK IT, TARZAN! I AM QUEEN OF THE JUNGLE!
REVENGERS
BLAM
BLAM
BLAM
HEY!
OOONF?
LOOK, DOWN THERE! IT'S--

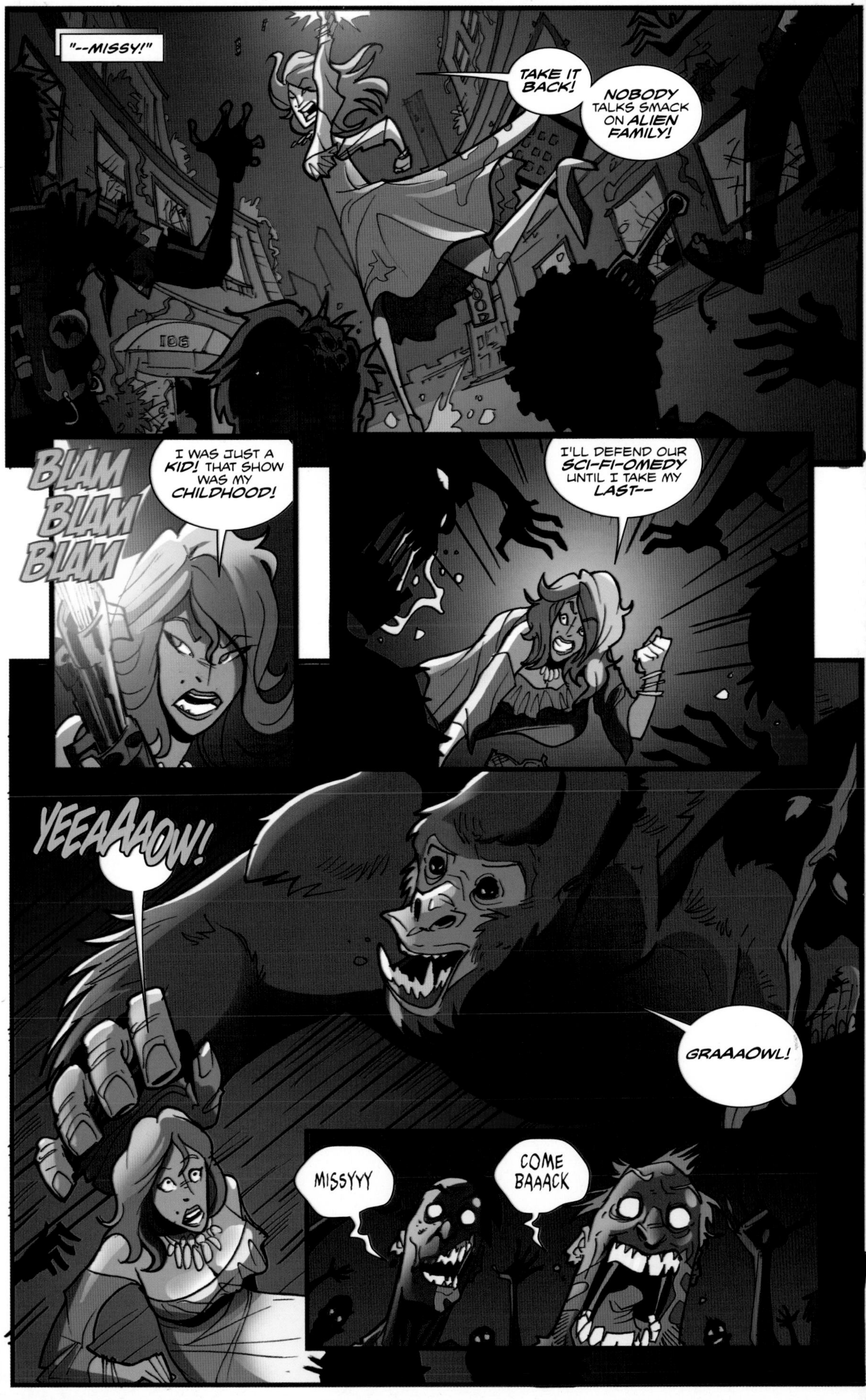
"--MISSY!"
TAKE IT BACK!
NOBODY TALKS SMACK ON ALIEN FAMILY!
BLAM BLAM BLAM
I WAS JUST A KID! THAT SHOW WAS MY CHILDHOOD!
I'LL DEFEND OUR SCI-FI-OMEDY UNTIL I TAKE MY LAST--
YEEAAAAOW!
GRAAAOWL!
MISSYYY
COME BAAACK

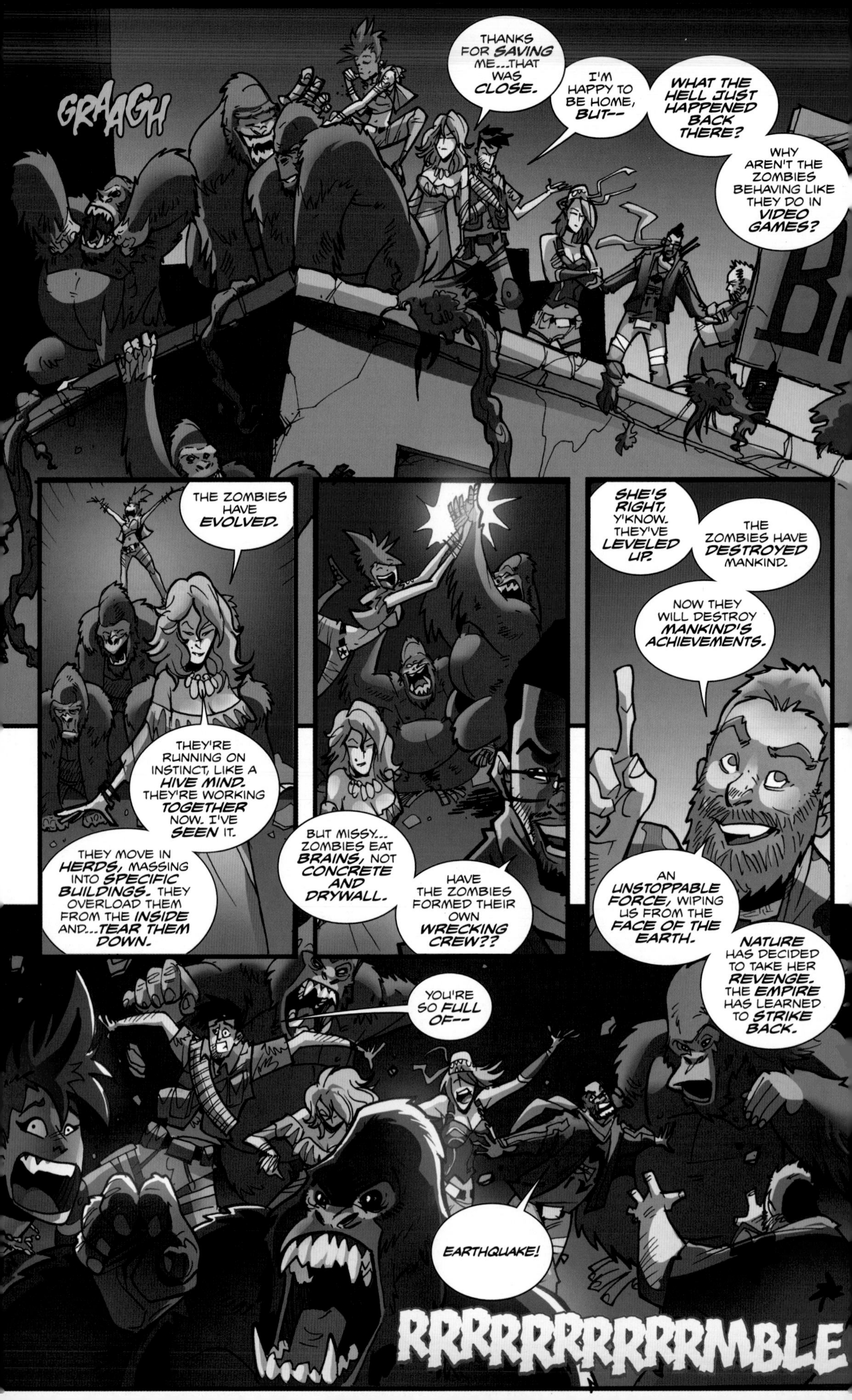
GRAAGH
THANKS FOR SAVING ME...THAT WAS CLOSE.
I'M HAPPY TO BE HOME, BUT--
WHAT THE HELL JUST HAPPENED BACK THERE?
WHY AREN'T THE ZOMBIES BEHAVING LIKE THEY DO IN VIDEO GAMES?
THE ZOMBIES HAVE EVOLVED.
THEY'RE RUNNING ON INSTINCT, LIKE A HIVE MIND. THEY'RE WORKING TOGETHER NOW. I'VE SEEN IT.
THEY MOVE IN HERDS, MASSING INTO SPECIFIC BUILDINGS. THEY OVERLOAD THEM FROM THE INSIDE AND...TEAR THEM DOWN.
BUT MISSY... ZOMBIES EAT BRAINS, NOT CONCRETE AND DRYWALL.
HAVE THE ZOMBIES FORMED THEIR OWN WRECKING CREW??
SHE'S RIGHT, Y'KNOW. THEY'VE LEVELED UP.
THE ZOMBIES HAVE DESTROYED MANKIND.
NOW THEY WILL DESTROY MANKIND'S ACHIEVEMENTS.
AN UNSTOPPABLE FORCE, WIPING US FROM THE FACE OF THE EARTH.
NATURE HAS DECIDED TO TAKE HER REVENGE. THE EMPIRE HAS LEARNED TO STRIKE BACK.
YOU'RE SO FULL OF--
EARTHQUAKE!
RRRRRRRRRRRMBLE

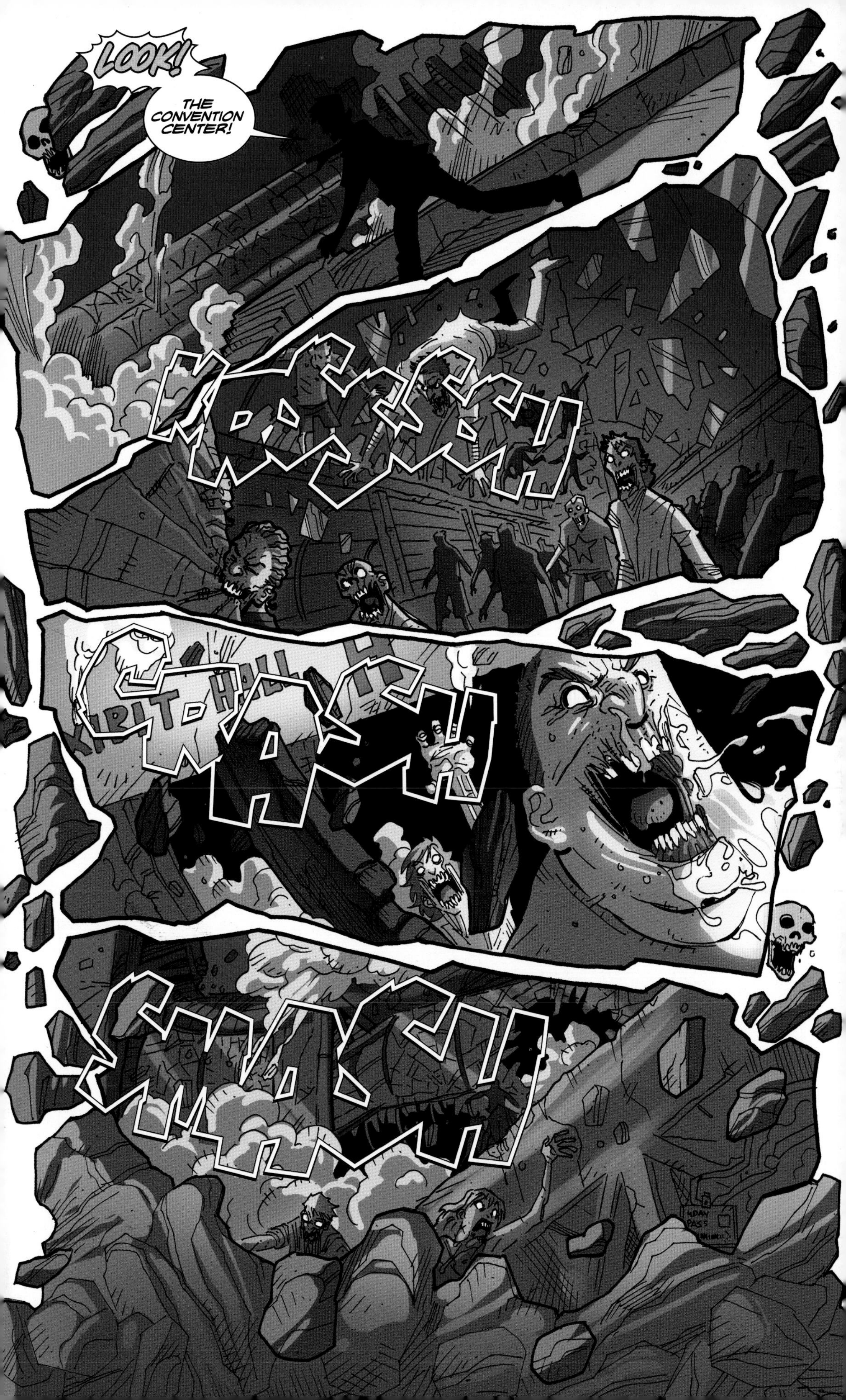
LOOK!
THE CONVENTION CENTER!
KRASSH
CRASH
SMASH
4DAY PASS

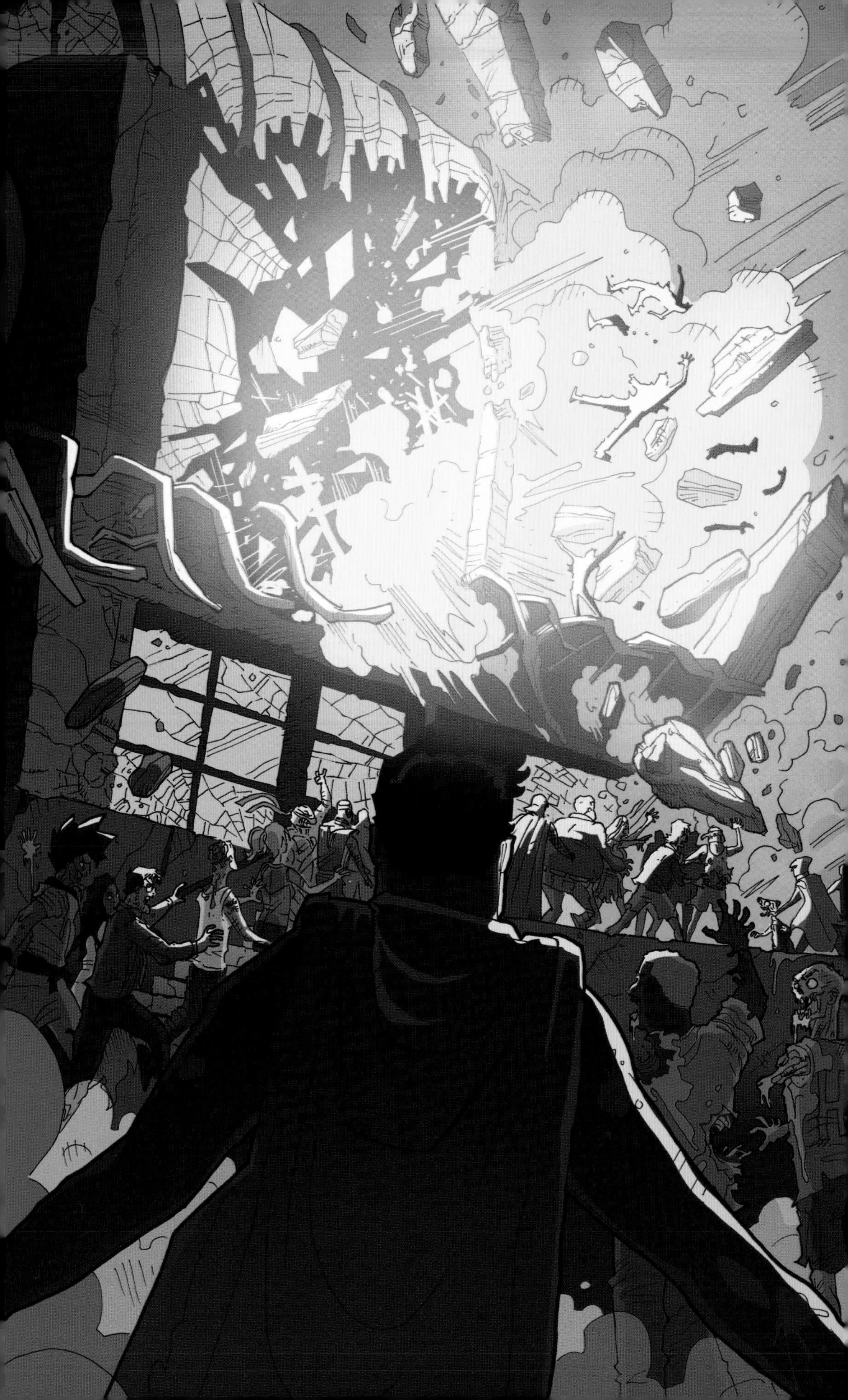

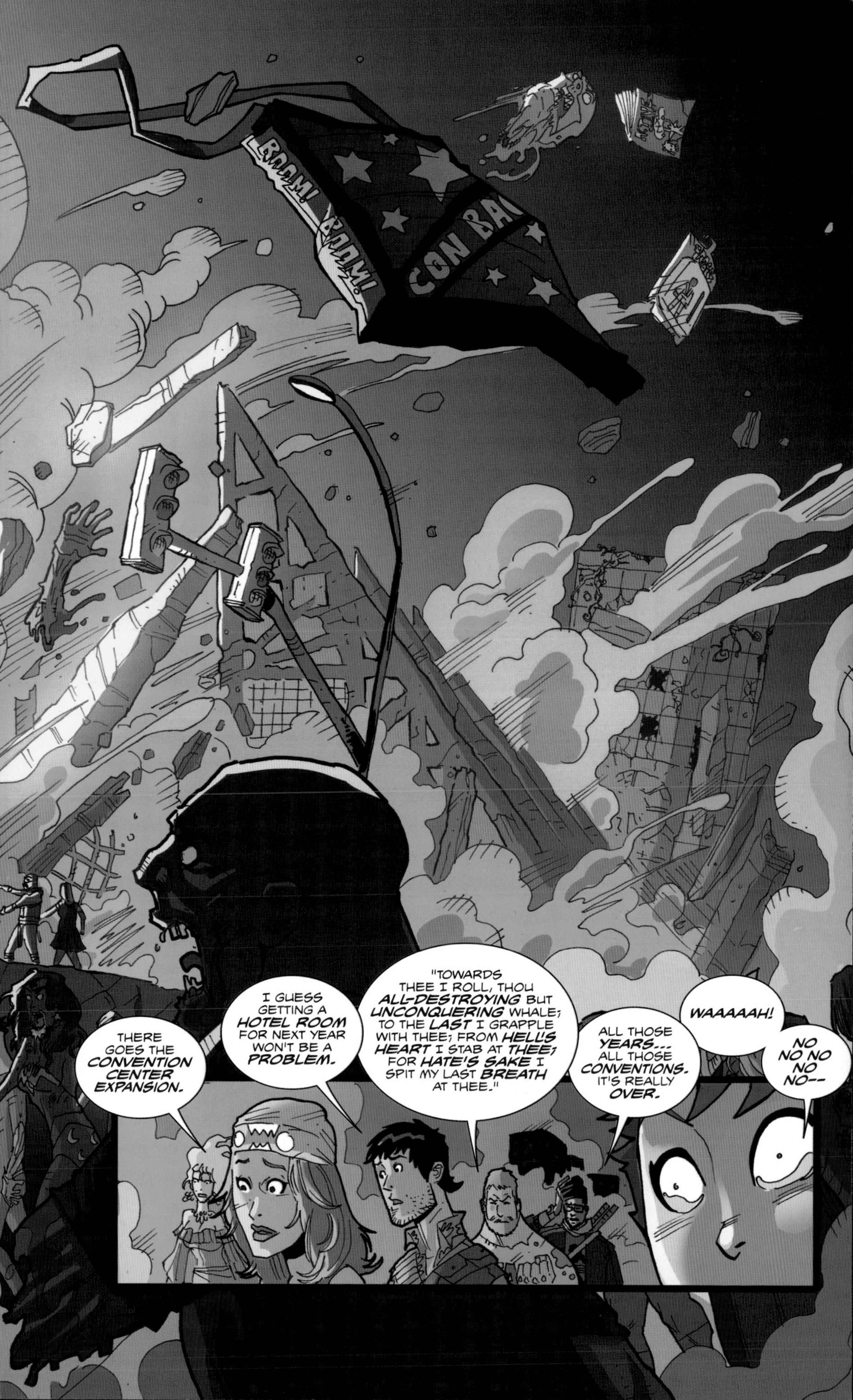
BOOM!
BOOM!
BOOM!
CON BA
THERE GOES THE CONVENTION CENTER EXPANSION.
I GUESS GETTING A HOTEL ROOM FOR NEXT YEAR WON'T BE A PROBLEM.
"TOWARDS THEE I ROLL, THOU ALL-DESTROYING BUT UNCONQUERING WHALE; TO THE LAST I GRAPPLE WITH THEE; FROM HELL'S HEART I STAB AT THEE; FOR HATE'S SAKE I SPIT MY LAST BREATH AT THEE."
ALL THOSE YEARS... ALL THOSE CONVENTIONS. IT'S REALLY OVER.
WAAAAAH!
NO NO NO NO NO--

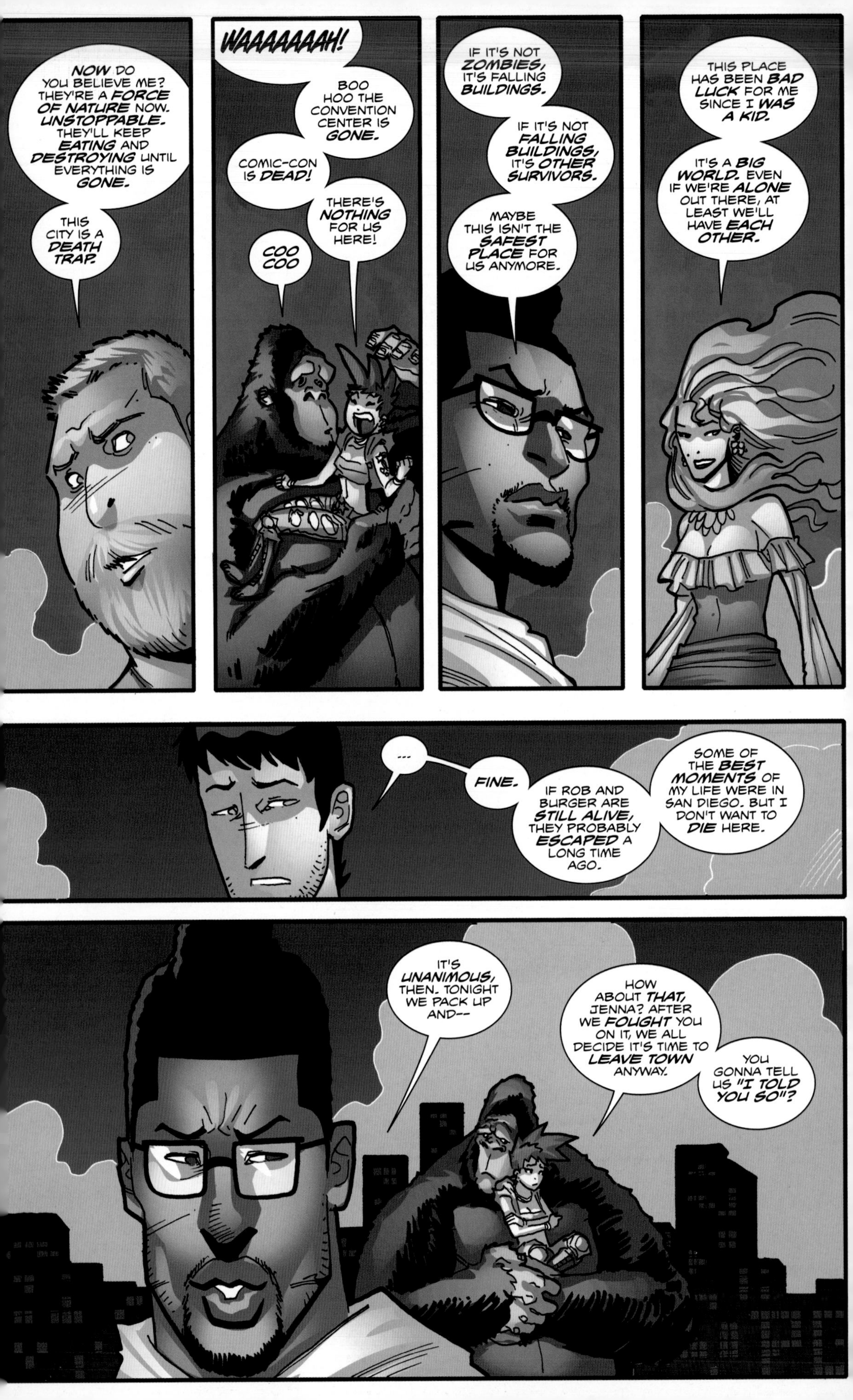
NOW DO YOU BELIEVE ME? THEY'RE A FORCE OF NATURE NOW. UNSTOPPABLE. THEY'LL KEEP EATING AND DESTROYING UNTIL EVERYTHING IS GONE.
THIS CITY IS A DEATH TRAP.
WAAAAAAAH!
BOO HOO THE CONVENTION CENTER IS GONE.
COMIC-CON IS DEAD!
THERE'S NOTHING FOR US HERE!
COO COO
IF IT'S NOT ZOMBIES, IT'S FALLING BUILDINGS.
IF IT'S NOT FALLING BUILDINGS, IT'S OTHER SURVIVORS.
MAYBE THIS ISN'T THE SAFEST PLACE FOR US ANYMORE.
THIS PLACE HAS BEEN BAD LUCK FOR ME SINCE I WAS A KID.
IT'S A BIG WORLD. EVEN IF WE'RE ALONE OUT THERE, AT LEAST WE'LL HAVE EACH OTHER.
...
FINE.
IF ROB AND BURGER ARE STILL ALIVE, THEY PROBABLY ESCAPED A LONG TIME AGO.
SOME OF THE BEST MOMENTS OF MY LIFE WERE IN SAN DIEGO. BUT I DON'T WANT TO DIE HERE.
IT'S UNANIMOUS, THEN. TONIGHT WE PACK UP AND--
HOW ABOUT THAT, JENNA? AFTER WE FOUGHT YOU ON IT, WE ALL DECIDE IT'S TIME TO LEAVE TOWN ANYWAY.
YOU GONNA TELL US "I TOLD YOU SO"?

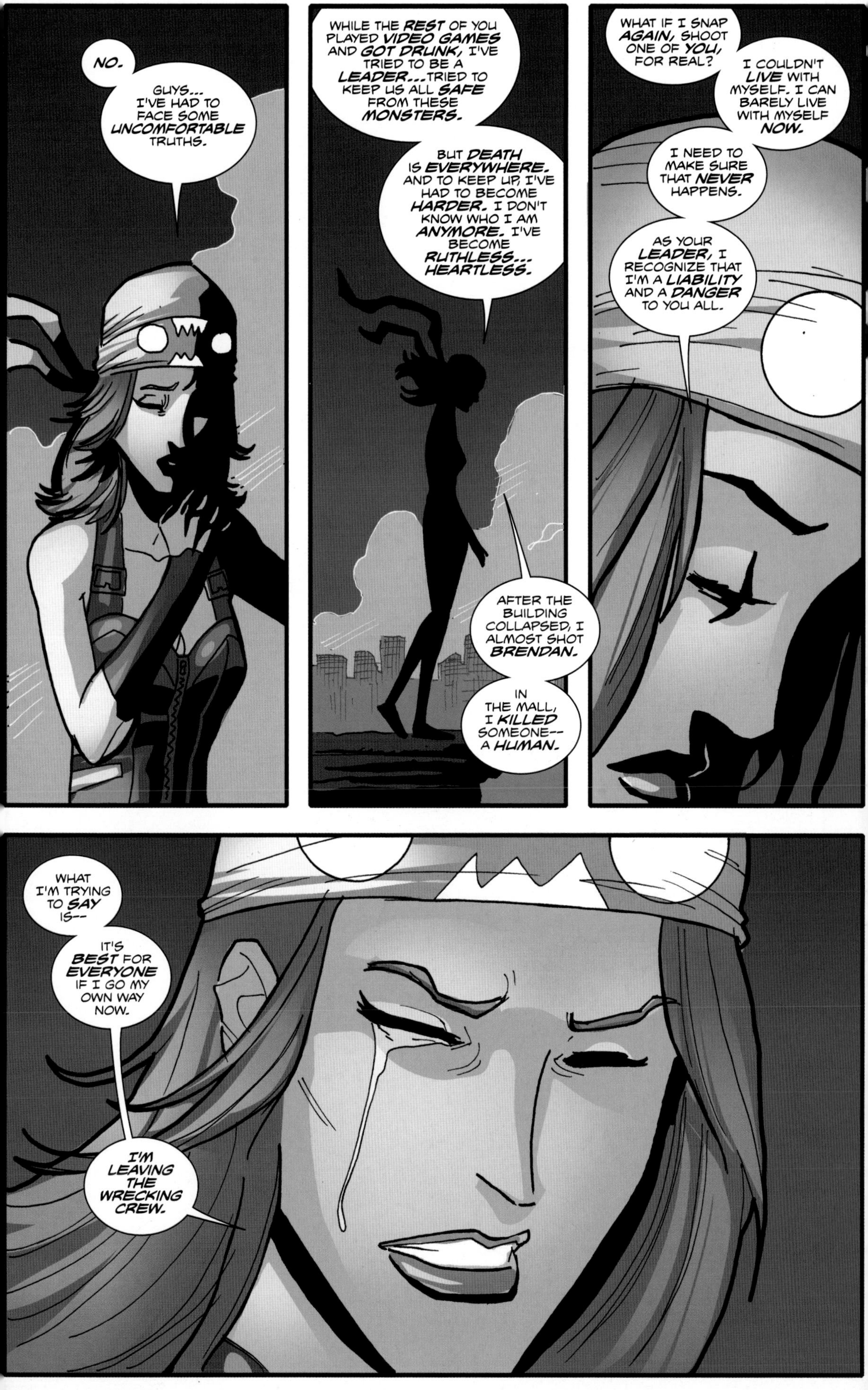
NO.
GUYS... I'VE HAD TO FACE SOME UNCOMFORTABLE TRUTHS.
WHILE THE REST OF YOU PLAYED VIDEO GAMES AND GOT DRUNK, I'VE TRIED TO BE A LEADER... TRIED TO KEEP US ALL SAFE FROM THESE MONSTERS.
BUT DEATH IS EVERYWHERE. AND TO KEEP UP, I'VE HAD TO BECOME HARDER. I DON'T KNOW WHO I AM ANYMORE. I'VE BECOME RUTHLESS... HEARTLESS.
AFTER THE BUILDING COLLAPSED, I ALMOST SHOT BRENDAN.
IN THE MALL, I KILLED SOMEONE-- A HUMAN.
WHAT IF I SNAP AGAIN, SHOOT ONE OF YOU, FOR REAL?
I COULDN'T LIVE WITH MYSELF. I CAN BARELY LIVE WITH MYSELF NOW.
I NEED TO MAKE SURE THAT NEVER HAPPENS.
AS YOUR LEADER, I RECOGNIZE THAT I'M A LIABILITY AND A DANGER TO YOU ALL.
WHAT I'M TRYING TO SAY IS--
IT'S BEST FOR EVERYONE IF I GO MY OWN WAY NOW.
I'M LEAVING THE WRECKING CREW.

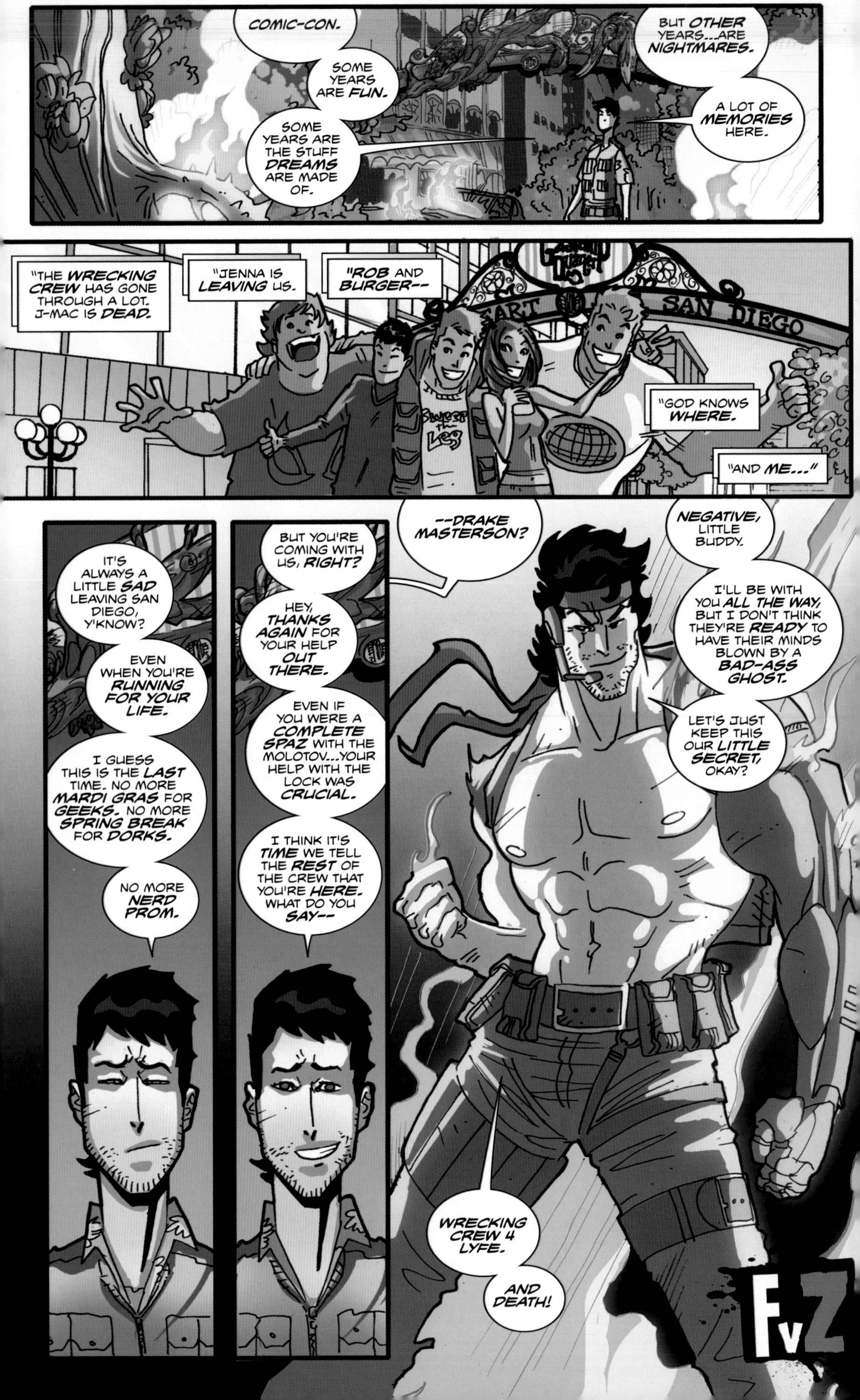
COMIC-CON.
SOME YEARS ARE FUN.
SOME YEARS ARE THE STUFF DREAMS ARE MADE OF.
BUT OTHER YEARS...ARE NIGHTMARES.
A LOT OF MEMORIES HERE.
"THE WRECKING CREW HAS GONE THROUGH A LOT. J-MAC IS DEAD.
"JENNA IS LEAVING US.
"ROB AND BURGER--
"GOD KNOWS WHERE.
"AND ME..."
SAN DIEGO
IT'S ALWAYS A LITTLE SAD LEAVING SAN DIEGO, Y'KNOW?
EVEN WHEN YOU'RE RUNNING FOR YOUR LIFE.
I GUESS THIS IS THE LAST TIME. NO MORE MARDI GRAS FOR GEEKS. NO MORE SPRING BREAK FOR DORKS.
NO MORE NERD PROM.
BUT YOU'RE COMING WITH US, RIGHT?
HEY, THANKS AGAIN FOR YOUR HELP OUT THERE.
EVEN IF YOU WERE A COMPLETE SPAZ WITH THE MOLOTOV...YOUR HELP WITH THE LOCK WAS CRUCIAL.
I THINK IT'S TIME WE TELL THE REST OF THE CREW THAT YOU'RE HERE. WHAT DO YOU SAY--
--DRAKE MASTERSON?
NEGATIVE, LITTLE BUDDY.
I'LL BE WITH YOU ALL THE WAY, BUT I DON'T THINK THEY'RE READY TO HAVE THEIR MINDS BLOWN BY A BAD-ASS GHOST.
LET'S JUST KEEP THIS OUR LITTLE SECRET, OKAY?
WRECKING CREW 4 LYFE.
AND DEATH!
FvZ

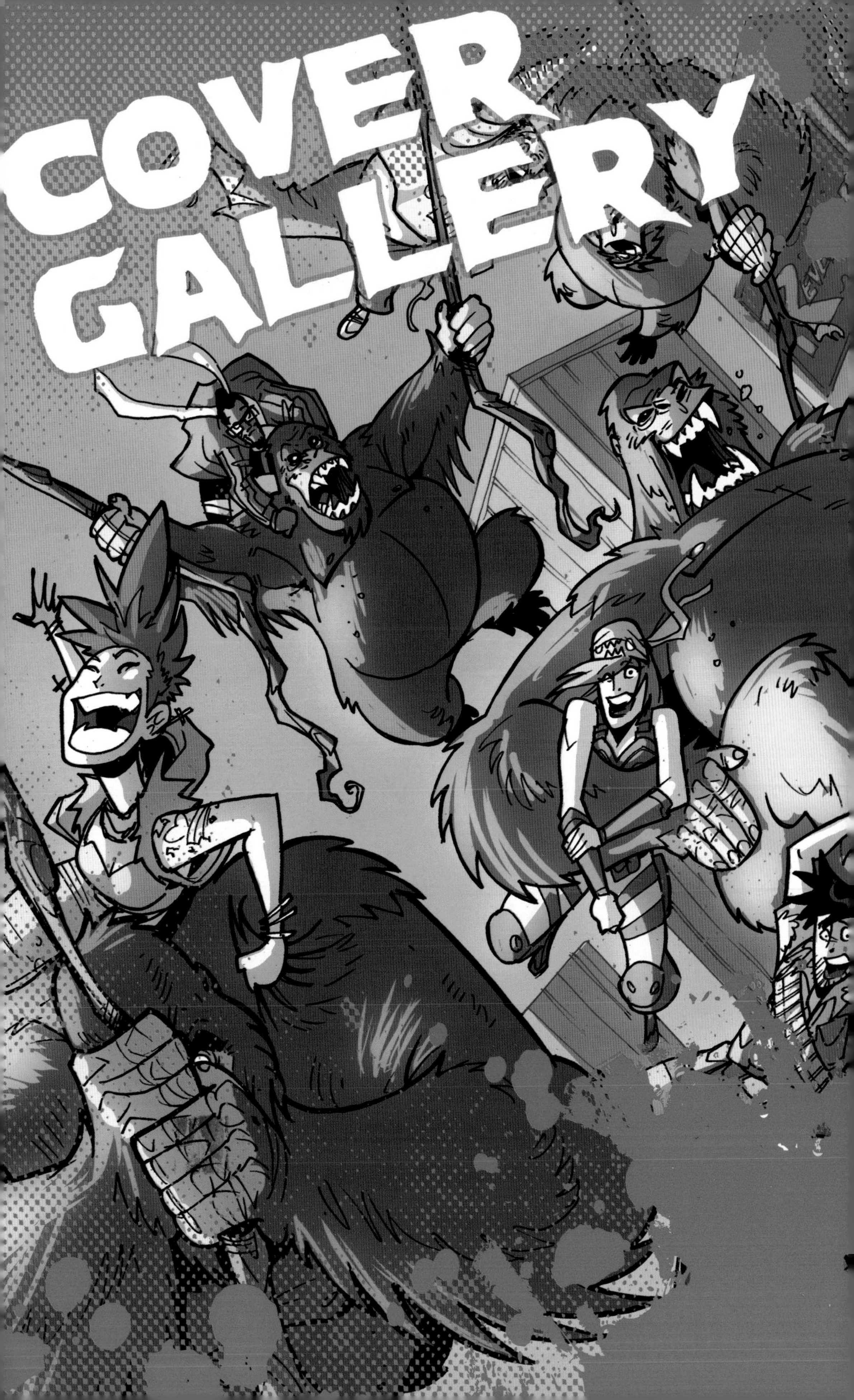
COVER GALLERY

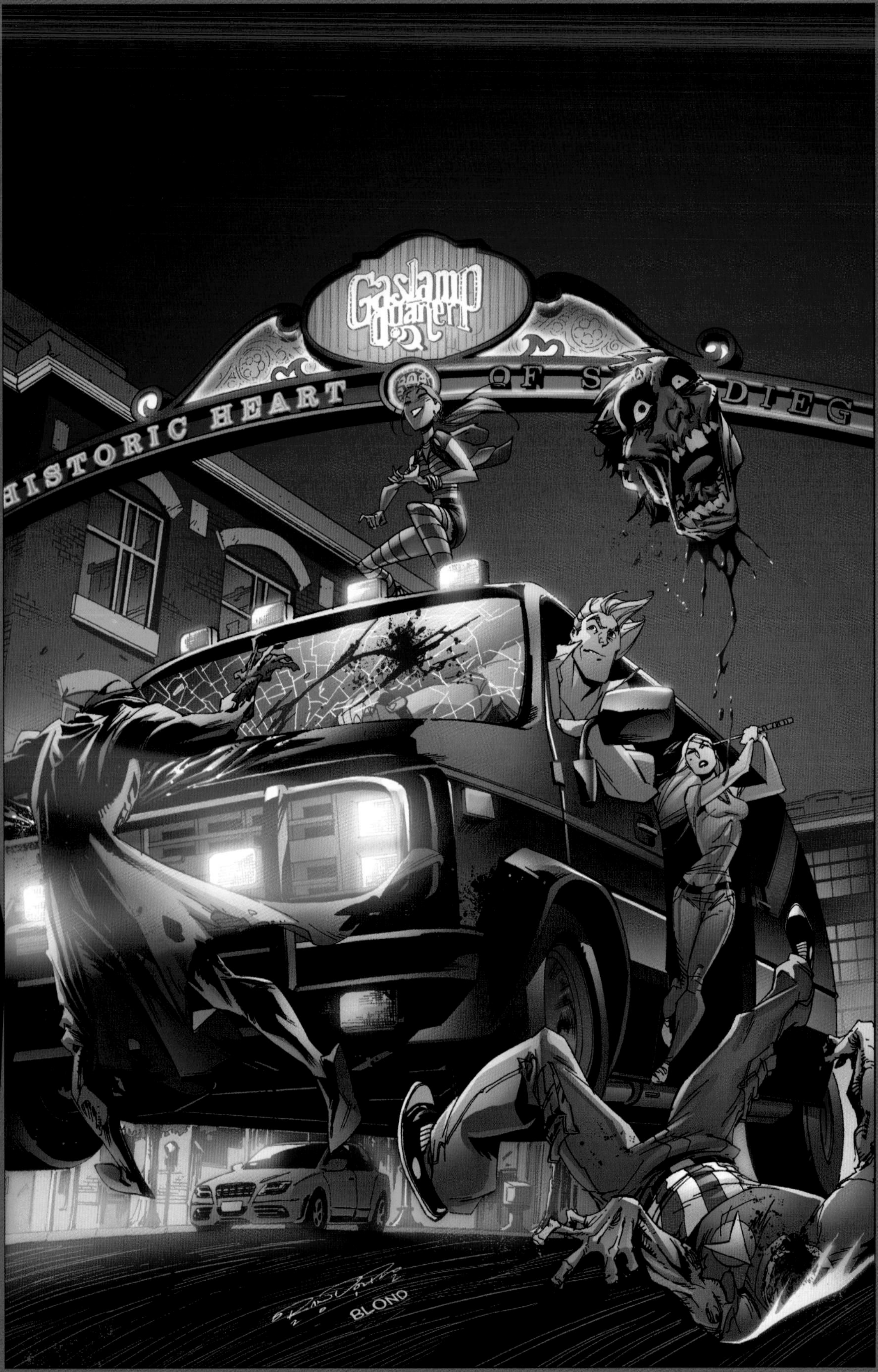

Gaslamp Quarter
HISTORIC HEART OF S DIEG
BLOND


**ISSUE FIVE: KHARY RANDOLPH**
**WITH COLORS BY BLOND**

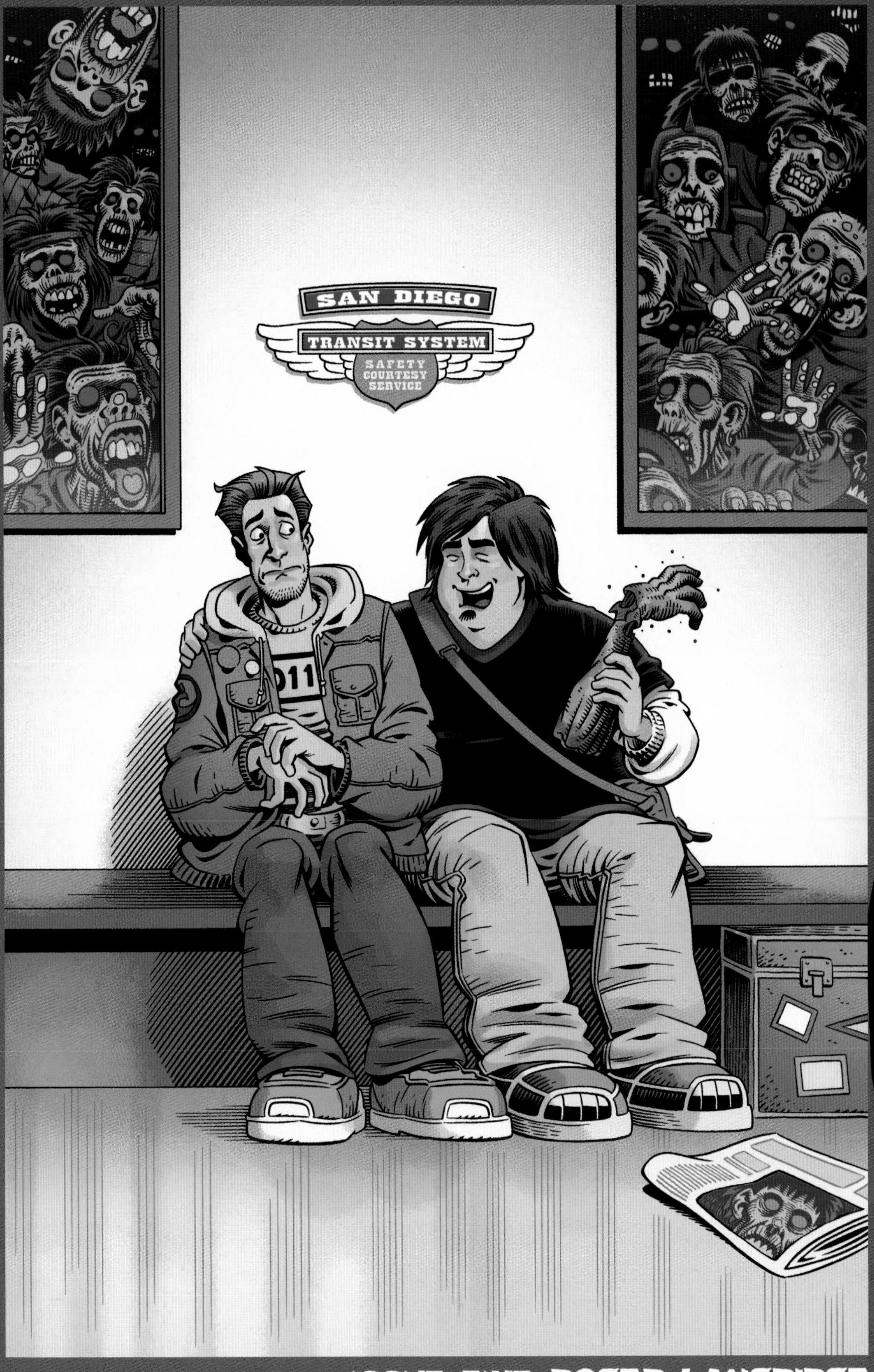
SAN DIEGO
TRANSIT SYSTEM
SAFETY
COURTESY
SERVICE

ISSUE FIVE: ROGER LANGRIDGE
WITH COLORS BY MATTHEW WILSON

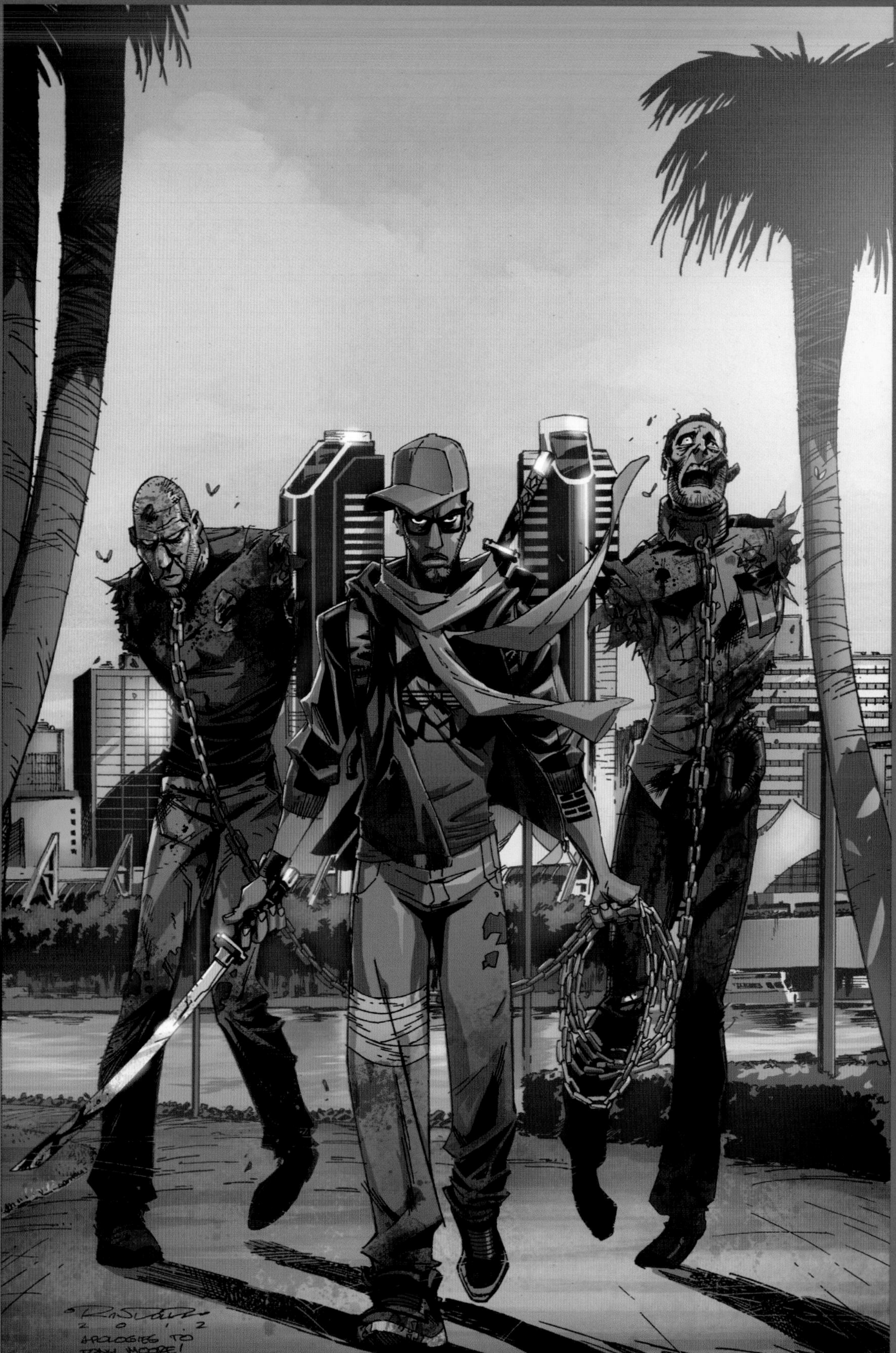
2012
APOLOGIES TO TONY MOORE!

ISSUE SIX: KHARY RANDOLPH
WITH COLORS BY EMILIO LOPEZ

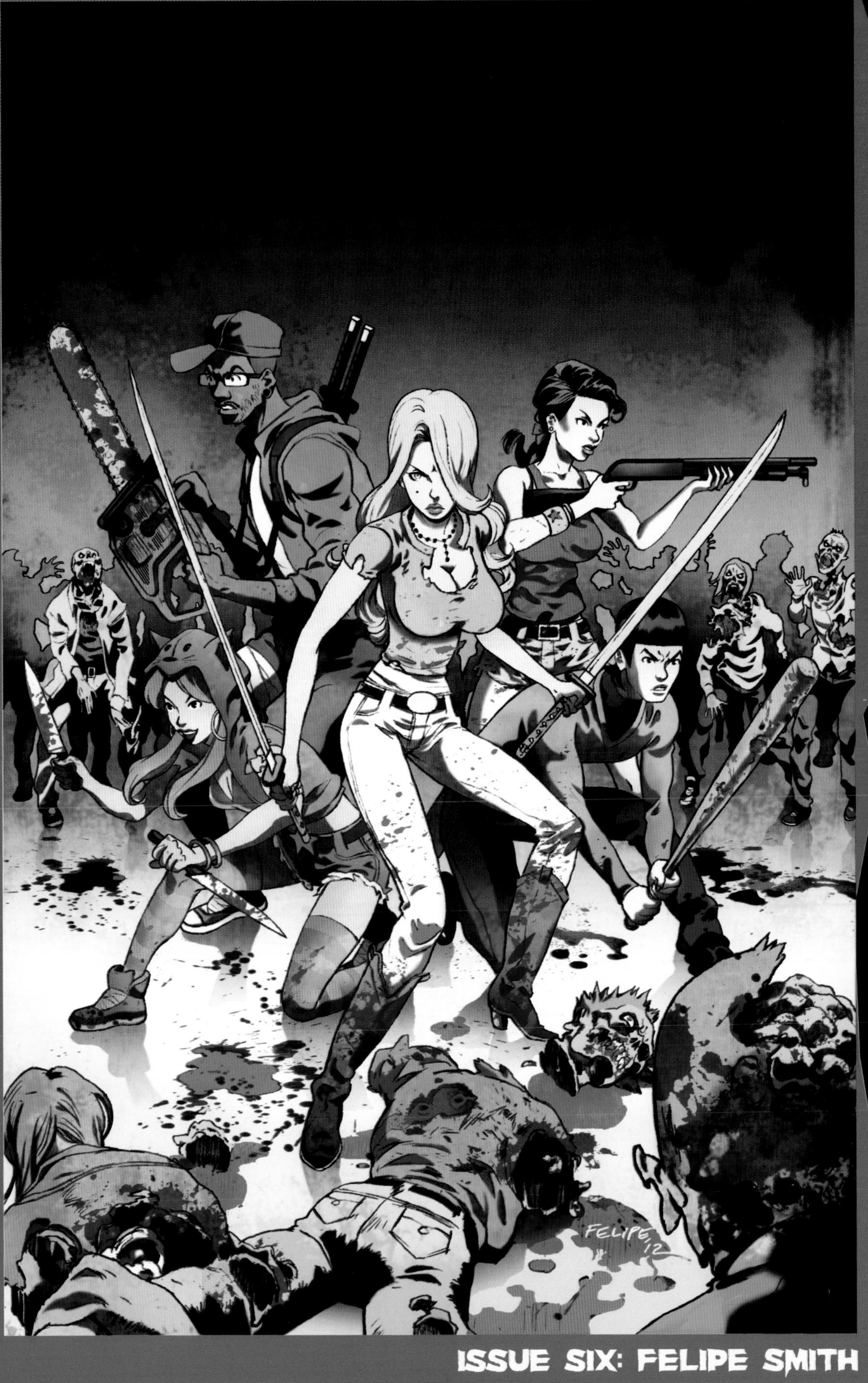
FELIPE '12

ISSUE SIX: FELIPE SMITH

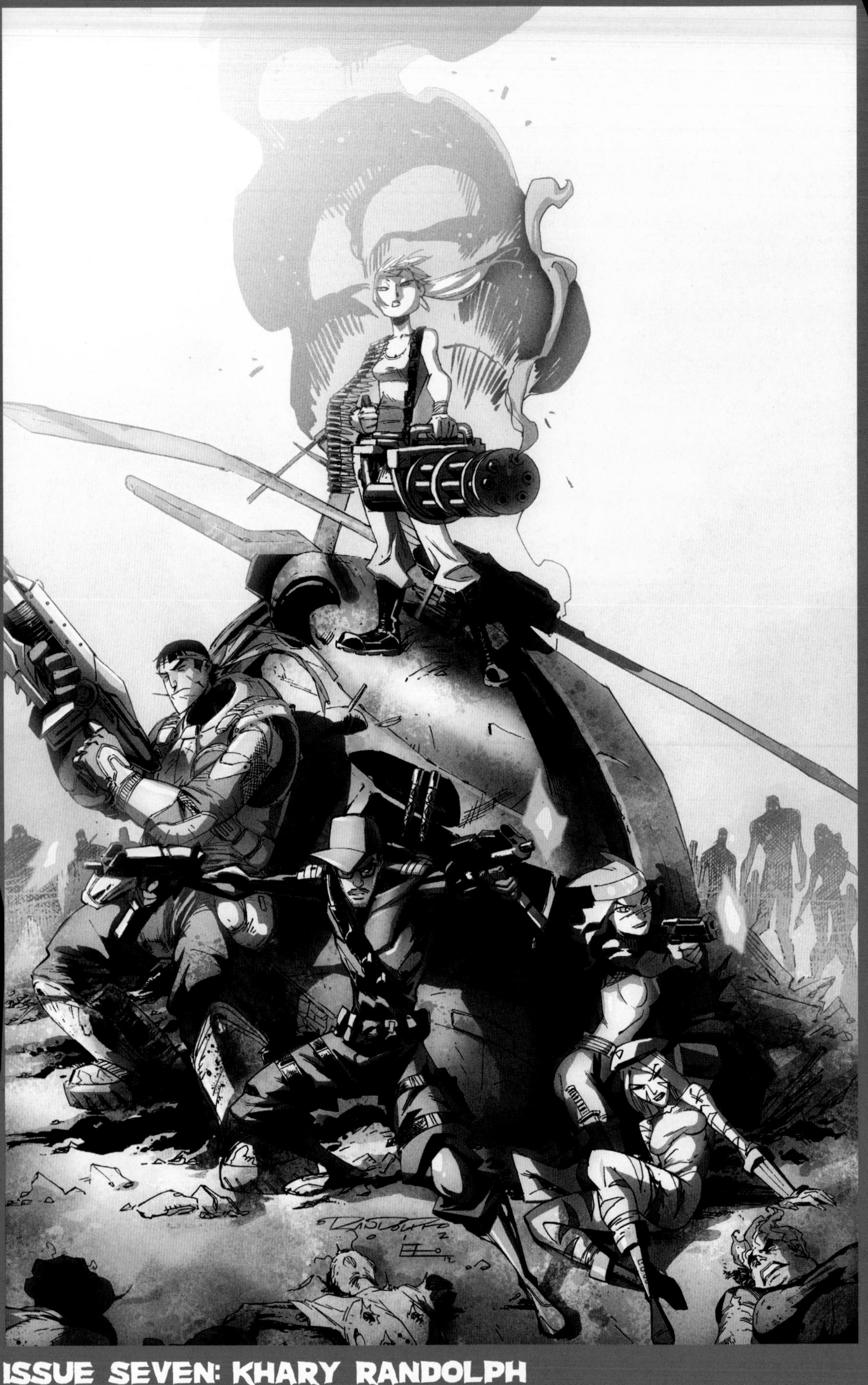

**ISSUE SEVEN: KHARY RANDOLPH**
**WITH COLORS BY EMILIO LOPEZ**

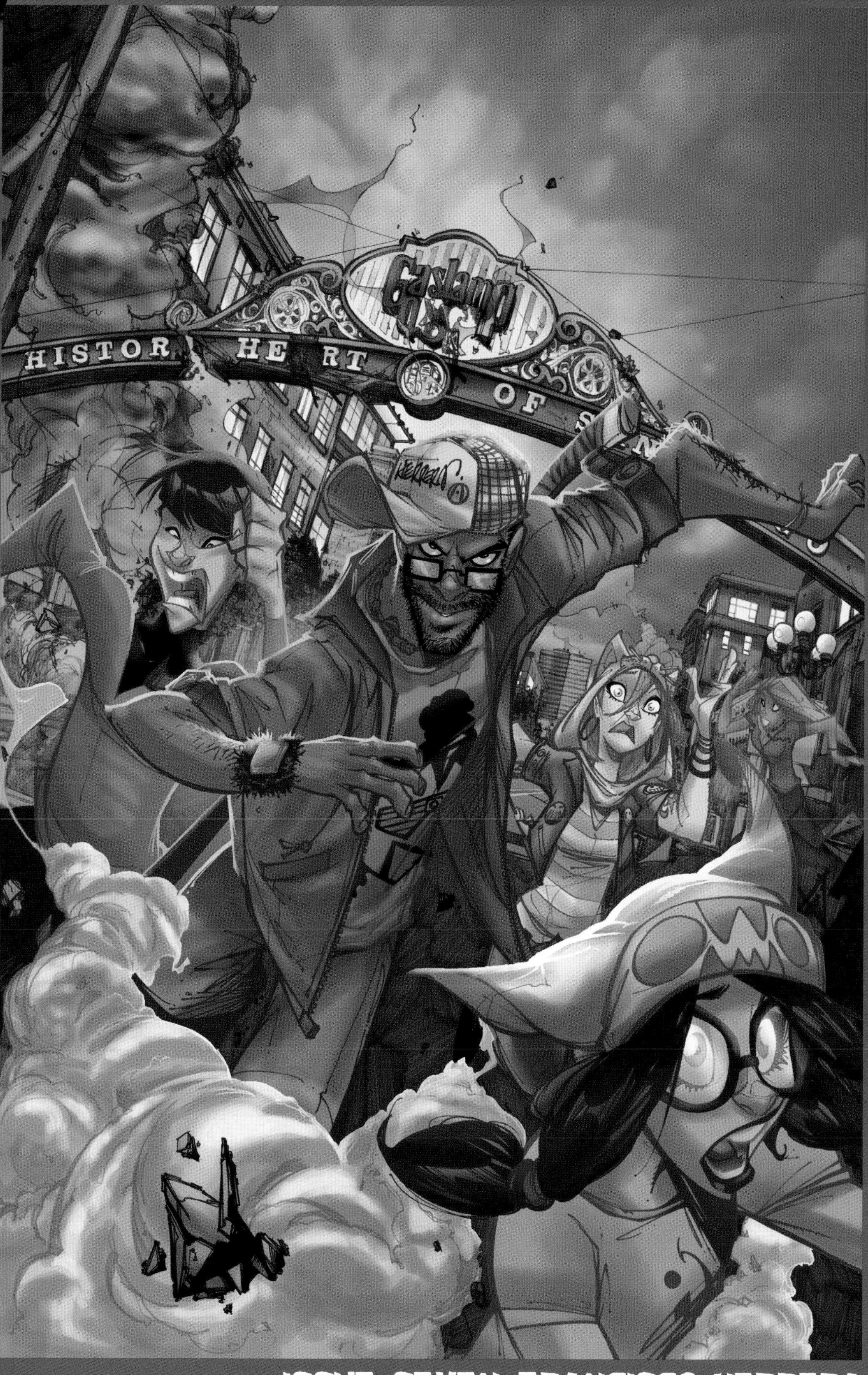
Gaslamp
HISTOR HE RT OF

ISSUE SEVEN: FRANCISCO HERRERA
WITH COLORS BY LEONARDO OLEA

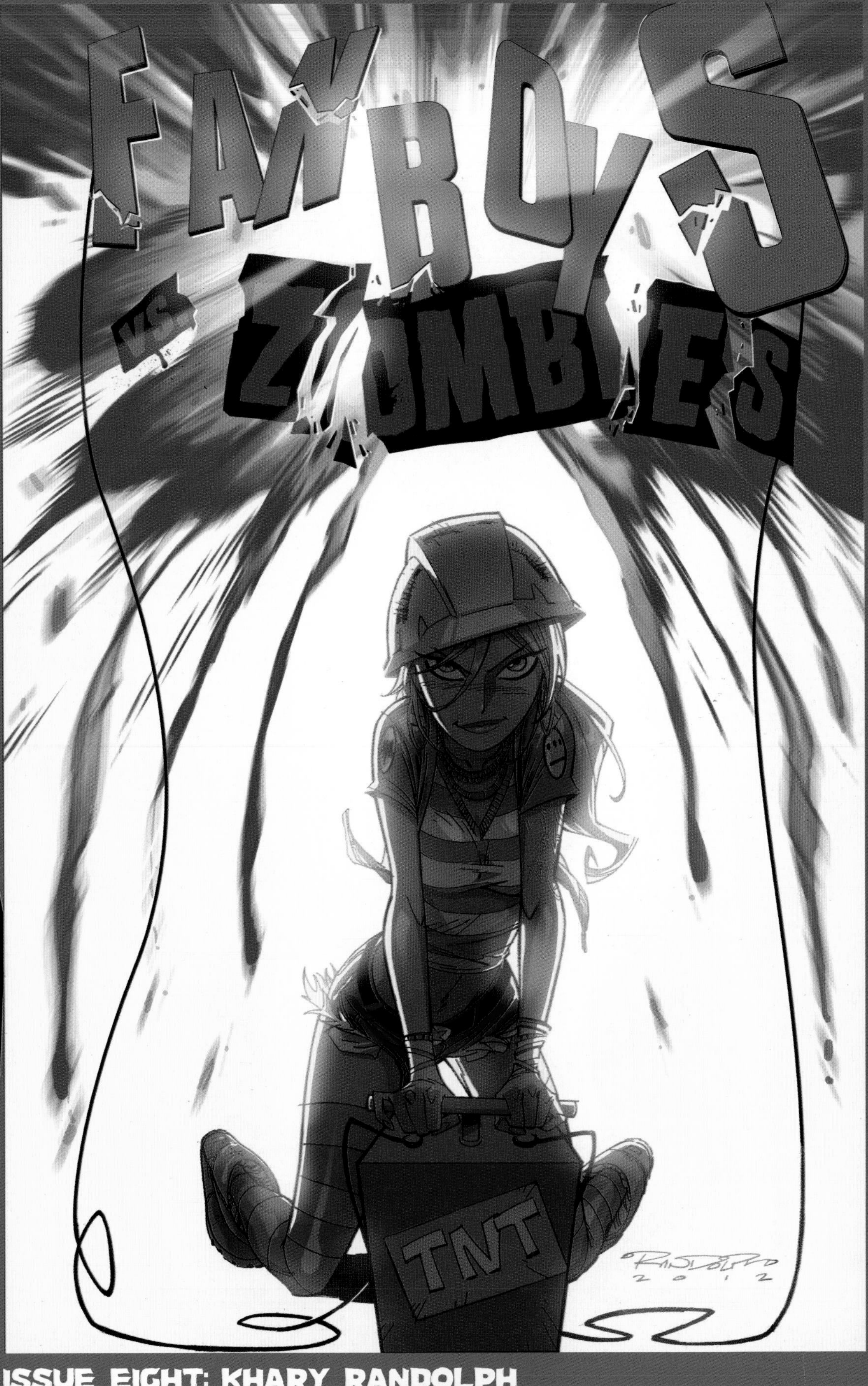
FANBOYS
VS.
ZOMBIES
TNT
RANDOLPH 2012

ISSUE EIGHT: KHARY RANDOLPH

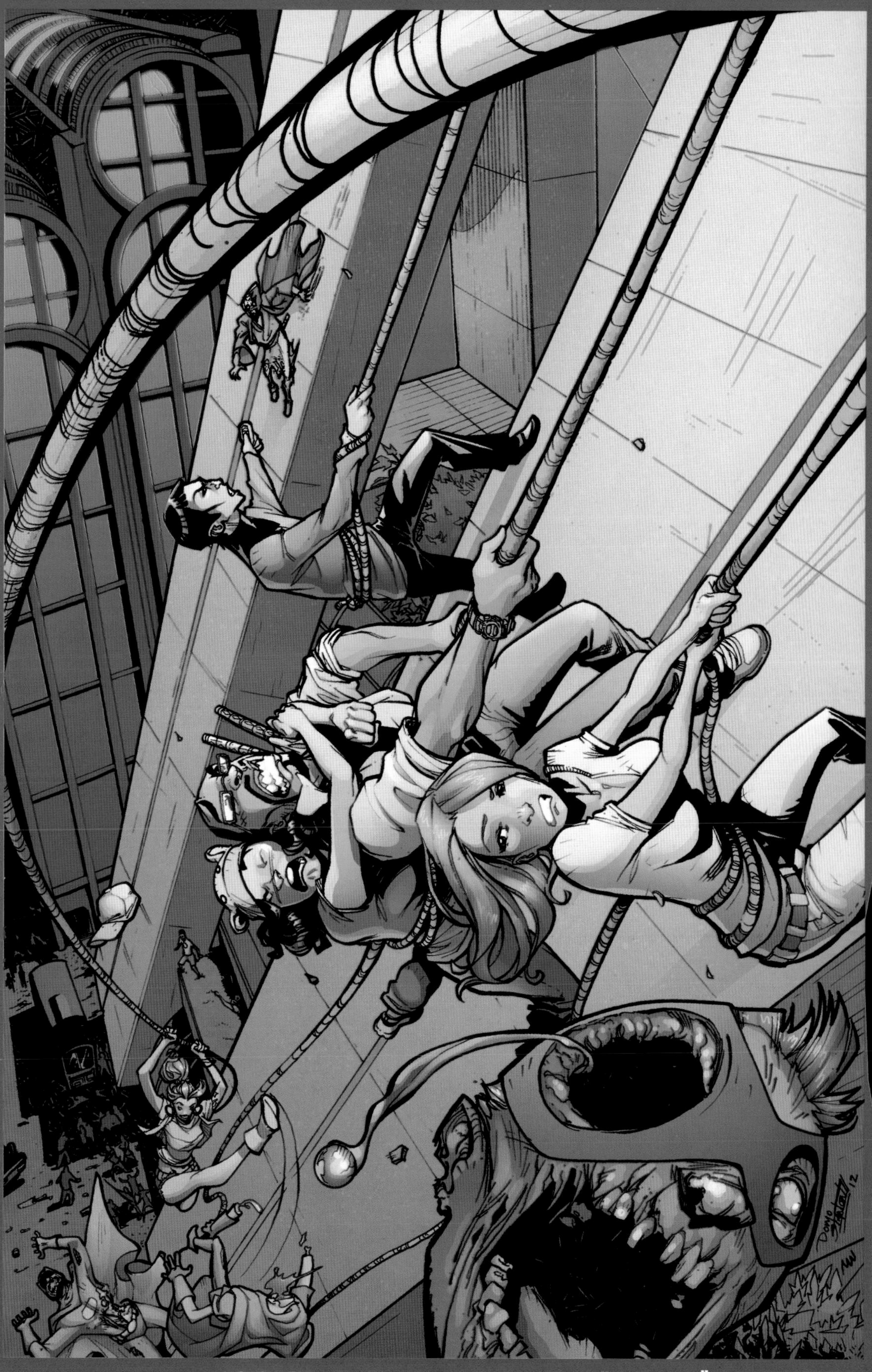
DOMO STANTON '12
NW

ISSUE EIGHT: DOMINIKE "DOMO" STANTON
WITH COLORS BY NOLAN WOODARD

**ISSUE FIVE: EDDIE NUNEZ**
**WITH COLORS BY BLOND**

**ISSUE SIX: EDDIE NUNEZ**
**WITH COLORS BY**
**ALEX DELIGIANNIS**

**ISSUE SEVEN: EDDIE NUNEZ**
**WITH COLORS BY BLOND**

**ISSUE EIGHT: EDDIE NUNEZ**
**WITH COLORS BY BLOND**

COMING SOON!

# FANBOYS
## vs. ZOMBIES

## VOLUME THREE
### ESCAPE FROM SAN DIEGO